INDUSTRIAL RELATIONS IN DEVELOPING COUNTRIES

The Case of Nigeria

ABEL K. UBEKU

LL.M. (London), D.Phil. (Sussex)
Managing Director, Guinness (Nigeria) Ltd

Foreword by Guy Routh
formerly Reader in Economics, University of Sussex

St. Martin's Press   New York

© Abel K. Ubeku 1983
All rights reserved. For information, write:
St. Martin's Press, Inc., 175 Fifth Avenue, New York, NY 10010

Printed in Hong Kong

Published in the United Kingdom by The Macmillan Press Ltd.
First published in the United States of America in 1983

ISBN 0-312-41512-5

Library of Congress Cataloging in Publication Data

Ubeku, Abel K.
  Industrial relations in developing countries.

  Bibliography: p.
  Includes index.
  1. Industrial relations—Nigeria.   2. Industrial
relations—Developing countries—Case studies.
I. Title.
HD8831.U23 1983   331'.09669   83-13994
ISBN 0-312-41512-5

INDUSTRIAL RELATIONS IN DEVELOPING COUNTRIES

The Case of Nigeria

By the same author

PERSONNEL MANAGEMENT IN NIGERIA

To my wife, Beatrice Obiageli,
I dedicate this book

Contents

List of Figures and Tables

FIGURES

TABLES

Foreword

Guy Routh

A few days in Nigeria are enough to convince the visitor that it is a country on the move. Its population is increasing at more than 3.5 per cent per year, a rate not unusual for an African country, but its economic growth of between 5 and 10 per cent has been able to cope with the rise in population and, in addition, to institute those changes which, by the end of the century, will have transformed the country into a modern industrial state. The transformation is, of course, oil-powered, with one million barrels per day producing, at 1982 prices, $13 billion per year. The current collapse of oil prices has necessitated a rethinking of priorities, but the ebullience and enterprise of the Nigerian people remains an unmistakable asset. They struggle to seize their opportunities and grapple with their problems under the interested gaze of the rest of the world. Unfortunately, the country's economic growth was slowed down by the world-wide economic recession leading to a reduction of oil production output in 1983. As oil is responsible for nearly 95 per cent of Nigeria's foreign exchange earnings, the impact was dramatic. The reduction in the posted price of oil early in 1983 was a logical consequence, and in order to conserve foreign exchange certain economic measures had to be taken. However, those who know Nigeria well are optimistic. Dr Ubeku points to the fact, that although the country fought a thirty-month civil war, its economy remained intact. He argues that, as the world economy picks up again, Nigeria will be once again on the path of economic progress.

Oil comes from the bounty of nature; the use to which this bounty is put is a matter for the Nigerians themselves. It might be squandered on current consumption; it might, as the planners conceive, be used to transform the country – but this will require Herculean labours for many years to come. It is in this context that industrial relations are of particular importance, and it is for this reason that Dr Ubeku's book is to be welcomed. It is of the greatest importance that trade unionists, government and employers should have for their reference and as a basis for discussion a reasoned exposition of the field, an account and analysis of its origin and development, and an identification of the problems that will arise now and in the future. His conclusions and recommendations merit close consideration by all concerned.

The practical value of the work must not be allowed to obscure its theoretical interest. Nigerian systems of industrial relations (of which several have been tried in this experimentally inclined country) are placed in context with those in other parts of the world. 'Industrial relations' exist wherever there are employers and employees. Their interests, as Adam Smith remarked, are by no means the same, the one desiring to get as much, and the other to give as little, as possible. Thus it is that, along with the curious differences between countries, there are curious similarities that persist over the centuries and in countries with contrasting social and political systems. For most of the working day, and the working year, the parties must accommodate one another, respect one another's foibles and agree to differ on those things upon which neither party can be compelled to yield. Without this accommodation, life would be intolerable and nothing would get done; with it, each can make a living, and a living that becomes less irksome and more rewarding with the advance of method and the passage of time.

Within Nigeria itself, we are taken through the colonial period, when British industrial relations were being transplanted to a very different setting; then independence and parliamentary rule, which, again, reflected the British way; then military rule and civil war, followed by the 'bloodless *coup*' of 1975 that led to the return to civilian rule but now on an American rather than a British model. These phases have been accompanied by sweeping changes in trade-union law and structure, demonstrating a degree of government power and discretion that ministers or secretaries for labour in democratic capitalist countries might well envy. There now exist the institutions and statutes upon which a system of industrial relations may be built that will accord with the needs of industrial development. I say 'may', for, as this book demonstrates, there remain discords awaiting resolution.

Dr Ubeku has qualifications, academic and empirical, that enable him to treat his subject with impressive insight. His bachelor's and master's degrees at the University of London were in law; his work has been in personnel management, in which he took the Institute of Personnel Management Diploma at the London School of Economics.

More recently, he has completed his academic work in the Labour Studies Division of the Graduate School at the University of Sussex. Thus he is able to apply interdisciplinary techniques to the interpretation of the wealth of clinically derived data that have enriched his experience. The result is a study that will be of interest to students of industrial relations across the world.

Brighton, Sussex, England

Preface

One common feature in the developing countries is the extent to which their institutions, social, economic and political, have been influenced and indeed modified by developed countries. This is particularly marked in the case of those countries which were, for a time, under colonial rule. The developed countries, in the process of exploiting the economic opportunities available, brought with them their own systems and values and superimposed these on the existing customs and traditions. Thus they imported their own legal systems, methods of government, and their approach to labour relations, among other things, and superimposed these on those practices already in existence, in the colonial territories.

Before the advent of the modern industrial sector in Nigeria, there were already in existence employer-employee relationships with systems of work and reward based on the culture and traditions of the people. In general, the employer was an individual and his workmen were essentially members of his household or of the extended family, including cousins, nephews and nieces. In the circumstances the approach was paternalistic in respect of monetary rewards and other welfare facilities.

However, the modern industrial sector brought with it the modern concept of collective relations as manifested in the collective bargaining process. This new approach in employment relationships was predicated upon the British system, the metropolitan country at the time. That system had developed during the *laissez-faire* period in Europe, had matured over the years, and was based essentially on the voluntary principle.

The voluntary approach to industrial relations presupposes the existence of certain factors for its viability. These include:

1. *A democratic way of life.* This makes it possible for the various parties and interest-groups to respect each other's rights. Accordingly, the system is unlikely to thrive in a situation where opposition is not tolerated or where trade unions are seen as working against national goals.

2. *The balance of power between employers and employees.* Where that balance tilts in favour of the employers, and the workers' organisations are weak and poorly led, as is common in a number of developing countries, the system is not likely to be viable.

The experience of developing countries like Nigeria is that in their approach to economic development they rely mostly on development plans based on specific objectives. To achieve those objectives necessarily implies a strict adherence to the strategy agreed upon for their achievement. This means that opposition, dissent and suggestions for deviation from the agreed path are not likely to be looked upon with favour. Accordingly, strong virile labour movements are considered to be working against the interests of the nation. This has been the position in Nigeria. It becomes questionable, therefore, whether the British model of industrial relations is appropriate in a country like Nigeria.

The literature on the subject of industrial relations in Nigeria is very scanty. Yesufu's work, *An Introduction to Industrial Relations in Nigeria,* was published in 1962, two years after Nigeria attained her independence from Britain and at a time when the government, though independent, was still sustaining most of the institutions of the colonial era. As a result, the book describes the system of collective relations based mainly on joint consultation as collective bargaining was not widely practised in the country at the time. Furthermore, by 1962 no new labour legislation had been passed to reflect the 'indigenous' situation following Nigeria's independence in 1960.

Peter Kilby[1] has argued that the colonial administration's legislative and administrative measures on industrial relations in Nigeria represent a reproduction of the metropolitan institutional framework, corresponding to a mature system of industrial relations and wage determination which had developed over a long period. Although the government, after independence, had shown its adherence to the British model, it failed to honour the voluntary principle in respect of wage determination in the public sector. Here, wage and salary changes have occurred, not as a result of collective bargaining, but on the recommendations of specially constituted tribunals. He therefore came to the conclusion that the imported British system of industrial relations in Nigeria had failed. However, Kilby's article is not concerned with the specific question of whether a new system of industrial relations had developed in Nigeria or not. Similarly, although a few other writers, including Damachi[2] and Diejomaoh,[3] have focused on some aspects of industrial relations in Nigeria, we are still left with the question of what system of industrial relations has developed there. Our aim in this study is therefore to trace and analyse critically the development of industrial relations in Nigeria, and specifically to determine what system has developed in Nigeria and to evaluate its prospects. Although we are concerned with labour relations in all enterprises in Nigeria, ranging from the very small to the very large, our main focus will be on the upper end of the scale from where most of our examples will be drawn. We do so for two reasons.

First, many of the companies in the first two categories are owned by private individuals, mainly Nigerians. The owners operate these enterprises on a one-man basis. Generally, in spite of the provision in the Labour Act 1974 which stipulates that within three months of a worker taking up employment he should be supplied with written particulars of his employment, these businesses are run on a completely casual basis without the conditions governing employment being stipulated in writing. As the enterprises are small, with the number of workers generally below fifty, and because of fear of termination of employment, many of these enterprises are without unions. Even where the enterprises are foreign, as in the case of certain restaurants or certain companies that drill for oil on contract to the main oil companies such as Shell–BP and Mobil, most of their workers are considered to be, and are treated as, casual. Only a few of the staff who are skilled or are supervisors are kept on a permanent basis. Again, trade unionism does not thrive in these circumstances.

Second, the Trade Unions Act 1973 provides that a trade union may be formed by at least fifty members. This means that the law itself recognises that an enterprise with less than fifty workers need not have a union. The Minister of Labour is, however, empowered to authorise that a union be formed by a lesser number of workers if he is satisfied that such workers are not members of an industrial or general union. In spite of that exception and in spite of the grouping of unions into industrial unions discussed later in the study, there are still many small enterprises, including hotels, drinking and catering establishments and garages, which have no house unions. The labour relations in these enterprises are determined by the owners or proprietors on a non-systematised, casual basis.

However, the fact that these small enterprises do not have unions does not mean that the workers suffer in absolute silence without redress. Workers in these organisations do in fact exercise their rights. They may resign their appointments or in some cases just walk off the jobs if they feel that they are not being fairly treated. Some have even embarked on strike action, as was the case of the workers of the K. Chellarams' Supermarket and the workers of the Quo Vadis Restaurant, both in Lagos. Both strike actions took place even though the workers had no organised unions. Similarly, six workers employed by a sewing mistress in Ikeja, near Lagos, went on strike because 'madam is always accusing us falsely'. Therefore, notwithstanding what we have said about focusing on fairly large and large enterprises, where we refer to the behaviour or reaction of the Nigerian worker in this study, we include all workers whatever the size of the enterprise they work for.

The study has six chapters. In Chapter 1 we review industrial-relations systems in various countries. These systems have been grouped into four categories: namely, the Anglo-Saxon model, the West German model, the communist model and the model in developing countries. In Chapter 2 we take a look at the economic, political and social aspects of the Nigerian scene, as a background to the theme of our study. The history and development of trade unions and employers' associations together with their role and that of the government are discussed in Chapter 3. Chapter 4 deals with the dynamics of the Nigerian industrial relations system. Here we analyse the machinery for the collective bargaining process at the enterprise and national levels. In Chapter 5 we discuss the machinery for dispute settlement. The discussion covers the voluntary internal procedures and the statutory procedures including conciliation, arbitration, the industrial court and inquiry. In Chapter 6, the final chapter, we summarise our findings and draw conclusions.

In carrying out this study I have been helped by a number of people. It is not possible for me to mention all of them here but there are a few of them who deserve to be singled out. I am grateful to Dr G. C. Routh of the University of Sussex, Brighton, who supervised this study. Without his encouragement and guidance I would not have been able to complete it. My gratitude also goes to Dr K. J. McCormick, again of Sussex University, who gave me valuable advice and showed considerable interest throughout the period of the study. I wish to express my thanks to my close friends who gave me encouragement and practical assistance. In particular, I am grateful to Professor U. G. Damachi, formerly of the International Institute for Labour Studies, Geneva, and now Dean of the Faculty of Business, University of Lagos, who started me off on this enterprise. I thank Dr I. C. Imoisili, formerly Lecturer at the University of Lagos and now the Executive Secretary of the Food, Beverage and Tobacco Employers' Association, who assembled a lot of source materials for me and provided useful suggestions. I am also grateful to Mr G. C. Okogwu, formerly Director of Labour, the Federal Ministry of Labour, and now the Director of the Nigeria Employers' Consultative Association, Lagos, who, drawing upon his experience in government, made available to me old government policy papers, reports and records. To all others who helped me in various ways, I am most grateful.

Lagos, Nigeria   ABEL K. UBEKU

1 A Review of Industrial Relations Systems in Various Countries

1.1 INTRODUCTION

Originally, the Nigerian industrial relations system was based on the Anglo-Saxon model with its emphasis on voluntarism. The adoption of this model had been necessitated by the fact that Nigeria was, for the period 1914–60, under British rule. The colonial power had imposed the models of its institutions on its colonial territories including Nigeria. However, after independence and following the upheavals caused by the army *coup* of 1966, the civil war that followed (1967–70) and the military administration which lasted for thirteen years, radical changes occurred in the socioeconomic and political spheres. Many established traditions and institutions were changed in the process. It was during this period that Nigeria moved away from the voluntary ethic in industrial relations into one of government involvement and intervention.

The question therefore is, to what extent has Nigeria abandoned the voluntary approach to industrial relations? What are the essential features of the current system? As we shall see in the study, the Nigerian industrial relations system is an amalgam of many systems. It has borrowed elements from the various systems being operated in different parts of the world. As a background to the study of the Nigerian system therefore, we shall examine some of these systems in this chapter. We start our analysis with a review of the Anglo-Saxon model as typified by the British system. Also included in this model is Australia to highlight its uniqueness in compulsory arbitration and to illustrate how the history of a country can make it depart from the original model. Moreover, the Nigerian system has some elements of compulsory arbitration and a comparison of the two systems is considered useful. We have also included the American system to illustrate a situation where the law plays a significant role and yet allows the unions and employers sufficient latitude to decide their own issues within procedures laid down by themselves. This element is present in the Nigerian system.

The German model with its system of labour courts has aspects that are similar to the Nigerian system. In both systems there is industry-wide collective bargaining. A comparison of the relevant aspects may be useful for our purpose. Government intervention in industrial relations in Nigeria has raised doubts as to whether the intention is to take complete control of the system as in the socialist states. Accordingly, we have included in our review the communist model, which is state-controlled and directed. We have chosen the Soviet Union to illustrate our point. However, we are aware of the variations in Yugoslavia and the recent changes that took place and are still taking place in Poland.

For comparison with other developing countries, we have chosen three countries which, like Nigeria, are ex-colonial territories of Britain. These are India, Tanzania and Ghana. It will be interesting to see whether or not these countries are developing their industrial relations systems on a different path from that of Nigeria. Finally, as the French approach to industrial relations in colonial Africa was based essentially on a Labour Code, we have included Senegal in this analysis. Although the Nigerian experience has been different, certain aspects of its industrial-relations system have been codified in the Labour Act of 1974 and the Trade Unions Act of 1973.

Before we start our review of the different systems of industrial relations, we shall first discuss the scope of industrial relations, and specifically to answer the question: What do we mean by industrial relations?

1.2   THE THEORETICAL FRAMEWORK

Different approaches have been canvassed as to what constitutes the scope of industrial relations. The *Marxist* approach insists that in capitalist societies, the state is always on the side of the employer in an attempt to protect the interest of the bourgeoisie. 'The executive of the modern state is but a committee for managing the common affairs of the whole bourgeoisie.'[1] Emphasis is therefore placed on the need to fight for democratic political institutions. These political institutions, however, could not be achieved without economic and social democracy. According to Miliband, the state stands for a number of institutions which together constitute its reality, including the government, the judiciary, the military, the police and other statutory bodies that are constantly used to harass and repress the trade unions. The state is therefore seen as a coercive instrument of the ruling capitalist class.[2] In the area of wage claims, the government under its income and deflationary policies interferes with the collective-bargaining position of wage earners. Thus, the state encourages employers to restrain workers' incomes, intensify work-pressure and work-discipline and reinforce managerial control at the point of production, thereby engendering conflict.[3] Conflict is therefore central in this approach. Richard Hyman argues that to define industrial relations exclusively in terms of rules and regulations is far too restrictive. Such interpretation confines industrial relations to the maintenance of stability and regularity in industry. The focus is on how conflict is contained and controlled, rather than on the processes through which disagreements and disputes are generated. In his view, therefore, industrial relations is the study of processes of control over work relations; and among these processes, those involving collective worker organisation and action are of particular concern.[4] The *pluralist approach* applies the analogy of pluralism in society to industrial relations. A society that encourages sectionalism, squabbling and conflict would be torn apart. However, if some societies prove relatively stable, as in the case of the developed countries of the West, then there must be some mechanism at work which binds the competing groups together and holds them back from rending their societies to pieces. This mechanism is the continuous process of concession and compromise.[5] Trade unionism as an interest-group in the society still bears the stigma of an alien and slightly disreputable force, acceptable only in its role of negotiating general wage rates and working hours, but of doubtful respectability when it comes to challenging management authority within the plant. But, 'the legitimacy and justification of trade unions in our society rests not upon their success, real or supposed, in raising the share enjoyed by their workers, but on social values which recognise the right of interest-groups to combine and have effective voice in their own destiny'.[6] The argument here therefore is for a more effective role for unions in the decision-making process and in the management of enterprises.

However, in the workplace the claims upon management consideration are many and wide-ranging. They include not only the work people but also its technical resources, its shareholders, the government and the local community within which the organisation operates. Consequently, management must maintain at least a necessary minimum concern with all these claimants and cannot, therefore, govern entirely in the interests of any one of them. In the words of Peter Drucker:

> the main function and purpose of the enterprise is the production of goods, not the governance of men. Its governmental authority over men must always be subordinated to its economic performance and responsibility .... Hence it can never be discharged primarily in the interest of those whom the enterprise rules.[7]

John Dunlop ('the systems model') has suggested that an industrial-relations system overlaps with the other sub-systems in the total social system; namely, the economic system and the political system[8]. In its development an industrial-relations system must comprise three groups of actors: the workers and their organisations, the employers and their associations, and the governmental agencies concerned with the workplace and work community; certain contexts, namely, technology, the market or budgetary constraints, and the power relations and status of the actors; and an ideology that binds the industrial-relations system together. Of the actors in the system, the government agencies in some systems may have such a broad and decisive role that they can override the hierarchies of managers and workers on almost all matters. Yet in other systems, the role of the agencies may be so minor and constricted as to permit consideration of the direct relationships between the two hierarchies without reference to governmental agencies, while in other systems still the workers' hierarchy or even the managerial hierarchy may be assigned a relatively narrow role. However, in every system, these three actors together create the 'web of rules' to govern the workplace and work community. These rules are made within the constraints imposed by the contexts and their ideology, and take a variety of forms in different systems: agreements, statutes, decrees, regulations, awards, policies and practices and customs. The actors in an industrial relations system are seen as confronting an environmental context at any time. In Dunlop's view, the central task of any theory of industrial relations is to explain why particular rules are established and how and when they change in response to changes affecting the system.

Allan Flanders ('Oxford approach') has described industrial relations as a study of the institutions of job regulation.[9] He argues that the only aspect of business enterprise with which industrial relations is concerned is the employment, the relations between the enterprise and its employees and among these employees themselves.

One way of identifying these relationships is to place them in their legal setting. They are all either expressed in or arise out of controls of employment (or service) which represents in common speech – jobs. The study of industrial relations may therefore be described as a study of the institutions of job regulations.[10]

The approach provides that the rules of any industrial relations system are either procedural or substantive. These rules are determined through the rule-making process of collective bargaining, which is regarded as a political institution involving a power relationship between employers and employees. A distinction is made between internal and external job regulation, the essence of the difference being whether the rules can be changed automatically by the firm and its employees without the consent of an outside authority.

Margerison takes issue with Flanders's conception of industrial relations.[11] He contends that industrial relations is a complex field of study which requires understanding at the behavioural, as well as institutional levels. As conflict is inherent in industrial society, there is a need to resolve it through agreed rules between the contending parties in order to avoid the use of violence or other non-legitimate measures. To this end, he identifies two conceptual levels of industrial relations. The first is the intra-plant level where most of the conflict is generated. Here, situational factors, such as job content, work task and technology and interaction factors, produce three types of conflict: distributive, structural and human relations. The second is outside the firm and in the main concerns the conflict-resolution mechanism for conflict not resolved at the intra-organisational level. But the framework is not so neat. Not all industrial-relations conflicts start at the intra-plant level, neither does all resolution occur within the formal structure.

The various theories discussed above have highlighted certain characteristics common to any industrial-relations system. These are

(a) *the key actors:* the trade unions, employers' associations and government and its agencies;
(b) the interaction of the actors and the conflict thus generated;
(c) the rules and regulations established through the collective

bargaining process, to regulate relationships including conflict resolution; and

(d) the role each actor plays or should play in an industrial-relations system.

Having analysed the theoretical framework for industrial relations, we now examine the four models of industrial relations.

1.3 THE ANGLO-SAXON MODEL

In this section our discussions will cover the systems in Britain, Australia, and the USA. Great Britain became industrialised first in the eighteenth century, while the other two countries became industrialised in the nineteenth century. Both countries were founded by immigrants from Britain. It is to be expected, therefore, that the developments which took place in the sphere of employer–employee relationships in Britain would naturally affect both countries. However, as we shall see, the history of each of these countries has shaped its industrial relations in a unique way.

In Britain, industrialisation came at a time when the philosophy of *laissez-faire* underlay all economic affairs. Consequently, this philosophy influenced employer–employee relationships in the free enterprise system. Even today the role of the state still exhibits the characteristics of that philosophy. Another important general point to note is that because these countries have been industrialised for a long time, a large proportion of the citizenry constitutes the wage labour force. This point is important in industrial relations when it is remembered that, in contrast, in the developing countries, only a small proportion of the total population forms part of the wage-employment labour force. Even then, that small proportion constitutes the growth part of the economy.

Other factors that influence industrial relations in these countries include the high level of literacy and the involvement of citizens in the democratic process, such as voting at elections, etc., which make it possible for the workers to want to have a say in the way things are done in their place of work; industrial discipline and commitment, attributes that were acquired over a long period; and the easy mobility of labour. All these factors distinguish the situation in the developed countries from developing ones.

1.3.1 Great Britain

In Britain, the Industrial Revolution led to the breakdown of the domestic system of manufacture and the growth in its place of entrepreneurial enterprises, which established the necessary conditions for the development of trade unions. These conditions were twofold:[12]

(a) the creation of an employer–employee relationship; and
(b) the congregation of numbers of employed workers in a common place of work and engaged on common or closely related tasks.

The situation was further accompanied by the accepted principles of a *laissez-faire* labour market, which replaced the long-established practice of state and customary regulation of economic relations. Labour became a commodity to be bought and sold at a price determined by the law of supply and demand, established through the higgling process of the market. In order to re-establish certainty and security, it became necessary for workers to combine against new methods and new values that had undermined the old. Thus, in the first stage, trade-union organisation arose as a protest against change in the organisation of production and exchange.[13] Thereafter, it sought to cushion the impact of the new system of production on the workers and to make it tolerable to them by the adoption of common rules of employment and mutual assistance. Also, groups of workers were persuaded to combine because organisation offered them the opportunity to improve their lot at the expense of other groups who were not allowed access to employment in the organised industries and occupations. In the view of the Webbs, the unions were called into being because of 'the economic revolution through which certain industries were passing (industries in which the great bulk of the workers) had passed into the conditions of lifelong wage-earners'.[14] Thus, it was the growth of industry, and the new methods of manufacture, mining and transport, which stimulated open and wide-embracing (as well as closed and narrowly limited) trade unions to seek to achieve improvements in the economic and social conditions of their members by the exercise of industrial and political pressure through mass membership.

The early part of the nineteenth century in Britain saw a vast movement of resistance to the traditional power of employing classes and the suspicious attitude of the courts. During this period trade unions were regarded as unlawful combinations. The attitude is reflected in the observation of the Duke of Portland, who was then Home Secretary: 'If nothing injurious to the safety of the government is actually in contemplation, associations so formed contain within themselves the means of being converted at any time into a most dangerous instrument to disturb the public tranquility.'[15] That view reflects accurately the thinking at the time and the confirmation that 'the first twenty-five years of the nineteenth century witnessed a legal persecution of trade unionists as rebels and revolutionists'.[16] The courts gave numerous judgements against combinations of workers, holding that such combinations were in restraint of trade and therefore illegal at common law. Finally, the Combination Acts of 1799–1800 provided for a general prohibition of combinations in all trades.

However, by 1824, the situation in England had changed to such an extent that Sir Robert Peel was able to say: 'Men who ... have no property except their manual skill and strength, ought to be allowed to confer together if they think fit, for the purpose of determining at what rate they will sell their property.'[17] Consequently, the Combination Laws Repeal Act of 1824 was passed to legalise trade societies. The Act provided that workmen or others entering into combination for the purpose of regulating wages and conditions of employment should not be subject to proceedings for conspiracy or otherwise. The immunity thus granted led to the widespread formation of unions.

In spite of the shift in thinking and attitude, the trade unions did not secure effective rights under legislation until the Acts of 1871–1906 were passed. Under these Acts, trade unions were legally recognised and protected. Trade unions were no longer illegal at common law because of their purpose in restraint of trade. The Act of 1875 permitted peaceful picketing and excluded from indictment as a conspiracy any agreement or combination to take any action in furtherance of a trade dispute unless such action by an individual would have been punishable as a crime. The Trade Disputes Act 1906 gave protection from civil proceedings to acts done by agreement or combination in contemplation or furtherance of a trade dispute. The Act also forbade courts to entertain an action against a trade union in respect of any tortious act alleged to have been committed by or on behalf of a trade union. These Acts together with subsequent laws that have been passed have established the unions' position in the industrial-relations system.

Meanwhile the unions, realising the role that politics and law had played in their development, decided to involve themselves in these processes. This decision led to the formation of the Labour Party and the election of workers' representatives into Parliament, with the sole aim of ensuring that the interests of labour were fully protected and catered for. Although the unions were thus highly concerned with political issues, the core of their purpose and activity was from the beginning to be found in the narrow context of improving wages and working conditions.

The three normative principles of the British system of industrial relations have been well stated by Allan Flanders. These are:[18]

(a) a priority is accorded to collective bargaining over other methods of external job regulations;
(b) the system has accorded a priority to voluntary over compulsory procedural rules of collective bargaining; and
(c) the parties to collective bargaining have generally preferred to build their relations more on their procedural than on their substantive rules.

On the second principle the Ministry of Labour's *Industrial Relations Handbook* says:

It has been continuous policy for many years to encourage the two sides of industry to make agreements and to settle their differences for themselves. The over-riding principle is that where there is a procedure drawn up by an industry for dealing with disputes, that procedure should be followed. Even where there is no agreed procedure of this kind it is desirable that the parties themselves should make an endeavour to reach a settlement. In either case some evidence of the use of procedure or an attempt to reach agreement must generally be forthcoming before the Ministry will accede to a formal request for its assistance.[19]

Kahn-Freund gives an explicit explanation of the third principle:

Compare the way collective bargaining is organised in a large section of the British economy with the methods used elsewhere. Here all the emphasis is on institutions such as joint industrial councils and the like, on the machinery, its constitution, above all its procedure. The substantive rules about wages, hours and other conditions are not, as they are in many foreign countries, built up as a series of systematically arranged written contracts between employers and unions. They appear as occasional decisions emanating from perma-

nent boards on which both sides are represented and sometimes they
are informal understanding, trade practices never reduced to writing. A very firm procedural framework for a very flexible corpus of
substantive rules, rather than a code laid down for a fixed time – such
is the institutional aspect of much collective bargaining in this
country.[20]

In other words, the British system is subject to little legal intervention
and tends to lean heavily on its procedural rules, the centrepiece and
most characteristic feature of the system.[21] With respect to the settlement of disputes the system relies upon voluntary agreements between
employers and unions as the means of settling labour disputes. Thus,
there exist statutory provisions for conciliation, arbitration and inves-
tigation or formal enquiry. Even in these cases, there is no compulsion
on the parties to submit to the statutory machinery.

Increasingly, however, the state is also assigning certain types of
disputes to specialised bodies. These include, but are not limited to,
industrial tribunals that have jurisdiction of individual disputes arising
under certain statutes; a Central Arbitration Committee (CAC),
which exercises a compulsory jurisdiction over collective disputes in
respect of the interpretations and application of specific statutes; and
the Advisory Conciliation and Arbitration Service (ACAS) which has
a number of roles, including recommending in appropriate circumstances that employers recognise and treat with trade unions, and
providing facilities for conciliation, mediation, arbitration and inquiry
in the context of both individual, and collective disputes involving
either rights or interests. Jurisdiction over still other kinds of cases
remains with the ordinary civil courts.[22]

Since the Second World War, and particularly during the last two
decades, voluntarism has been under attack as state intervention
continues to grow. The growth in state intervention has been the result
of two main factors. First, economic circumstances have driven both
Labour and Conservative governments into a series of incomes
policies. The implementation of such policies, especially the placing of
a limit on what the unions and employers may negotiate, is a negation
of the voluntary principle in collective bargaining. Second, there have
been attempts to control collective bargaining and trade unions by
direct legislative intervention. The ill-fated Industrial Relations Act of
1971 is a good example. Moreover, the present Conservative government under Margaret Thatcher, with its monetarist policies, shows
inclination to intervene in a more decisive way in industrial relations.

Thus, the system is gradually changing. As Flanders has correctly remarked, 'the voluntary tradition will have to be modified and public policy, even legislation is likely to have a hand in the matter'.[23]

1.3.2 The USA

The development of trade unions in Britain became a model for other countries as they industrialised. In the USA, the first trade unions were formed in the very early days of industrialisation by artisans. Drawing on the British experience the unions were strong supporters of radical political policies and pursued goals with the aims of reforming society. However, the American society founded on freedom and individualism did not take kindly to the new development; and it was not until workers concentrated on building trade unions with more narrowly defined occupational interests that they succeeded in establishing themselves as stable organisations.[24]

The unions met with considerable opposition from their employers, and they sought to achieve high wages and better working conditions by collective action. The employers' response was to attack the workers in the courts as engaging in combinations or conspiracies in restraint of trade. It will be recalled that a similar attitude had been adopted by the employers and government in Britain. But in spite of the vehement opposition from the courts towards trade unions, the union movement won its first victory in 1842. In that year the Supreme Court of the State of Massachusetts ruled that it could not be considered unlawful for workers to join a society whose purpose was to induce all those engaged in the same occupation to become members, or attempt to accomplish that purpose by refusing to work for any employer engaging a journeyman who was not a member. The legality of such an association would depend upon the means employed for its accomplishment. Thus, freedom of association for trade unions was for the first time given recognition by the courts.

However, trade unions only began to take firm root after the Civil War of 1861–5. As industry developed under the impetus of the construction of railways and the Civil War, unions likewise grew. During this period, some attempts were made to form national organisations but without success. The first successful attempt at creating a national labour organisation was the achievement of Samuel Gompers and others, who in December 1886 founded the American Federation of Labour (AFL). Later a split occurred in the Federation when a group disagreed with the Federation's policy of craft unions as opposed to their industry policy, broke away, and formed the Congress of Industrial Organisations (CIO) in 1938. But by 1955 the two federations had gained a new respect for each other following co-operation during the Second World War, which made it possible for them to merge into a single national labour organisation, the AFL–CIO, in that year.

In the USA the process of collective bargaining is a private system of industrial self-government, of which the collective agreement is only a part. The many rights of employers, unions and of employees that arise by virtue of the collective agreement often require litigation in the courts to resolve conflicts, as collective agreements are legally enforceable. Thus, the law occupies a prominent place in the labour–management relations in the USA. Originally, trade-union leaders – including Samuel Gompers and George Meany – had adhered strictly to the theory of voluntarism on the tradition that 'the state and the trade union could not complement each other; they could only co-operate'.[25] But later events changed that stand and the unions accepted the role of law in employer–employee relationships. Numerous legislative provisions exist in the country concerning not only the principle of freedom of association and protection of its exercise in practice, but also a wide range of trade-union activities. In addition to provisions relating to the right of workers to organise, and select representatives of their own choosing, there are provisions that affect trade-union activity in regard to collective bargaining, strikes, boycotts and the settlement of industrial disputes.

For example, the Wagner Act of 1935 provides that: 'The denial by employers of the right of employees to organize and the refusal by employers to accept the procedure of collective bargaining lead to strikes and other forms of industrial action or unrest, which have the intent or the necessary effect of burdening or obstructing commerce.' Accordingly, the policy of the USA was declared to be the elimination of these obstacles to collective bargaining, freedom of association and the workers' right to designate representatives of their own choosing. The Act thus formally recognised the collective-bargaining process. The Taft-Hartley Act of 1947 placed a new emphasis upon protecting the individual worker as opposed to the group. The Act placed a limit on certain union excesses and in particular identified unfair labour practices on the part of unions. There was thus an effort to reduce the power of the union over the individual, but at the same time no denial of the fact that the labour union was still the only effective means by which the working man could be represented in the workplace. The Landrum–Griffin Act 1959 recognised that in some unions the membership was prey to both gross and subtle forms of exploitation by entrenched officials. In response, the law specifies, among other things, that every member of a union shall have an equal right to participate in union meetings and elections. He is entitled to freedom of speech and association with other members in discussions including union affairs, both in and out of union meetings. No member of a union may be fired, suspended, expelled, or otherwise disciplined except for non-payment of fees, having been given every opportunity. Thus, the law regulates not only the relationships between unions and employers but also between unions and their members.

Although the law plays an active role in labour–management relations in the USA, it does not detract from, nor replace, the preponderant practice of voluntary labour–management relations. These relations are conducted without recourse to legal proceedings and without involving the procedures of the law. The provisions of the law, such as those of the Wagner Act, are supplementary to the voluntary system in that procedures are available at the request of the parties. The parties must file a charge or a petition to invoke the jurisdiction of the Board which administers the Act, wherever the voluntary machineries are inadequate or if the parties themselves desire the more formal procedure.

1.3.3   Australia

The development of the trade-union movement in Australia can be divided into three phases corresponding to the country's economic-development stages. The first period covers from the time of settlement in 1788 to the 1850s. This first period saw the development of small farmers and growth of a pastoral economy based on the vast expanse of land available. According to Kenneth Walker, this period saw the sporadic beginning of trade unionism, but no enduring organisation.[26] The second period is between the 1850s and 1890s. During this period the trade-union movement took shape as a powerful machinery for collective bargaining. An important corollary in this development was the gradual increasing interest in politics shown by the movement. This continued and, by 1901, all the states of the country were controlled by the workers' party–the Labour Party. Although agriculture was still the mainstay of the country's economy at this time, industry, especially mining, had started to make significant inroads. The third period starting in the 1890s saw the growth of manufacturing industry into a major sector of the economy, which in turn led to the development of an effective labour movement.

One significant factor in the Australian trade-union development is that the workers had the advantage of the British experience behind them. A number of the deportees were even trade unionists who were deported because it was felt that their activities constituted a threat to the state.[27] The country therefore had workers who knew about the role the labour movement could play in the economic and political life of their members.

Meanwhile, the democratic change in attitude towards unionism in Europe and the USA further helped the union movement in Australia to develop. Democratic revolutions were sweeping over Europe and the USA. The reverberations of all these happenings also reached Australia and this led to the development of effective trade unions. By 1880, craft unionism had developed a strong organisation along the British lines, and was bargaining successfully with employers in most of the skilled trades in building and manufacturing. This development led the government to establish a legal status for the unions by legislation that was patterned on the English Trade Unions Act 1871. The legal recognition of trade unions had become necessary for three main reasons. First, the vast wave of immigration to the country provided large numbers of new settlers who knew about, and were sympathetic to, trade unionism. Second, the long upswing of economic conditions created a labour shortage that gave labour sufficient bargaining power to build a strong organisation. Third, even with the gold depression that took place towards the end of the nineteenth century, the stranded miners could not be settled on the land as small farmers, and this accentuated the population in the towns. This concentration of population in the towns aided trade-union organisation.[28]

It will be seen therefore that the period after 1880 was a growth period for the labour movement in Australia. It is not surprising that the unions at the time felt strong enough to challenge their employers, which led to widespread strikes and dislocation in the country between 1891 and 1896. The disruption caused by the wave of strikes during the period had two important consequences for industrial relations in Australia. First, the country was compelled to introduce compulsory arbitration which, while recognising the unions' right to bargain collectively, nevertheless placed a check upon their power and thus restricted strikes. Second, the unions recognised the importance of legislative power as the law had been used to restrain its activities. As in Britain, they turned the labour movement towards politics.

It is only Australia among the countries of the West that has the distinctive and bold experiment in the social regulation of industrial relations through the compulsory arbitration system. The statutory machinery provides the framework for practically all industrial negotiations. The majority of employees in the country work under awards or agreements made under the arbitration tribunals.

At the national level the system consists of two distinct bodies: the Commonwealth Industrial Court and the Commonwealth Conciliation and Arbitration Commission. The Court exercises judicial function under the Conciliation and Arbitration Act 1904. This includes interpretation of awards and points of law, ordering of compliance with an award and imposition of penalties for breach of an award or other offence against the Act. It also covers the administration of the provisions of the Act dealing with registration of unions and employers' associations. The Court is the only final court of appeal in all judicial proceedings concerning the Act and its operation.

A significant aspect of the Commonwealth machinery on industrial relations is its emphasis on the relevance and importance of public interest in the matters concerning employers and employees. The Act defines 'industrial matter' to include: 'all questions of what is right and fair in relation to an industrial matter having regard to the interests of the persons immediately concerned and of society as a whole'.[29] Another provision bestows on the federal government the right to intervene in the public interest in any matter in which the Commission has jurisdiction. Similarly, the Commission is empowered to dismiss any matter or refrain from determining a dispute if further proceedings are considered to be against public interest. The role of the state in protecting the 'national interest' is very significant.

At the state level the form of machinery to be used differs in various ways among the several states and between the states and the federal government. Thus two states, Victoria and Tasmania, chose to establish wages boards, which are quasi-legislative tripartite boards for the direct regulation of wages and other conditions of employment. The other four states chose to establish arbitration tribunals, which involve the legal recognition of unions and employers' associations and procedures for settling disputes between them. Unions and employers' associations are obliged to register under the tribunal before they can be recognised. The effect of this system is that the collective bargaining process has become weakened. Unions have brought cases before the tribunals even when no real stoppage treatened, 'as a means of securing regulation ... the opportunity was seized of getting away from freedom of contract in the industrial field and of seeking the assistance of judicial tribunals to do what, in effect, was to make a contract of employment, with a statutory force behind it between the parties concerned'.[30]

In addition to taking cases to tribunals for decisions, the industrial relations machinery also makes provision, in varying degrees, for the making and legitimation of collective agreements. Under the law such agreements have little legal force unless registered with an arbitration tribunal. Under the state-arbitration systems, privately negotiated agreements may be registered without any prior reference to a tribunal, thereby becoming legally enforceable. Thus, of the three actors in the industrial relations system in Australia, the government and its agencies play a more dominant role than the other two actors – the workers and the employers.

1.4   THE WEST GERMAN MODEL

The Industrial Revolution not only spread across the Atlantic to the USA, it also spread across the Channel to countries of Western Europe. In the case of Germany, the early unions that came into being following the industrialisation of the country in the nineteenth century consisted of the free trade unions, Christian trade unions and Hirsch–Dunker trade unions, apart from the syndicalist unions.[31] However, the rise of the Nazis in January 1933 marked the beginning of the end for the German trade-union movement. The Nazi government ordered the occupation of all union offices and the arrest of union leaders, many of whom were sent to prison or concentration camps. Thus, at one blow the great unions built over fifty years, encouraged and strengthened by the Weimar Republic, were destroyed.

Modern trade unionism in Germany dates back to 1945 when, following the end of the Second World War, the trade unions started to regroup. This had to be done from scratch because there were no free trade unions between 1933 and 1945.[32] The efforts culminated in the emergence of sixteen industrial unions and the establishment of the German Federation of Labour, the DGB, at Munich in 1949. On formation, the Federation adopted a four-point charter stressing demands for full employment and maximum efficiency in the use of national resources, co-determination with management, nationalisation of key industries, a fair share in the national economic product and help for the elderly, the sick and the disabled. These principles were later to play a significant role in the industrial relations system of West Germany.

West Germany is the only country in the West that has the unique arrangement of co-determination in the management of enterprises. Co-determination was first introduced in the coal and steel industry in 1951 and a year later in all other industries. The object is officially stated to be to ensure that every citizen will be enabled to participate on a basis of full equality in every economic, cultural and political decision affecting his country because, as Professor Erhard put it, 'Labour, together with employers, have brought about the reconstruction of Germany.'[33]

The co-determination laws of 1952–76 provide for a 50 per cent representation of trade unionists on the board of directors (*Aufsichtsrat*) and the board of managers (*Vorstard*) of every individual plant. They also provide for works councils in every industrial establishment. The supervisory board decides basic over-all policy but its members do not intervene in day-to-day management. This is the responsibility of the management board, which includes a labour director, appointed with the approval of the worker members of the supervisory board.

The works council is an exclusive employee body elected by all plant employees regardless of union membership. The council plays an important part in the management of the enterprise. The employer must advise the council on the effects of personnel planning policies to be pursued by the company, and the council has co-decision rights in all such matters. The co-decision right also extends to other aspects of the business including the economic and financial condition of the company, the production and stocks situation, planned production changes and investment in new capital equipment, plans to rationalise the company's activities, and all other aspects of the company's operations and activities.

1.4.1 Collective bargaining

The usual collective agreement is the association collective agreement concluded between an employers' association and the relevant national union. However, a few organisations, including the Volkswagen Company, have special collective bargaining arrangements resulting in the enterprise collective agreements. Collective agreements are binding upon the parties that have concluded them. This is important in respect of the 'peace obligation' which is a necessary part of the agreement, although it is not formally expressed. The peace obligation is considered to be a part of the contractual section of the collective agreement and concerns only the terms of the individual collective agreement. What is not part of the agreement is not covered by the peace obligation. For example, a collective agreement on wages does not prohibit a union from striking for more time off, or even from engaging in a secondary strike.

The normative section of the collective agreement covers all matters concerned with working conditions. These conditions are binding upon the individual employers and employees who are members of the organizations that concluded the agreement. As these conditions become legally a part of the individual contract of employment, any waiver of his rights acquired in this manner by the individual employee is invalid unless the parties to the agreement have consented to it. The substitution of conditions of the individual contract of employment by those of the collective agreement enables the individual employee to bring suit in court. The trade union is not authorised to bring suit in its name, neither can trade unions confront the individual employer, because he is not considered a party to the collective agreement if it was concluded by the employers' association. If an employer fails to observe the terms of that agreement in his plant, the course for the union to take is to submit a complaint to the employers' association which must exert pressure on its members according to the so-called 'performance duty', another part of the contractual section of the collective agreement.

Collective agreements can apply to non-union members under two conditions. First, if they contain plant rules or if they change the constitution of the plant, for example the composition of the works council. These provisions are applicable to all plants owned by employers who are members of the employers' association that concluded the collective agreement and second, if they include joint institutions of the collective bargaining parties, for example, welfare plans, private-pension supplements, and wage-equalisation funds. Moreover, an employer may grant the same working conditions to all non-organised employees in individual contracts of employment. Also, the law provides that the Minister of Labour may, after formal procedure and under certain conditions, extend the terms of a collective agreement to such employees and employers.

In respect of collective bargaining, trade unions have been deprived of much of their influence within the plants by the introduction of the works councils, already referred to. These councils may take up all questions with the employer and handle grievances of the employees. They watch over the application of all statutes and collective agreements, as well as their own agreements favouring employees that have been concluded with the employer. Agreements between works councils and employers must be concluded with respect to social matters, such as the beginning of shifts, time and place of payment of wages, etc., but they may be voluntarily concluded for other purposes as well.

Employers and works councils are expected to co-operate with the employers' association as well as with the trade unions. They are prohibited from endangering labour and peace in the plant, especially from engaging in strikes and lockouts. This means that the works councils must represent the interests of the workers without the strike weapon. According to Professor Thilo Ramm, this explains their weak position if they are not backed by the unions. Consequently, everything depends on the strength of the union and the ability of the employer to keep it out of his plant. This is one of the factors responsible for the very slight influence of unions in small and medium-sized plants.[34] Works council–employer agreements may cover the same subject as do collective agreements, thus competing with the latter. However, in order to prevent the weakening of the unions' position, the Works Constitution Act of 1953 provides that works council–employer agreements are 'inadmissible' if wages and other conditions of work are usually regulated by collective agreement, except when a collective agreement permits a supplementary works council–employer agreement.

1.4.2 Dispute settlement procedures

The disputes settlement procedures are a combination of labour courts, arbitral process and works courts. These procedures are concerned with disputes over rights only, while disputes over interests are settled through other means including strikes and lockouts, etc.

(i) The labour courts

The labour-court system consists of three levels: the regular courts; the appellate labour courts which hear appeals on points of fact and points of law; and the Federal Labour Court which hears appeals on points of law only. The composition of all labour courts follows the same pattern: all panels are composed of two wingmen (laymen) and either one or three professional judges. The wingmen are chosen from the employers' and the employees' side. Together with one professional judge they form the panels of the courts at the two lower levels, and with three professional judges, the divisions of the Federal Labour Court. The one exception is the 'big division' (*Grosse Senat*) of the Federal Labour Court, a special institution established to provide uniform adjudication of the Court and to develop the law. The labour and appellate labour judges are appointed by the Ministers of Labour of the states from among groups of employers and employees for terms of four years. The federal labour judges are appointed by the Federal Minister of Labour.

Labour courts have exclusive jurisdiction over:

(1) individual disputes that include private disputes between an employer and an employee arising out of the employment relationship, over the existence or non-existence of an individual contract of employment or over obligations that remain after the contract of employment has terminated. It also applies to individual legal disputes among employees arising out of the employment of work gangs, for example, over gang piece-rate payment, or out of torts connected with the employment relationship. The exclusive jurisdiction does not apply to certain categories of persons employed – such as civil servants and legal representatives of corporations. However, such persons may contractually agree with their employers upon the optional jurisdiction of the labour courts;

(2) collective disputes that include parties to collective bargaining agreements and to works constitutions. This covers all disputes over the contractual section of the collective bargaining agreement, including the peace obligation and the interpretation of the normative section of the collective agreement. Only criminal and political matters, for example, political strikes, are excluded from the jurisdiction of the labour courts.

The Labour Courts Act of 1953 contains general provisions requiring these courts to attempt settlement of the legal dispute by compromise during the entire proceedings. To encourage compromise, the rules on court costs favour conciliation. If, for example, a compromise is reached before the labour court or an out-of-court settlement is reported to the court, fees are not charged at that level, even after a trial.

The law permits the appearance of a lawyer for a party in appropriate cases, especially in respect of proceedings before the appellate labour court and the Federal Labour Court.

(ii) Arbitration

The system of state labour courts can be excluded by arbitration only in a few limited cases. Only the parties to a collective agreement may provide, by means of a clause in that agreement, for arbitration, and then only in two types of cases: one involving disputes over the interpretation or application of the agreement, or over the existence of such an agreement; the other involving disputes arising out of contracts of employment of a small number of specialised occupations, provided that the labour relation is governed by a collective agreement. Otherwise, arbitration agreements concerning labour disputes, especially for normal individual claims and for all types of disputes arising out of the works constitution, are considered to be 'inadmissible'. This means that arbitration awards rendered under such agreements can be set aside by the courts.

Arbitration can take place at three levels:

(a) between the parties to the individual contract of employment;
(b) between parties to the collective agreement regardless of whether there is only one employer or an employers' association on the employer's side;
(c) between the employer and the works council within the enterprise.

Even then the state keeps an eye on this private arbitration through supervision by the labour courts.

The supervision by the labour courts is done in several ways:

(a) an award or a settlement before an arbitration board can be enforced only after the chairman of the labour court has declared it provisionally enforceable;
(b) a second possibility is by suit for setting aside the award. An award may be set aside for violating a legal norm, the so-called normative section of the collective agreement consists of legal norms. Thus, the legal interpretation of a collective agreement by an arbitration award may be fully supervised by the labour courts;
(c) if arbitration was not admissible; and
(d) if the award was based on criminal misconduct, such as false testimony, falsified documents, or deliberate miscarriage of justice by the arbitrator.

(iii) The works courts

These courts may be established either by collective agreement or by works council–employer agreement, dealing with specific 'social matters', that is, matters concerned with the order of the plant and the conduct of the employees. These private courts are tripartite boards composed of wingmen from the employers' and the works council's side and an impartial chairman. Their jurisdiction varies: they may settle cases of unjustified absence from work, drunkenness on the job, violation of fire regulations, damage to property in the plant, theft of plant and fellow employees' property, and of maligning or assaulting fellow employees. Sanctions usually are fines or dismissal.

It will be seen from the above analysis that the state plays a predominant role in industrial relations in West Germany. This predominance, argues Professor Thilo Ramm, is rooted in the country's history. According to him, the country's legal thinking is strongly influenced by the power of the state, 'rooted in the tradition of the feudal order, enriched by social legislation of the Weimar Republic and the dictatorship of the *Reichs* President in the last years of the Republic, perfected under the National Socialist regime, and finally assured by Adenauer's "chancellor democracy"'.[35] It is this legal attitude that may explain the attempts to incorporate unions and employers' associations into the structure of the state. In this regard, the interpretation of the terms of the collective agreements as legal norms is employed to consider unions and employers' associations law-making agents of the state, thus performing a function that is otherwise reserved for the state. Moreover, their participation in the labour-court system favours the trend to regard them as agents of the state. The attempt is to integrate all parties into the system, thereby minimising conflict and promoting economic development.

1.5   THE COMMUNIST MODEL

When the means of production are no longer privately owned as in the Soviet Union, the place of the workers changes radically because these means then become the property of the people, including the workers themselves. However, although there are no longer any private employers in factories and farms, the latter nevertheless need labour and the workers need employment. The work of the workers must still be organised and supervised, their working conditions must be settled and arrangements for their remuneration must be devised. In such circumstances, the workers who constitute the labour in the factories and farms and who also share in the ownership of the means of production must have a vital role to play.[36]

Another important point to remember is that the Soviet economy is centrally planned. The economic life of the nation is determined and directed by the state plan, and one of the aims of this plan is to raise the material and cultural standards of the working people.[37] Thus, the worker is not engaged in producing a return on capital invested by private enterprise but is considered to be taking part in an effort to promote the welfare of the whole population. Accordingly, whether he is employed in a factory or on the land, in mining or in forestry, on the railways or in an office or shop, he is either working on or making use of property that belong to the people.

Industrialisation did not come to Russia until the second half of the nineteenth century when machines began to oust the more primitive forms of manufacturing. From 1865 to 1890 the number of workers employed in the larger undertakings increased considerably, and the workers together with the intelligentsia demanded improvements in working and living conditions. But the absolute power of the Tsars and an oppressive political system tended to stifle independent thought and to forestall any attempts to improve the situation. However, a substantial proportion of the intelligentsia was in touch with European revolutionary movements and, convinced of the need for fundamental reforms in the economic and social system, became the organising force of the industrial and rural proletariat, for which it provided leadership. They organised strikes in several important factories, designed to drive home their demands.

The organised workers and their leaders, inevitably, came to accept that no significant improvement in the lot of the workers and peasants could be achieved unless the political system was changed. Political action and economic action were regarded as parts of the same process, and the conviction had grown that no solution to the economic problems could be found without the abolition of the political system.

The formation of trade unions was a part of the organised political drive and the clandestine left-wing parties had their cells in the various industrial centres of the country. Although the government applied a policy of repression, the workers' organisations had periods of legal existence and this enabled the clandestine parties to take firm roots among the workers and to carry on their activities under trade-union cover. This development shaped the character of the trade unions.

From the very outset, they were politically minded and constituted the main rank and file of the revolutionary parties.

1.5.1 The unions and the Communist Party

The right to organise is provided for in the law. The structure of the Soviet trade unions is uniformly industrial – everyone from the director to the lowest worker is a member. But membership is not compulsory, although non-membership involves the loss of many amenity rights including housing, holiday camps and even social insurance.[38] The central union organisation is the All-Union Central Council of Trade Unions (AUCCTU) while the grassroots organisation of the unions is based on factory union committees and their secretaries. The trade-union movement is obliged by law to receive its directives and guidance from the Party on the role it should play. In the opinion of Dr Schwarz, 'the Soviet trade unions have long since lost any trace of spiritual independence and have become accustomed to accept without question or discussion the directives issued by the Communist Party'.[39]

While the need for close links between the Party apparatus and the trade unions did not necessitate the keeping of the the unions as an integral part of the Party without an existence of their own, the principle was recognised that the unions had an educational part to play in the building of the communist society and that they should act as transmission belt between the Party and the masses, especially at the production level. Trade unions were essential for the purpose of building socialism and subsequently, as the state withers away, they would remain an 'educational organisation, an advising and training organisation ... a school of management, a school of communism'.[40] Thus, the trade unions were regarded as the link between the masses and the vanguard of the proletariat, namely, the Communist Party.

1.5.2 The unions and the state

The unions are regarded as standing between the state and the Party; at the same time remaining distinct from each other in order to be able to perform certain tasks that fell to them during the transition from capitalism to communism. The performance by the unions of major functions of a public character is not supposed to affect the independence of the union movement *vis-à-vis* the government or the free exercise of their trade-union right. Rather, it implies constant co-operation between the authorities and unions at all levels.

The trade unions must be looked upon as one of the mass organisations that go to make up the complex system of the dictatorship of the proletariat. The participation takes three main forms: independent activities; co-operation with state bodies; and direct discharge of certain functions which in other countries are functions of the state.

The first function includes the collective representation of workers at the factory level: union meetings, production conferences, negotiation and carrying out of collective agreements, etc., the organisation of socialist emulation; and the running of cultural and social activities.

Under the second type, the unions advise, assist and check the authorities in economic and social matters: production plans, output norms, scales of pay, and the application of labour legislation.

Lastly, the unions carry out certain functions which in other countries are performed by the state through a Ministry of Labour: social insurance, factory inspection, etc.

1.5.3 Collective bargaining

The collective bargaining process does not occupy the same pride of place as it does in the West. Indeed, the general attitude of the trade unions has been to leave the fixing of wages to the management in each enterprise. The rationale for this attitude was explained by N. M. Shevernik, Secretary of the AUCCTU in 1940: 'If the economic plan is the real base for the development of our national economy, the problem of concern to wage earners cannot be settled without reference to the plan or without taking its provisions into account. Thus, collective agreements have lost their *raison d'être* as a means of fixing wages.'[41]

Therefore, the negotiation of wages and other conditions of employment, which forms the basis of collective bargaining in the West, pales into insignificance under the Soviet system. However, the unions are active in other aspects, as we shall see below when we discuss the factory committees.

1.5.4 The role of the factory committee

The factory trade-union committee (*Zavkom*) is the most important trade-union institution in the plant. This committee has the responsibility for concluding collective agreements, directing the work of production conferences, supervising the observance of the labour laws, and generally for directing all union activities. As a standing body responsible for trade-union affairs, the factory committee is the principal operative organ of the trade-union movement and a vital link in its structure.

Moreover, the local union organisation has a significant role to play in three key areas: first, checking on the work of the management at all points; and ensuring that obligations under the production plan and protection of the members under labour legislation and the contract are carried out as fully as possible. Second, it also includes educating and leading the workers to know and fulfil their obligations and obtain their rights. Third, to serve the welfare of the plant's workers in a variety of ways.

In the case of labour disputes, where direct discussion with the management fails to achieve results, the disputes must be referred through the factory trade-union committee to the joint committee on labour disputes at the work-stage level. The worker may appeal against a decision of the latter committee to the factory joint committee and beyond that to the factory trade-union committee, which is also competent to hear cases on which the members of a joint committee have failed to agree. Both the parties to a dispute may appeal to the people's courts against the decision of the factory trade-union committee. However, disputes that arise during the negotiation of a collective agreement between factory trade union and management, fall within the jurisdiction of the regional economic and trade union councils.

There is no specific legislation that either grants the right to strike or bars strikes. Apparently, there are no strikes in the Soviet Union. The theory is that since the means of production belong to the workers, they do not have to resort to strike action as there is nobody for them to strike against. Some authorities confirm that the strike is used only at great risk, including risk of bodily harm.[42]

1.6   THE MODEL IN DEVELOPING COUNTRIES

The four developing countries we have selected for study, namely, India, Tanzania, Ghana and Senegal, differ from each other in many respects – location, size, population, natural resources, culture and political institutions. More significantly, not even the stage of economic development provides a common denominator. Indeed, one of the countries, India, is well over the hump on the road to industrialisation while the remaining three are still taking the first steps. In the light of the environmental variation in each country, it is not surprising that the institutions and practices of their labour markets show a significant diversity. However, on closer examination, certain uniformities can be discerned which, in spite of the fact that they do not fit into a neat theoretical pattern, nevertheless do throw some light on the labour-market arrangements prevailing in developing countries.

1.6.1 India

Trade unionism is a relatively recent development in most of the developing countries. In India, although the All-India Trade Union Congress (AITUC) was formed in 1918, the movement did not become effective until the Second World War when the leaders of the India National Congress used the movement to fight for independence. The immediate post-war period was one of violent industrial unrest. Faced with this unrest, the Congress Party – which had assumed control of the government of India at this time – promulgated the Industrial Disputes Act 1947. This Act, passed at the time of serious labour unrest, understandably embodied many of the features of the restrictive defence and emergency regulations which were in force during the war. None the less, the Congress Party in pursuance of its policy of moderating labour protest gave high-level official support to the labour movement. Indeed the labour movement was regarded as an arm of the Congress Party. In 1947, a conference of labour and management representatives was held in New Delhi, under the auspices of the government, to discuss the serious deterioration of industrial production because of strikes and to suggest ways of improving the situation. The conference unanimously adopted the 'Industrial Truce Resolution' calling on 'labour and management to agree to maintain industrial peace and to avert lockouts, strikes, or slow down of production during the next three years'.[43]

The Truce is significant in that it placed greater emphasis on the prevention and settlement of industrial disputes and on developing a system of mutual discussion and by resorting to the existing statutory and other machinery in a just and peaceful manner. In pursuance of government policy generally, and the recommendations of the Resolution in particular, the central and state governments passed a series of measures aimed at training the radicalism of labour leadership. Furthermore, it became clear to the Congress leaders that a rival national labour movement was the answer to what they regarded as AITUC's intransigence. In May 1947, with the full support of the Congress Party leaders, a new labour organisation, the Indian National Trades Union Congress (INTUC), was formed. In 1948 the government declared that the INTUC, and not the AITUC, was the most representative labour organisation in the country and supported its members to the ILO.

Meanwhile, disagreements erupted between the socialists and the communists in the AITUC over ideology. These disagreements came to a head at the conference held in Calcutta in December 1948, as a result of which the Hind Mazdoor Sabha (HMS) was launched. This was followed in 1949 by the establishment of yet another federation, the United Trades Union Congress (UTUC). The UTUC was formed by a group of left-wing socialists who broke away from the HMS, in order to 'conduct union unity free from sectarian party policies'.[44] Thus, four trade-union centres each with a different ideology claim to represent the workers in India.

In the area of employer–employee relations the government has been most active. In 1946 the government passed the Industrial Employment (Standing Orders) Act. The Act required employers of industrial establishments employing 100 or more workers to define in detail the conditions of employment which should be certified by a government officer after consultation with the workers. Meanwhile, the Industrial Disputes Act 1947 prohibited workers from striking without giving fourteen days' notice pending conciliation and adjudication proceedings. Compulsory adjudication became the cornerstone of labour-dispute settlement procedures. The Acts of 1946 and 1947 were substituted for the normal collective bargaining. Thus in India, the government is the pivot on which the whole industrial-relations system revolves. Not only did the government establish a legal framework for collective relations, it is also actively involved in determining the level of wages and other conditions of employment through its many agencies including tribunals and wages boards.

1.6.2 Tanzania

The first trade-union legislation in Tanzania (formerly Tanganyika) was passed in 1932. But as the colonial administration itself admitted, the trade-union ordinance was passed 'merely because it was the desire of the Secretary of State for the colonies to comply with certain international obligations'.[45] Even with the quickening of the economic tempo brought about by the Second World War, the government and its agencies did not consider it necessary to encourage unionism as a channel for dealing with the workers. They felt that 'in the present early stages of the development of industrial relations in the territory, it is preferable to fix the remunerations and conditions of employment in industry by statutory authority rather than by any system of collective bargaining in which neither side of industry is as yet experienced'.[46]

The dock strike of 1947 led to a change in attitude and the resultant efforts culminated in the formation of the Tanganyika Federation of Labour (TFL) in 1955. Thereafter, both the ICFTU and the British TUC helped the unions in the field of industrial relations.[47]

After independence in 1961, the government became totally involved in industrial relations. The political link that existed between the TFL and the Tanganyika African National Union (TANU) had continued after independence. Rashidi Kawawa, who had been president of TFL, was appointed Minister of Labour and continued to retain his union position. Two seats in the National Executive Committee of TANU were made available to TFL; while trade unionists were given government posts.

Meanwhile, the government introduced laws giving substantial benefits to the workers. However, these were followed by increased control by government. The government introduced legislation similar to that adopted in Ghana, under which the Minister of Labour had power to designate a sole federation to which all unions must belong. Strikes and lockouts were made illegal in certain circumstances. But in 1964, following the abortive army *coup*, the TFL and all other unions were disbanded and the National Union of Tanganyika Workers (NUTA) was established.

The establishment of NUTA ushered in a new system of industrial relations. The administrative structure of the union was centralised, and the day-to-day functioning of the organisation was remote from the elected representatives. The general secretary and his deputy were appointed by the President of Tanzania. All other administrative officers of the union, including the assistant general secretaries of the industrial divisions, the financial secretary, and the directors of the organisation and of Economics and Research, were to be appointed by the general secretary. These officers formed the Executive Council, responsible for the day-to-day administration of the union.

The first general secretary was Kamaliza, who was then the Minister of Labour. For all practical purposes the union became a constituent part of the Ministry of Labour. The projected functions of the new union were collaboration with government and employers in the development of a national wage policy; to enforce and to assist in the enforcement of collective agreements and awards and a disciplinary code; and to provide benefits for its members.

At the enterprise or plant level, the new system under the Security of Employment Act of 1964 provided for workers' committees that were supposed to be forums for discussions on production and productivity; however, the aims and objectives of these committees were so vague that they remained ineffective. Moreover, the over-centralisation of the industrial relations machinery militated against their effectiveness, as officials became remote from the workers. Following the report of an ILO mission to the country in 1967, the government established a Permanent Labour Tribunal, which was empowered to vet all collective bargaining agreements in accordance with a wages policy which placed limitations on annual wage increases. Apart from the internal structural problems of NUTA, the establishment of the PLT very much reduced NUTA's role in wage bargaining, and this again further reduced the changes of the union being close to the workers' representatives. Thus, an active government role weakened the role of the other actors in the industrial relations system.

1.6.3 Ghana

In Ghana trade unionism did not become a practical reality until 1941, when the then Gold Coast government passed a trade-union ordinance. The ordinance was passed at the instance of the British government which was interested in keeping the labour movement in the colonies primarily concerned with economic matters and thus not with nationalistic politics.[48] This legislation gave legal recognition to unions and a few unions registered under it.

The period between 1941 and 1956 was one of growth and development of the trade-union movement. The Department of Labour, which was established in 1938, had the specific responsibility of ensuring the development of responsible trade unions and to encourage good industrial relations generally. In 1943, the railway union, with the active encouragement of government labour officers, took the initiative in forming the Trades Union Congress of the Gold Coast. However, in spite of the active support given by the officials of the Department of Labour, the TUC did not accomplish much at the initial stage. This was the result of lack of experience on the part of the union leaders. Second, the principal constituent unions, namely, the Mines Employees Union and the United Africa Company Workers' Union, were only registered in the period 1945–8.

In 1950, the TUC called a general strike. It is significant to remember that at the time the TUC called the strike, political excitement was already running high and the newly formed Convention People's Party (CPP), led by Dr Kwame Nkrumah, was pressing for constitutional reforms. The day following the outbreak of the general strike, the CPP decided to initiate a 'positive action' campaign to further its demand for immediate self-government, and the two movements became inextricably mixed. Damachi and others believe that the general strike was a political strategy designed to coerce the colonial government.[49] It would appear that even the colonial government shared this view because the strike was broken by vigorous action which resulted in the imprisonment of some of the strike leaders and CPP leaders, among whom was Dr Kwame Nkrumah. As a result of these developments, the whole union movement went into a state of eclipse. By 1951 the TUC had been reformed with the aid of the Department of Labour, and individual unions also began to reorganise.

After Ghana attained independence in 1957, the government was anxious to have industrial peace so that it could implement its economic development and pan-African policies. To that end, it wanted complete control of the labour movement. It supported proposals that the sixty-four unions then affiliated to the TUC should be constituted into sixteen national industrial unions, and that each of these – while enjoying complete autonomy in negotiations – should operate subject to the over-all policy to be decided by the TUC which was closely associated with the government. The government backed its position up by the enactment of the Industrial Relations Act 1958. The Act abolished the TUC and set up a new one with facilities for check-off, and it also provided that for a union to operate as such, it must be certified by the Minister of Labour; and application for certification must be made through the TUC. Evidently, the TUC could use the big stick on any recalcitrant trade union. Thus, the Act assisted in the development of a centralised trade-union movement which now had to be controlled and guided by the CPP. The 1958 Act, with later amendments, today constitutes the statutory industrial-relations machinery in Ghana.

Unfortunately for the government, it assumed that once it had convinced the executives of the new TUC on any issue, it would have the support of all workers in Ghana. Thus, even when the effect of the worsening economic situation was being felt by the workers, the government was not able to see the storm that was gathering. That storm broke in 1961, when a general strike engulfed the whole country.

In 1971 the government passed a new Industrial Relations Act, which abolished the TUC. Consequently, the only unions that remained in existence were the national unions originally affiliated to the TUC. The unions, thus deprived of direction from the centre, acted independently of each other and for self-interest. The Act also placed a ban on strikes and lockouts and empowered the Minister of Labour to call off or suspend any strike or lockout he considered would endanger the national economy, the defence of Ghana, and the lives and property of a substantial number of people. In such a situation, the Minister could issue an order for the settlement of the dispute, which was to be binding on the employers and employees concerned in the strike or lockout. Such a settlement overrode the provisions of any existing contract or collective agreement.

The developments initiated by the government in Ghana have been based on the interrelated principles of compulsory negotiation, definition of and statutory remedies for unfair labour practices, provisions for compulsory check-off facilities and, between 1960 and 1969, there was compulsory trade-union membership. In the words of Professor Roberts, the trend in Ghana has been to restrict rather than protect the freedom to associate.[50]

1.6.4 Senegal

In Senegal trade unionism developed just before the Second World War. The first trade-union law for French West Africa was passed in 1937, but there were certain restrictions placed on union membership. To be a member of a union, for example, it was necessary to be literate in French and have the equivalent of an elementary school diploma. This restriction and the prohibitions of the wartime government prevented any real beginnings until 1944.[51] In that year it was decided that one aspect of the 'new deal' to be offered to a post-war Africa would be the encouragement of trade unionism. By a decree of 7 August 1944, literacy requirements for membership of unions were abolished and all the wage earners became lawfully organisable for the first time. As civil servants were very conscious of discrimination, the most educated elements among the African workers – the clerks and civil servants – spearheaded the movement. The administration was agreeable and Europeans from France were eager to help the Africans get under way. Consequently, labour organisations mushroomed in all parts of French West Africa and it is believed that a third of all those unionised were in Senegal.[52]

An interesting development of the trade-union movement in Senegal and other former French territories was the affiliation of local unions to trade-union federations in metropolitan France. The unions in Senegal, for instance, belonged to the French Confédération Générale de Travailleurs (CGT) from which they received constant help. This integration into the French trade-union structure had certain consequences. First, it led to pressure on the French government to legislate improvements in the conditions of work and the rights of trade-union delegates. Such pressures were reinforced by African representatives in the French Assembly. A good example of this type of politics was the passing of the Overseas Labour Code in 1952. This extended the French labour legislation to the colonies.

Second, it made the Africans insist on equality of treatment with their European counterparts. The railway strike of 1947 was fought over the issue of common conditions of work for Africans and Europeans. African trade-union leaders, especially of the white-collar unions, used the French colonial government's pronouncements of assimilationist idealogy against it in negotiations. The 'equality lever' was based upon the 1946 Constitution's expressed egalitarian principles. The use of the lever consisted of demanding alignments in wages and conditions of employment between (i) African civil servants and French ones, (ii) auxiliary and temporary public employees with permanent ones, (iii) employees in the private and public sectors. In this way, unions tried to extend wage increases for French public employees in France to African workers in Senegal.[53] Clearly, the situation could not continue and, by the Loi-Cadre of 1956, the African civil service conditions were established separate from those of France. In that year also, the local unions severed their relations with metropolitan organisations to assume their autonomy.

The industrial relations system is regulated by the Labour Code of 1952. The Labour Code is the main source of labour legislation in the country and collective bargaining plays a subordinate part in the regulation of the employment relationship. Individual firms may conclude plant-level agreements with their staff on secondary matters only; while individual employment contracts are standardised and conform to the Code.[54]

The role of the government in affecting the labour market by means of its policy of a wage-determination system is very significant. The wage policy is to link actual wages to the national minimum wage rate which is determined by the administration alone. Neither trade unions nor employers' associations have any direct means of influencing decisions of the administration in this matter. The trade unions at the enterprise level have therefore devised the strategy of raising wages by (i) category changes, that is, in all firms delegates present periodic lists of requested category changes for selected personnel, which are then presented with justification, (ii) delegates also try to raise take-home wages by increases in bonuses and premiums.

With regard to industrial disputes, individual disputes arising between employers and employees are settled by labour inspectors acting as conciliators and by labour courts, which were created under the 1952 Code. The main features of the labour courts are total absence of cost for either party for their use, extreme rapidity of the procedure and the presence throughout the procedure of a professional magistrate.[55] The right to strike is expressly recognised by the Senegalese Constitution 'within the laws that rule it'.[56] On the other hand, it is the policy of the government to contain strikes. In this regard, the procedure for settling collective disputes is complex. The procedure has three phases: (i) conciliation by the labour inspectorate, (ii) arbitration in the first instance by one arbitrator chosen from a list of personalities by the Minister of Labour, (iii) arbitration in the second instance by a council of arbitration; this council is presided over by the President of the Cour d'Appel and other members are: one civil servant, magistrates and experts selected from the list mentioned previously. Altogether, cases must be dealt with within sixty-five days. The procedure subordinates the exercise of right to strike to a decision taken by the Minister of Labour. Unless authorisation is given, strikes can break employment contracts of those on strike.

1.7 SUMMARY

Under the Anglo-Saxon model of industrial relations, there is recognition that the employers and the workers are the best judges of their problems and that the state, as one of the parties, should merely establish the framework to ensure success in the collective-bargaining process and in the resolution of conflicts. To that end, the government and its agencies do not play a direct role in these systems. Labour disputes, following from the recognition of the right to strike, are left to the parties themselves to settle through their own voluntary internal machinery. The statutory machinery for the settlement of disputes is only invoked when such voluntary machinery does not exist or where it is inadequate to deal with the particular dispute. In almost all cases, the statutory machinery is invoked at the instance of the parties. However, there is a trend towards state intervention under this model. Thus, in Britain a number of labour laws passed in recent years and the adherence to incomes policies by successive governments have increased state influence. In the USA, the system – though voluntary – accords a significant role to the law while in Australia the compulsory arbitration system is a complete departure from the model.

The West German model is a combination of state intervention, the collective bargaining process and the system of works councils. Co-decision-making at the plant level is a unique feature of this model. In dispute settlement, the system assigns a very dominant role to labour courts and a very modest one to arbitration. The labour courts are empowered to supervise the settlement of disputes by arbitration boards under collective agreements. Under this system, therefore, the state is predominant in industrial relations. The aim here is to integrate unions and employers' associations with the state in the industrial relations system, as a strategy of economic and social development.

Under the Soviet system, some salient features stand out. First, while unions exist as separate bodies they cannot act except on the directive of the Communist Party. Accordingly, what happens at the enterprise level is dictated by third-party economic planners. Second, wages, the negotiation of which forms the corner-stone of the collective bargaining process in the West, is left to management and government authorities to fix. The state knows what is best for the workers whose interest must be subordinated to that of the state. Third, unions administer social security and factory inspection, thus effectively fulfilling the role that would normally be assigned to a Ministry of Labour in the West. While collective bargaining takes place, the scope is restricted and is concerned more with the fulfilment of production targets rather than the improvement of the economic lot of the workers. The system is state-controlled and directed.

In the case of developing countries, the industrial relations systems are being shaped by their contemporary economic and political circumstances more than by the experience and influence of developed countries. Therefore Marx's assertion that 'the country that is more developed industrially only shows, to the less developed, the image of its own future'[57] now appears questionable. Of the three actors in the industrial relations system identified by Dunlop, the government plays a dominant role. Although there is collective bargaining, the process is hedged about with constraints. Such constraints include the significant role of the law and wage-determination policies of the governments. On the resolution of conflicts, again the state plays a leading role. In some cases there is outright ban on strike action and where it is allowed, there are arduous legal requirements to be fulfilled. The compulsory statutory machinery of dispute settlement is the norm and the parties are expected to comply: the underlying philosophy being that the unions together with the employers and government must ensure economic progress for the country. The model therefore has both elements of voluntarism and elements of state control. Our model for evaluating the Nigerian industrial relations, therefore, is as shown in Figure 1.1.

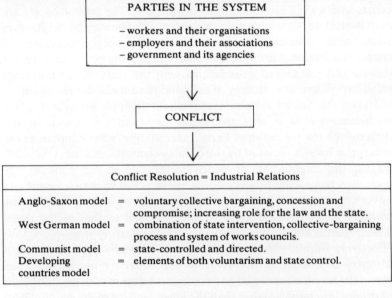

FIGURE 1.1　The industrial relations model

2 The Environmental Background

We define environment to mean those factors and events in Nigeria that have helped to shape the country's industrial relations. These include the historical and political development and the economic changes that have taken place over the years. They also include the sociocultural factors affecting attitudes and behaviour at work. It is within this milieu of interrelated factors that the parties in the industrial relations system interact.

2.1 HISTORICAL DEVELOPMENT

2.1.1 The period before 1960

Following the discovery in 1830 that the River Niger entered the sea through what is now known as the Niger Delta, many British merchants who had hitherto confined their commercial activities to the delta areas carried these activities into the hinterland. During the succeeding seventy years, the trade in palm oil and other agricultural products grew rapidly. It was first conducted by private entrepreneurs, but later – between 1886 and 1900 – these activities were taken over by the Chartered Royal Niger Company. The company had been formed under the leadership of Sir George Goldie as a result of his amalgamation of all rival companies.[1] Meanwhile, the Berlin Conference of 1885 on Africa had conceded British claims to the Niger Basin, whereupon the British government empowered the Royal Niger Company to administer, make treaties, levy customs and trade in all territories in the basin of the Niger and its affluents.[2] In the eastern parts of the country, the flag had also followed trade. Trade in oil had flourished in these parts since the 1830s and the British Government had appointed a consul in 1849 to supervise trading activities in the Niger Delta.

Again, following the Berlin Conference, the areas were proclaimed the Oil Rivers Protectorate. In 1893, having extended the protectorate over the hinterland, the British government renamed it the Niger Coast Protectorate.

In the western part of the country, Lagos was the centre of activities. It had been annexed by the British in 1861 and administered by a governor. In 1900, the Niger Coast Protectorate became the Protectorate of Southern Nigeria and in 1906 it was amalgamated with Lagos under the title of Colony and Protectorate of Southern Nigeria. These piecemeal changes came to an end in 1914 when the northern and southern protectorates were amalgamated to form the Colony and Protectorate of Nigeria, under British rule. The piecemeal approach had its implications for the development of the country and Coleman summed it up thus: 'The fact that such acquisition was piecemeal and occurred in successive stages accounts in part for the extreme uneven-ness in the degree of social change and modernization among the various groups and areas of Nigeria.'³

As a result of the activities of nationalist movements, it became obvious that political reforms would follow that would eventually lead to independence. The end of the Second World War saw an accelera-tion of constitutional reforms towards self-government. The first of these reforms was the Richards Constitution of 1946, which created three regional assemblies in the west, north and east, even though the country had not been formally divided into regions. The division of the country into regions did not come until 1951, when another constitu-tion was introduced which divided the country into three regions and brought elected government into Nigeria. The year 1951 is significant for our purpose because in that year three main political parties contested and won elections, each in its home base. Thus, the Action Group (AG) controlled the Western House of Assembly; the National Council of Nigeria and the Camerouns (NCNC)⁴ controlled the East-ern House of Assembly; and the Northern People's Congress (NPC), the Northern House of Assembly. Each of these parties was so entrenched in its region and the major ethnic groups in each that loyalty to the ethnic group transcended loyalty to the ideals of a labour movement, as we shall see later. Consequently, the idea of all the workers voting for a single party could not and did not arise, even though the labour movement had become a force in the urban centres of the country.

In 1954, a federal constitution was introduced for the country. That constitution spelt out the division of powers between the federal and regional governments. A significant aspect of this constitution was that the regions were given a reasonable degree of autonomy in political and economic matters. Internal self-government was granted to the Western and Eastern Regions in 1957 and the Northern region in 1959. Finally, with the experience gained in self-government, the British government granted political independence to Nigeria on 1 October 1960.

2.1.2 The period after 1960

Many people welcomed independence day with feelings of trepidation. The federal elections of 1959 that ushered in independence had been inconclusive. Two parties, the NPC and NCNC, had to form an alliance in order to form a government with a workable majority. Even then the alliance was shaky and this led to a feeling of instability in the country. Moreover, the division of the country into three regions by the colonial administration had been completely arbitrary and the regions were unequal both in land area and in population. This bred a lot of ill-feelings and frustrations.

The federal elections of 1964 and their aftermath brought these frustrations to the fore. There were accusations of open corruption and the political system was being wrecked by confirmed reports of open rigging of elections and the falsification of census results. The whole population was demoralised and it was a relief to all when the army staged a *coup* in the night of 15 January 1966. However, after the dust settled down, it became clear to everyone that the *coup*, as shown by those killed, was carried out in a parochial manner and there was a strong feeling that those who carried it out were attempting to install men of their own ethnic group in power. Thus, an action that had all the ingredients of unifying the masses had collapsed on the altar of ethnic loyalty. The lack of trust and faith in those who carried out the *coup* in January precipitated the *coup* of July 1966. The consequences of this second *coup* were more severe than those of the first. There were disturbances in all parts of the country resulting in the death of thousands of people. Many workers, especially those from the Eastern Region, left their places of work for the security of their homes. This posed a problem for the employers as many of their staff – most of whom were skilled – left. Moreover, the *coups* and riots had a shattering effect on the labour movement. It was no longer possible to talk of a labour movement as loyalty was to the individual's place of origin. When the civil war broke out in 1967, the employers came to the conclusion (as they did not know how long the war would last) that all workers who left their places of work should have their contracts formally terminated. Many of those whose jobs were terminated were reinstated at the end of the civil war in 1970, but a large number who returned to their places of work could not be absorbed. Meanwhile, the harsh effects of the civil war were being felt throughout the country. Oil exploration was disrupted, goods were scarce and inflation was high. The workers became restless and there was a spate of strikes in many organisations during 1968. As a result of this and in order to stem the tide of unrest, the federal government promulgated the Trade Disputes (Emergency Provisions) Decree 1968, which established compulsory arbitration and banned strikes and lockouts. It also provided that no changes may be made to wages and salaries unless by the approval of the federal military government. Thus collective agreements were made subject to the approval of the government.

One important constitutional change made by the military in 1967 was the division of the country into twelve states. The fear of one region dominating the others had been a source of friction, and the administrative changes that took place were clearly in the right direction.

When the civil war ended in 1970, it was expected that the military would arrange for a quick return to civil rule. Indeed, a promise was made that the country would be returned to civil rule in 1976. However, the military later changed their mind on the grounds that the original target date for handing over to a civilian administration was 'unrealistic', as former politicians had shown by their utterances that they had not 'learnt their lesson'.

The 'bloodless' *coup* of July 1975 was expected as things had deteriorated. The Wages and Salaries Commission whose report was published that year and the huge arrears paid brought chaos into the country's economy. The military administration that took over in 1975 gave itself a four-year term that it kept to rigidly. The country was further divided into nineteen states and the presidential system of government was introduced in October 1979. In the centre, the president is the chief executive while the Senate and the House of Representatives constitute the legislature (the National Assembly).

Each state is governed by a governor who is the chief executive, while the State House of Assembly is the legislature. Labour matters are on the exclusive list, i.e. those matters of federal nature and which should be dealt with at the national level only. When the military

handed over the reins of power to a civilian president, a workers'
delegation paid him a goodwill visit, hoping once again that things
would be better for them in the Second Republic.

2.2 THE NIGERIAN ECONOMY

The history of the economic development of Nigeria has been divided
into four phases.[5] The first phase covers the pre-colonial and early
colonial period and was characterised by economic stagnation. The
second phase was one of pronounced economic expansion during the
first thirty years of the present century, but this was interrupted by the
Depression and the economic crisis caused by the Second World War.
The third phase was therefore one of economic stagnation, especially
during the years 1929–45. The fourth and final phase was one of
renewed economic expansion following upon the end of hostilities in
1945.

Before the advent of Europeans on the Nigerian scene, economic
activities were restricted to the production of goods for local consumption. However, there is evidence of international trade between Northern Nigeria and North Africa, and the impact of this 'caravan' trade on
the development of the economy in that part of the country was quite
substantial.[6]

2.2.1 Agriculture

With the abolition of the slave trade, European merchants turned to
raw materials and trade developed rapidly in the Niger Delta areas of
the country. Originally, this trade was dominated by oil-palm products
that were mainly from the eastern part of the country. These were later
followed by cocoa which was produced in the western part of the
country, and groundnuts, cotton, and hides and skins from Northern
Nigeria. Thus Nigeria moved from the era of production of goods for
local consumption into the export market.

An important point in the economic development process of Nigeria
that is relevant to our study is the fact that while in some colonial
territories in Africa – such as the Camerouns and Tanganyika (now
Tanzania) – it was the Germans who owned the huge plantations and
the British did the same in Kenya, Uganda and other East African
countries which included Tanganyika after the First World War, in

Nigeria the export crops were the sole handiwork of the peasant farmers, whose motivation was the wealth generated by the sale of cash crops.

The economic depression that hit the world in 1929 also had its shock waves in Nigeria. Nigeria's exports fell drastically from ₦35.2 million in 1929 to ₦17.2 million in 1931, a drop of 48.8 per cent in two years.[7] The situation was not helped by the onset of hostilities in 1939, and in 1945 the value of Nigeria's exports was the same as in the year 1929. Ludwig Schatzl believes that as only minor growth in incentives came from other sectors of the economy the per capita income of the Nigerian population probably remained unchanged for almost two decades.[8]

The decline in economic growth brought about by the Second World War was replaced by steady economic growth on the termination of the war in 1945. In 1954 the International Bank noted that Nigeria's economy had in less than ten years since the war ended grown and strengthened to such an extent as to bear little resemblance to the pre-war economy.[9] Yesufu says that the initial impetus for the growth at the time came from wartime and expanded post-war world demand for Nigerian export produce, mainly cocoa, groundnuts, rubber, palm produce and timber.[10] The post-war boom also led to expansion in other sectors – in commercial transport undertakings, commercial banking, manufacturing industries, including cement, textiles, cigarettes, beer, paper, plastics, motor assembly plants, among others.

Meanwhile, to help in the development process and to enable agricultural products to be transported to the coast for easy shipment to Europe, the colonial government had embarked on the development of the infrastructure. In 1896 work started on a narrow-gauge railway line, which eventually reached Kano, the centre of the groundnut growing area, in 1911. Following the discovery of coal in Enugu, a second line was started from Port Harcourt which reached Enugu in 1916. This line was later extended to Kaduna and Jos, the latter city being the centre of the tin mines. However, while agricultural products for export were solely in the hands of local indigenous farmers, mining – the earliest industry in the country – was in the hands of foreign entrepreneurs, who employed capital-intensive production methods in extracting the minerals.

Until the second half of the 1960s, the economy of the country depended mainly on agricultural products, including cocoa, groundnuts, rubber and palm oil. In 1960 agriculture accounted for 70 per cent of the GDP,[11] but agricultural products were and still are subject to the violent fluctuation in prices in the world market. Accordingly, earnings from that source were not very reassuring. At this time the petroleum industry was still in its infancy.

During the first five years of independence, finance was a great constraint and the government found it difficult to carry out its development projects. All this led to general dissatisfaction, including unemployment in the urban areas. With the development of the petroleum industry in the country, the contribution of agriculture to the national economy began to decline. The contribution of agriculture to GDP at current factor prices fell from 61.2 per cent in 1962 to 28.2 per cent in 1976/77.[12] Similarly, the growth rate has been declining. So, while industry had a growth rate of 5.2 per cent in 1972, agricultural growth fell to 6.3 per cent. Even then agriculture accounted for 70 per cent of the total labour force in 1970 and current estimates put the figure at about 64 per cent.[13] The decline of agriculture, with its many economic disadvantages, has implication for school leavers who are forced to move into urban areas to look for industrial employment. Even for those who are fortunate enough to be employed, there is the problem of the high cost of foodstuffs, occasioned by too few people working the land.

2.2.2 The manufacturing industry

Although West European countries, especially Britain, had carried out commercial activities in Nigeria since the early part of the nineteenth century, industrialisation did not start until the mid-1950s. At the time of Nigeria's First Development Plan in 1946, there was scarcely any modern industrial enterprise in the country. In spite of the abundance of raw materials which could have made such a process possible, real industrialisation had to wait until just before independence.

A view has been put forward regarding the late take-off of industrialisation in the country. It is believed by some that the non-industrialisation of the country was a deliberate policy of the then colonial rulers, the British. According to this theory, Britain wanted Nigeria, like its other colonial territories, to be merely a source of raw materials to be processed in the metropolitan country, and then exported back to these same countries.[14] Thus, in spite of the dominating role of the British commercial activities in the country, industrialisation was not considered essential. This policy was adopted by other European merchants also who merely carried on the business of purchasing and export of raw materials and the importation of goods and their distribution throughout the country. The rejection of industrialisation by the foreign enterprises in order to protect their own trading interests had other important consequences for the labour situation in the country. First, as the organisations were only concerned with commercial activities, their workers were scattered throughout the whole country, a condition hardly conducive to the formation of worker organisations. Thus, although trade unions were in existence during the decade 1940–50, they were few, ineffective and confined to government establishments. Second, the non-industrialisation of the country early in the century deprived the nation of that industrial tradition and discipline which might have speeded up today's efforts if workers had been exposed to industrial discipline for the last fifty years.

However, changes were bound to occur and they did occur. After the Second World War, the process of industrialisation was actuated by the competition of foreign enterprises for the huge Nigerian market and accelerated by the industrial policy of the government as the country moved towards independence. The competition to import and sell various items had become intense during the decade 1945–55. The situation was no longer a monopoly of European companies. Asian, Greek-Cypriot, Lebanese and Syrian merchants, among others, joined in the struggle but, more significantly, Nigerians were not left behind since all that was involved was to import and sell. The signals became loud and clear: there had to be a switch to industrialisation. Moreover, government policy was deliberately devised to encourage the trend. The most important of these was the Aid to Pioneer Industries Act 1952. Under the Act, any industry that satisfied the provisions – basically that the industry was favourable to Nigeria and thus in its interest to assist – was declared a pioneer industry and relieved from the payment of company tax for a period of up to five years. Other benefits under the Act included generous depreciation rates, and a great variety of tariff concessions.

Other legislation exempting pioneer companies from income tax include the Industrial Development (Income Tax Relief) Act 1958; while the level of depreciation for such companies was regulated by the Income Tax (Amendment) Act 1958, and the Income Tax (Admendment) Act 1960; and the tariff concessions were regulated by the Industrial Development (Import Duties Relief) Act 1957, Customs Duties (Dumped and Subsidised Goods) Act 1958, and Customs (Draw Back) Regulations 1958. Thus by a whole series of fiscal measures the government hoped to stimulate industrialisation. As a result of these measures, a number of industries were established in the decade beginning in 1960, essentially all geared to import substitution.

The manufacturing industry has been dominated by foreign enterprises led by Britain. This domination has not been confined to the manufacturing sector only, but also the commercial, including banking and insurance and the distributive and retail trade. In 1977 the federal government enacted the Nigerian Enterprises Promotions Act.[15] Under this Act foreign enterprises are required to concentrate their activities on manufacturing and not to operate in such areas as retail and distribution. In areas where they are allowed to operate, it had to be on a partnership basis with Nigerians. The enterprises are expected to sell a substantial proportion of their equity shareholding to Nigerians, the actual ratio being determined by the nature of the business as classified under Schedules II and III of the Act. The 'indigenisation' of equity was supposed to be followed by the 'indigenisation' of managerial positions. Thus, Nigeria and Nigerians will be placed at the 'commanding heights of its economy'.[16]

2.2.3 The petroleum industry

In the financial period 1970–1 the share of oil in the GDP was 33.1 per cent, while in 1974–5 it was 45.5 per cent.[17] The growth rate of the GDP in real terms rose from an average of 5 per cent in the 1960s to 7.6 per cent during the period 1970–5 and to 10.3 per cent in 1976–7. In 1976, earnings from oil were 93 per cent. The projected contribution from the industry during the third Development Plan 1975–80 to the GDP was 40 per cent, while its contribution to government revenues and foreign exchange was estimated at 85 per cent.

The importance of the oil industry is further reflected in Nigeria's external reserves, its annual budgets, and the major projects undertaken in recent years. Table 2.1. shows the dominant role of the industry's foreign exchange earnings compared with the traditional agricultural products. As can be seen from this table, the growth in the oil sector has had implications for industrial and commercial development. Because money was available, the Nigerian potential was quickly spotted by entrepreneurs who, having sized up the opportunities, moved in. Furthermore, the 'oil boom' enabled the government to engage in modernisation of the country's infrastructure, roads, telephones and other public utilities. The construction and building industry in particular flourished. These in turn created employment and acted as a stimulus to industrial development. More importantly, as

TABLE 2.1 Nigeria's external trade: exports (₦ million) 1970–80

Description	1970	1971	1972	1973	1974	1975	1976	1977	1978	1979	1980
1. Oil sector											
Petroleum (crude)	510.0	953.0	1176.2	1893.5	5365.7	4563.7	6321.6	7072.8	5401.6	10166.8	13523.0
2. Non-oil sector											
Cocoa	133.0	143.2	101.1	112.4	159.0	181.8	218.9	311.1	377.9	432.2	311.8
Groundnuts	43.6	24.4	19.1	45.5	6.8	—	0.2	0.1	—	—	—
Palm kernels	21.8	25.8	15.7	18.9	43.7	13.5	27.0	32.6	12.7	11.8	11.5
Rubber (natural)	17.4	12.4	7.4	19.4	33.2	15.2	14.4	11.1	12.6	13.0	11.8
Timber (logs and sawn)	6.2	5.2	8.1	1.5	11.2	4.6	0.9	0.5	0.1	—	—
Tin metal	33.8	24.2	19.1	15.5	26.4	20.4	15.5	13.3	9.4	10.8	9.8
Other exports	199.6	105.2	87.5	171.7	148.8	122.7	152.6	189.1	187.7	147.2	147.0
	455.4	340.4	257.4	384.9	429.1	358.2	429.5	557.8	600.4	615.0	491.9

— = no exports.

Source: Nigeria's Principal Economic and Financial Indicators, 1970–80, issued by the Central Bank of Nigeria.

money was no longer a constraint, the government was not contented only with providing the infrastructure and right atmosphere. It undertook direct investment in industry, either alone or in association with private enterprise. Thus, examples of the federal and state governments' initiative in that direction abound in the country, including textiles, meat processing, hotels, cement factories, beer breweries, transport companies, glass manufacturing and mineral extraction. Consequently, the governments of the country are today employers of labour not only in the public sector but also in the private sector. This is one reason why it is difficult for the federal government not to intervene constantly in employer–employee relationships, even if such disputes originate from the private sector.

In the area of direct employment, however, the expansion of the petroleum industry has had relatively little effect. In 1956 the oil industry employed about 3000,[18] and this rose to over 17 000 in 1965.[19] As at the end of 1978 the number directly employed was estimated at 23 000. In comparison with its contributions to the national revenue, that number is insignificant. However, while the direct consequences on employment may be slight, the industry has achieved other growth promotion factors which usually constitute constraints in developing countries. These include capital, adequate foreign reserves and skilled labour. The availability of these resources, which are associated with the development of the industry and the linkage effect of the petroleum companies, is particularly significant. Thus in 1965 a new refinery was opened at Port Harcourt, and this was followed by two more, one at Warri (1978) and the other in Kaduna (1980). Again, the Ajaokuta Steel Mill, the steel plant at Warri and the huge electric plant at Sapele all flow from the 'effects' of the oil industry. In addition to the very many uses that natural gas may be put to, including electricity and cooking gas, the industry is likely to generate many other industries, including plastic products, caustic soda and nitrogenous fertilisers. These government investments, financed from petroleum revenue, have the effect of stimulating the growth and development of the industrial labour force.

The implication of these developments is that the government was led to believe that salvation lay in oil, especially following the role oil played in the crisis of 1973 during the Middle East conflict. Therefore, when economic recession, which was world-wide, started in 1982, followed by the 'oil glut', Nigeria was completely unprepared for the shock. In telling the nation about the problem in a nationwide television in April 1982, the President said:

The inception of the civilian government in October 1979 brought with it a desire on the part of all governments of the Federation to meet the rising expectations of our people. The Federal Government embarked upon, in good faith and in the expectation that the flow of revenue from oil will continue, development programmes and import liberalisation aimed at improving the standard of living of our people. Unfortunately, in the midst of the implementation of these schemes, we suffered some economic setbacks of which the present is the most severe.

The President then sought to remedy the situation by the enactment into law, of the Economic Stabilisation Act, 1982. The Act gave him powers to impose whatever legitimate measures that were necessary. Under these powers the Federal Government introduced measures which had three aims:

(a) to reduce the level of imports and conserve the scarce foreign exchange
(b) to encourage and protect local industries
(c) to ensure strict adherence to government priorities.

Also, the government reduced the price of its premium oil by $5.50 to $30 a barrel.

In a nutshell, the measures became necessary because Nigeria had become an oil-dependent nation that had not planned for the day there would be no oil, and had embarked upon development projects which were beyond her means, fuelled by preference for foreign goods to the detriment of locally assembled or manufactured goods.

However, although it is too early to make an accurate forecast of how Nigeria will weather the economic crisis, there was general agreement with the President when he said in his 1983 Budget Speech:

I am pleased to say that these measures are yielding expected results. Already imports are down by 20 per cent and the indications are that they will go down further by the end of the year. Furthermore, there is encouraging indication that the business community is beginning to enjoy the benefits of these measures. Also it is hoped that the measures will lead to the mobilisation of domestic savings, investments, reduction in the rate of inflation and substantial improvement in the balance of payments position. Ultimately, we expect these measures to produce a growth rate of not less than 3 per cent in the Gross Domestic Product and an increase of ₦900 million in our external reserves.

The optimism expressed in the budget on the recovery of the Nigerian economy is not entirely misplaced. The economy has always been resilient, as evidenced by the fact that in spite of the difficulties the country experienced during the thirty-month civil war (including low output of oil) the economy was intact by the time the war ended in 1970. The general belief is that as the economic crisis in Nigeria is due mainly to world economic recession, as the world economic situation improves, Nigeria will be once again on the path of economic progress.

Development projects which were delayed or abandoned will once more be resuscitated and this will have far-reaching impact on the demand, supply and utilisation of resources, human and financial. Expanding employment opportunities will increase the intensity of competition by employers for the scarce skilled and managerial personnel. That situation helps the bargaining position of the workers and may lead to higher wages and fringe benefits. Education expansion and increased output from all levels in the education system can be expected to produce a more educated and skilled work-force. This category of workers can be expected to be very articulate in demanding their 'right' in what is expected to be a boom situation. As Nigeria becomes developed and transformed into a modern industrial society, the traditional aspirations will expand to include job security, participation in work decisions, etc. The educated work-force is fully aware of events around them, and with the change in the economic environment the workers will seek to achieve and maintain a sense of personal worth and importance, and to receive recognition and reward for what they do.[21] This will throw a direct challenge to the employers, the other actors in the industrial relations scene, in trying to balance the competing interests of the workers, the shareholders and the society.

2.3 SOCIO-CULTURAL FACTORS

The social and cultural factors which constitute the structure of a society have an important role in the development of an industrial relations system in any country. These factors affect and influence the behaviour of people and their general attitude to work and to leadership, to group cohesion and to their individual role in an organisation.

In this section, we shall examine certain of these societal factors in the Nigerian scene and determine their impact on the Nigerian worker. In this connection, the relevant question to ask is: what is the background of the industrial worker in Nigeria? As industrial workers migrate from the rural to the urban centres, we now take a brief look at life in the village.

2.3.1 The rural background

Nigeria is still essentially rural. The bulk of the population is unskilled in the modern sense of the word and is engaged primarily in agricultural pursuits, as we have already seen. The hub of activity in the village is the family,[21] the immediate social unit regulating the life of the individual – both socially and economically. The economic activities of the people are exclusively on the land, the mainstay of their livelihood. Land does not belong to an individual; it belongs to the family and is managed on behalf of all by the oldest male member of the family. The head of each household is allotted a piece of land for farming by the head of the family acting on behalf of the family. The farmer, his wife and children then work the land, with the farmer directing the farm policy. He is responsible for the decisions as to how income realised should be spent. Generally, wage payment is not involved but the farmer provides the needs of his wife and children.[22] Where members of a household are in difficulty, the family comes to their aid. Thus, a system of social security exists, designed to ensure the survival of the family and its members.

The pace and continuity of rural life is quite different from that of an industrial enterprise. In the village there is generally a low level of demand which is easily satisfied. Life is regulated not by the clock but by seasons and the individual's discretion. Wells and Warmington, commenting on the situation in Nigeria and the Camerouns, state the position as follows:

> sustained effort for set period of time is not required. Specialization merely involves the allocation of duties according to sex and age, and is sanctioned by custom. The same tribal authority governs the entire way of life, in which there is no sharp dichotomy between work and other activities.[23]

In the past the rural agricultural workers would all be illiterate, but with the expansion of educational facilities during the past twenty-five years, a substantial proportion of the workers between the ages of 20 and 30 would be literate, holding at least primary school certificates. This then is the heritage that the agricultural worker brings to his new industrial job in the urban centres.

2.3.2 The effect of societal factors on the Nigerian worker

The background discussed above which is common to workers in developing countries has led to the popular belief that workers in these countries come to modern industry with a handicap. The theory holds that as the whole background is the rural subsistence economy, where the tempo is regulated by farming seasons and is characterised by the informal and traditional life on the land, the job seeker who comes to the urban area for industrial employment with no experience of modern machinery and a general lack of rigid discipline which modern industrial employment demands, is at a severe disadvantage. Furthermore, having been 'pushed' from the land in the village into the urban areas, there is again the 'pull' towards the village and to the family to which the individual belongs. Consequently, it is believed that such workers refuse to commit themselves to life in the city and the discipline of factory work, while yet others return to the village to take up family responsibilities.[24] As a result, it is assumed that productivity is low and absenteeism and labour turnover are high. It is further assumed that the period of work is sporadic and that the workers are not really interested in the work but the money it provides, and that as soon as reasonable amounts have been accumulated such workers give up their jobs, thus creating high labour turnover problems.

This assumption has been completely eroded and must now be abandoned, because of recent findings in a number of developing countries, including Nigeria. In his study of the Egyptian situation, Harbison confirms that Egyptian employers identified their principal labour problem as one of lack of freedom to discharge rather than one of ability to recruit and commit workers to industrial employment.[25] In all cases, absenteeism and slack discipline in the factory appear to be more a function of poor management than of any inherent characteristics of the labour force. As labour is relatively cheap, there is a tendency to use it wastefully, 'a practice which does not breed careful habits in the labourer himself'.[26] Berg's studies in the former French West African territories also confirm that workers seem to be quite responsive to the economic incentives that are customary in advanced countries.[27] He found for example that many employers justified the low wages they were paying by the theory of the backward bending labour supply function. On closer inquiry, Berg found that the labour available to an employer was directly related to wages and conditions of employment and that the supply curve of labour was positively inclined throughout its relevant portion. Lack of economic motivation by workers did not appear anywhere as a serious consideration.

In the case of Nigeria, most of the arguments used to prove the case that the so-called lack of labour commitment in the developing countries is not universal are apposite. It is our submission that the mere fact that workers in the urban centres of Nigeria pay occasional visits to the village and to their families should not be seen as a negative factor. Indeed, it may well be a positive one. The social problems of overcrowding, lack of water, hospital care, etc., in the urban cities in Nigeria (especially Lagos) where most industries are located, have so much induced tensions that an occasional visit to the village may help relieve the strain. In fact, there is generally an exodus from Lagos every Friday afternoon, of employees of all grades and categories, including white-collar workers and senior civil servants and managers in industry, who originate from the nearby states. During festival occasions such as Easter, Christmas and Muslim festivals, many employees take the opportunity of going to their villages. This is an escape from crowded cities and, in our view, has nothing whatsoever to do with lack of commitment to their jobs to which they return on Monday morning.

Moreover, we think that the positive side of village and family ties has been overlooked. We believe that in the context of Nigeria, these ties contribute greatly to the stability of the industrial labour force and not the other way round. First, the family constitutes security to the individual and the individual has a defined role to play in it. Second, there is high regard for age and experience and the individual is prepared to accept the leadership of the older and more experienced person. Third, following the second point, the individual in the rural family is subject to a rigid discipline and family (team) cohesion and is prepared to contribute to ensure the survival of that family. Therefore, the individual who comes to the urban centres to look for a job is not completely 'green', as he comes with ingredients of respect for properly constituted authority (his manager, for example), respect for a more knowledgeable and experienced person (e.g. his supervisor), and has the discipline demanded by the group (such as a union). These attributes are not very different from those that are needed in the modern industrial sector. The foundation on which to build the new industrial discipline already exists. It is an exaggeration to insist that these attributes are not relevant.

Furthermore, there is no evidence to show that the Nigerian worker lacks commitment to his employer either in the form of low productivity, or a high rate of absenteeism and/or labour turnover. Hans Seibel has argued that it is without foundation to assume that there is something inherent in the African worker that produces this result.[28] Rather, the process is that of social change. In Seibel's view, wage labour has become fully integrated into normal life, it has replaced agriculture or craft work carried out in the village and it has become a socially recognised section of life. There is a positive attitude to migration into cities, because for many, 'wage labour is not only a means of earning one's living but has become an end in itself'.[29]

Peter Kilby, who has studied the Nigerian workers closely, has been able to establish that the Nigerian worker is capable of producing as much as his counterpart in Europe, but that the limitational factors were a number of management functions, namely, the provision of adequate incentives, adequate supervision and the proper organisation of work.[30] Where these improvements were made, productivity was as high as it could be. With regard to the question of absenteeism and high labour turnover, he found the incidence of these to be very low. Commenting on limited wants and the quest for leisure – supposedly common features of workers in the developing countries – he said of the Nigeria workers: 'Clearly the limited wants and high valuation on leisure postulated in the traditional portrayal are incompatible with the empirical findings.'[31] Kilby published his research findings about two decades ago but they are as valid today as they were then. Absenteeism and labour turnover, factors that would tend to support a low level of commitment, do not constitute a problem in the organised private sector today because the incidence is generally so low that it is negligible. Recently, we made surveys in two firms – the Nigerian Tobacco Company Limited with three factories, in Ibadan, Port Harcourt and Zaria and employing over 3000 workers, and Guinness (Nigeria) Limited with three breweries, one in Ikeja and two in Benin and employing 3800 workers – to determine the level of absenteeism and labour turnover. The survey covered the years 1976–8. We found that although the six factories are located in different parts of Nigeria, the pattern was the same. In respect of labour turnover the average rate was 0.4–3.0 per cent per annum, while in the case of absenteeism it was 0.2–4.5 per cent. With the exception of Zaria, where both rates were over 10 per cent during certain months of the year, the figures are so low that they certainly do not point to a problem. In any event, from our own experience as participants in the industrial relations system, we can confirm that absenteeism and high labour turnover have not constituted a problem for the Nigerian employer.

2.4   EMPLOYMENT AND THE LABOUR FORCE

In 1963 about 52.7 per cent of the population, estimated to be 55.7 million, fell within the working ages of 15–55 years. The Labour Force Sample conducted by the National Manpower Board in 1966–7 revealed that the population of working age was about 51 per cent of the total population.[32]

However, according to the estimates in the Third National Development Plan, the labour force was estimated to be 29.22 million in 1975 and this is expected to grow in absolute terms, by about 704 000 per annum during the plan period 1975–80 as shown in Table 2.2.

TABLE 2.2   Labour-force estimates, 1975–80

Year	Labour force estimates (millions)	Increase in labour force (millions)
1975	29.22	—
1980	32.74	3.52

Source: *Third National Development Plan, 1957–80.*

A significant aspect of the Nigerian labour force is the fact that it is a relatively young one, reflecting the age structure of the population. The major component of it, about 70 per cent, is persons aged between 18–40 years. On the estimated population of 70 million in 1980, about 70 per cent live in the rural areas.[33] Of this, approximately 44 per cent constitute the rural labour force drawn from the age group 15–55. In absolute terms the agricultural sector is the primary source of employment in the country. However, as the Third Development Plan notes, the sector is characterised by general underemployment owing to the seasonal nature of agricultural activities and the division of labour between the sexes. Equally characteristic of agriculture is the seasonal shortage of labour at peak periods of land clearing, planting, weeding and harvesting.[34]

2.4.1 Unemployment and underemployment

One major problem in Nigeria today is unemployment in the urban centres and underemployment in the rural areas. The problem that Professor Damachi refers to as 'unemployment trap'[35] constitutes a major headache for the country's economic planners. The causes are many but the principal reasons include a high rate of population growth, excessive migration to the cities, educational programmes not being related to the country's manpower needs, high wages in the modern sector and, at least until recently, the slow rate of economic growth and industrialisation. A recent labour force sample survey conducted by the National Manpower Board shows that urban unemployment remains a serious problem in the country. According to that survey, urban unemployment rates in November 1974 ranged between 1.5–22.3 per cent. By 1976 the situation had improved slightly. The urban centres that experienced the highest unemployment rates were Calabar, Port Harcourt, Benin, Enugu and Lagos. The relevant figures are shown in Table 2.3.

TABLE 2.3 Urban unemployment rates, 1974–6

| Urban centre | Unemployment rate (%) | |
	November 1974	March 1976
Lagos	7.2	6.2
Ibadan	5.7	4.1
Benin	13.1	8.6
Enugu	11.5	9.0
Ilorin	1.5	1.6
Kano	2.2	3.3
Maiduguri	5.0	6.1
Sokoto	2.0	2.8
Kaduna	6.1	n.a.
Jos	6.2	5.6
Port Harcourt	13.3	8.6
Calabar	22.3	13.5

Source: National Manpower Board, Lagos 1977.

As can be seen from Table 2.3, there has been some decline in the unemployment rate as revealed by the 1976 figures, and the situation appears reasonably satisfactory. This optimism is confirmed by the country's economic planners who estimated in the Third Development Plan that the country's unemployment rate in 1975 would be 4.5 per cent, with the anticipation that the figure would drop to 3.0 per cent in 1980, a figure that would suggest, at least in the case of a developing country like Nigeria, full employment.

However, it is our view that even if the unemployment rate in the urban centres were to drop to 3.0 per cent that would not really tell the whole story, for two reasons at least. First, as we have already pointed out, because of the seasonal nature of agricultural activities and the division of labour between the sexes, there is generally underemployment of able-bodied persons in the rural areas. Second, in the urban areas workers who are supposedly unemployed do derive some income from casual employment, and in some cases such income may be greater than would have been earned in regular employment. Accordingly, in Nigeria and especially in the cities, it is difficult to draw a clear distinction between those unemployed and those employed in the sense of income. What can be distinguished, however, is the level of those employed on a regular basis in the organised private sector.

2.4.2 The significance of the industrial labour force

Although the industrial labour force at present forms only a small proportion of the total labour force, its role in the economy of the nation is significant. First of all, it constitutes the growth part of the economy, and with the determination with which Nigeria is today tackling industrialisation, this role will become more and more important. Second, in comparison with the rural agricultural labour force, and others in commercial activities who are scattered and diffused, the urban industrial labour force is concentrated and thus easier to organise. Consequently, workers' organisations developed early around the industrial organisations in the country. In this connection, trade-union activity has a long history in the Nigerian railways, the ports, the coal mines at Enugu and the tin mines in Jos. The local unions in these organisations have not only brought about changes in their own organisations but have also influenced changes in other areas of the economy, including the public-service sector.

While trade unions in Nigeria have not been directly involved in political activities, their constant protests during the colonial era at employers who were from the metropolitan country of the colonial rulers gave some fillip to the nationalists who rode on the back of the union's economic agitation to fight colonialism generally. Strikes against employers were construed to mean disapproval of government action. Thus, the vocal agitation of the unions for economic improvements for their members indirectly contributed to the liquidation of colonialism.

Another important aspect of the industrial labour force is that it dictates the pace in the level of earnings through the collective bargaining system with the private employers. The government, which has no similar machinery, has to institute Wages and Salaries Commissions in order to improve the conditions of workers in the public sector. In the wake of one such commission in 1975, substantial increases in wages and salaries were awarded first to the public sector and ultimately extended to the private sector.[36] Thus, the effectiveness of the role of industrial labour must not be assessed solely with regard to numbers but should rather be judged on the impact it makes on the government and the economy generally. Indeed, one area where the impact on government is pronounced is that of labour legislation. It is the recognition of the strategic role of the labour force that has led the government to establish an elaborate statutory machinery for the settlement of industrial disputes, with the sole aim of preventing strikes and other forms of industrial disruptions, as we shall see later on in this study.

Finally, in Nigeria, the average worker in the modern wage-earning sector is typically the bread-winner for his family. It is not inconceivable that one worker may cater for as many as five or six other persons all dependent on him. In a survey conducted by Professor Yesufu in the Nigerian Tobacco Company Limited's factory in Ibadan in 1967, he found that although only 65 per cent of the 1000 + workers were married, 91 per cent maintained households of at least two persons, and the average size of the household was 4.5.[37] This dependency burden is not limited to the maintenance of members of the household only but extends to others left behind in the village, who either visit regularly to collect money or otherwise have money posted to them. Therefore when the worker struggles for a better level of wages and fringe benefits, he is not being influenced only by what can sustain him, his wife and children, but he takes into account the total financial burden that his privileged position as a wage earner places on him. These then are the environmental factors that have helped to shape Nigerian industrial relations. In Chapter 3 we shall discuss the development and role of the parties in the industrial relations system.

3 The Parties in the Industrial Relations System

We have already identified the parties (actors) in an industrial relations system to be: the workers and their organisations, the employers and their associations, and the government and its agencies. These parties create the institutional framework that develops a 'web of rules' which govern the industrial relations system in any country. In this chapter we shall examine the development, role and impact of these parties and determine the contribution of each to the evolution of the industrial relations system in Nigeria.

3.1 TRADE UNIONS

There had been organisations of workers in Nigeria before the advent of modern trade unionism. These organisations were essentially concerned with crafts and other skilled and professional trades and were generally based on local communities. Roper seems to believe that there was transition from these associations to modern unionism in certain parts of West Africa when he says:

> The transition from the guild of self-employed handicraft workers to the trade union of employed workers took place with differences of detail between different countries. In some cases, there was a sharp break between the decline of the guilds and the birth of the trade union. In other cases, there was a gradual and organic change from one to the other.[1]

However, there is no evidence to show that transition from these associations or guilds to modern trade unionism took place in Nigeria.

According to Yesufu, the main function of the associations was to organise material aid in cases of difficulty and to regulate trade practices.[2]

There is a general belief that trade unions in the former British colonies, including Nigeria, were not natural developments as in the metropolitan country but rather a creature of the then British Colonial Office. That view was shared by the Fitzgerald Commission of 1950, which was appointed by the British government to look into the disorders at the coal mines in Enugu in 1949. The Commission said: 'Trade Unionism in Nigeria was not of native growth. It was deliberately planted on the people by the British administration as part of the industrial system. There was therefore a special obligation on the Government to build it up on proper lines.'[3]

In spite of these claims, there is no evidence to show that the British deliberately imported trade unionism into Nigeria. It would appear, however, that the development of trade unionism in Nigeria may have been influenced by events elsewhere. Indeed, Yesufu believes that experience in Sierra Leone greatly influenced the development of trade unionism in Nigeria. According to him, the first union was not formed by a group of disaffected workers who wanted a platform from which to fight for amelioration of grievances, or for the improvement of specific conditions of employment. Rather, it was formed just to conform to what workers in Sierra Leone had done.[4] But what Yesufu did not explain is why, in the first place, the workers in the civil service in Nigeria were prepared to combine just as the workers in Sierra Leone had done. Surely, they must have had an aim for so doing. Indeed, in 1893 there existed in Lagos a Mechanics Mutual Aid Provident and Improvement Association, and we know also that there was a large-scale strike by artisans and labourers in the Public Works Department, Lagos, in 1897.[5] These developments were not confined to the public sector. In 1911 the Lagos Mercantile Clerks Association was formed to safeguard the interests of clerks working for the merchant houses in Lagos.[6] The reasonable inference to be drawn from the circumstances of the formation of the first unions in Nigeria is that in an attempt to protect themselves against the uncertainties of employment, the workers in a number of government establishments started to form themselves into associations. They certainly had an aim and they probably only drew on the Sierra Leonean experience.

The first of the formal unions to develop was the Civil Service Union, founded in 1912. This was followed by others including the Nigerian Railway Native Staff Union in 1919. Admittedly, the aims of these unions or associations were vague at the initial stage but there was no doubt that they were formed for the protection of the interests of their members and the word 'native' is clearly indicative of the implied struggle against the 'foreign' employer. The declared aim of the railway union was stated to be: 'To promote official interests and welfare of the members of the staff and to inculcate in them the principles of devotion to duty and loyalty to Government. The Union will also undertake to seek redress for grievances by constitutional means.'[7]

In 1931, the Nigerian Union of Teachers came into existence. This was particularly significant because it required a lot of effort to organise such a nation-wide union at a time when communications were very difficult. However, once trade unionism started to grow in Nigeria, the British government wanted to make sure that its development was channelled in the right direction. That was one of the intentions behind Lord Passfield's circulars of 1930 and 1946 whose purpose was to persuade the colonial administration to allow the development of workers' organisations. The circular of 1930, for example, had stated that the advances made in the economic and social conditions in the colonies had created a situation favourable to the development of unionism. As the idea of coming together for economic purposes was novel to the workers in the developing countries, sympathetic supervision and guidance would be needed. Otherwise, the unions might fall under the dominance of disaffected persons, by whom their activities might be diverted to improper and mischievous ends.[8] This theme was echoed years later by the Tudor Davies Commission of 1945 which said:

> the Trade Unions should receive every help and encouragement from Great Britain to develop along proper trade union lines. The alternative will be their being swallowed up and converted to political uses in a wider demand for self-government and independence, i.e. their drifting finally and irrevocably into the hands of the politicians.[9]

It is probably this heavy involvement by the British government in the development process of the unions that some may have confused with actually bringing them into being. With the passing of the Trade Union Ordinance in 1938, the existence of trade unionism was formally recognised. That law laid down the mode of registration of trade unions, and prescribed the rights and obligations of unions in the employer–employee relationships. Thus, the law was prepared to recognise the existence of a workers' organisation that fulfilled the minimum standards stipulated in the law. This gave impetus to trade-union development in the country. Within two years of the passing of the law, registered trade unions had increased to fourteen with a membership of over 4000. Although the unions were small, the trend in union development in the country had begun.

3.1.1 The growth of unions

Once the legal basis for unions has been established, three major events helped in the rapid growth of trade unionism, in that they gave a sense of oneness to all the workers and encouraged them to get closer. The first of these was the grant of a cost-of-living allowance (COLA) to government employees in June 1942, the second was the General Strike of 1945, and the third was the Enugu shootings of 1949.

(i) The COLA unions

The prosecution of the Second World War by the British and the involvement of the colonies in the war effort, including conscription of workers into the army, had created economic difficulties in these territories – especially for the working classes in the urban centres. This led the railway unions to demand a cost-of-living award in 1941. The demand was turned down and a crisis ensued. The government then appointed the Bridges Committee to look into the situation. As a result of the Committee's report, the Government granted a cost-of-living allowance (COLA) to all its workers. According to Tokunboh, in order to claim this allowance, many unions came into existence.[10] The strategy of these COLA unions, as they were called, was to apply quickly for registration and, once that was secured, they would organise celebrations marking the receipt of their certificates. The employer would be invited to the celebration, thereby committing him to the recognition of the union. Soon after, the union would apply for the awards on behalf of their members. As a result of this strategy, the total number of unions registered jumped from thirty-six in 1941 to seventy-seven in 1942, while in the same period the membership increased from 17 144 to 26 346. However, the unions came into existence for one purpose only: to get the allowance. Once the allowance was granted, many unions quickly became moribund and eventually dissolved.

There was one other important development from the COLA agitation. It underscored the need for an organisation that would speak for all sections of organised labour. Accordingly, in November 1942, the Federated Trades Union of Nigeria (FTUN) was established. In July 1943 the FTUN was changed to the Trades Union Congress of Nigeria, whose aims included the unity of all trade unions in one organised body and the protection of the legal status and rights of trade-union organisations.

(ii)   The General Strike of 1945

We have seen that the COLA agitations of 1941 were a result of the hardships created by the war. At the end of the war, the workers expected a change in their economic fortunes, but this was not realised. Prices of commodities were high, and the economic conditions of the time were so harsh that the unions, having realised their economic power during the COLA agitation, demanded a cost-of-living increase over the awards that the government had made in 1942. The government refused the demand and a general strike was called. As usual, the strike was engineered by the railway unions. The strike, which lasted forty-five days, was successful in its economic aims. All economic activities were paralysed and the government was forced to appoint the Tudor Davies Commission. On the basis of the Commission's report, the government awarded substantial increases based on the cost of living. The success in this respect again confirmed to the workers the important lesson that there was an advantage in going with the masses whenever strike action was called because, in the end, economic gains were bound to accrue.

However, in respect of trade-union development, the strike created some problems. The government declared the strike illegal, because the notice of twenty-one days required by the Defence Regulations before strike action could take place was not given by the unions. Realising the illegality of the strike, the union president advised that the strike action should be suspended so that the appropriate notice might be given. But it was already too late, the executive refused and the president resigned. The General Council of the Trade Union Congress then dissolved the executive body of the union and in 1946 a conference was held during which a new executive and president were elected. Thus although the strike helped to bring the workers together under the banner of trade unions, government reaction led to schism in the movement.

(iii)   The Enugu shootings of 1949

In 1949 a tragic incident occurred when coal miners at the Iva Valley in Enugu went on strike. Armed policemen were called in and twenty-one miners were killed. This tragedy was significant for trade-union development. The schism that had crept into the labour movement following the strike of 1945, was temporarily patched up when efforts were made by the main unions to form one central body. The unions felt that their salvation depended on their coming together. Accordingly, the TUC, the African Civil Servants Technical Workers Union and the Nigerian Federation of Labour (the latter two having come into being in 1949) formed the Nigerian Labour Congress. Although splits did occur, as we shall see later, there is no doubt that the incident encouraged the growth rate of trade unionism. Table 3.1 shows the growth of unions between 1947 and 1951. It is in the light of the miners' tragedy that the jump in trade-union membership between 1948 and 1951 must be appreciated.

TABLE 3.1   Growth of trade unions, 1947–51

Year	No. of unions	No. of members
1947	109	76 362
1948	127	90 864
1949–50	140	109 998
1950–1	144	144 358

Source: Department of Labour, Annual Reports, 1947–51.

The growth of unions both in number and membership continued over the years.[11] By 1957–8 unions had increased to 298 with a membership of 235 742. During the year 1962–3, the number of unions increased to 435 with the total membership of 324 203. A sudden jump occurred in 1968–9, the first year of the civil war when, although the total number of unions dropped from 662 to 659, membership increased from 393 671 to 648 060. The sudden upsurge was the result mainly of the economic problems created by the Nigerian civil war. This had tended to bring all workers together and, as we shall see in Chapter 5, there were very many strikes during the years 1968 to 1969, a situation that led to positive government regulation of industrial relations.

However, the growth of unions as revealed by the above figures must not be interpreted to mean the effectiveness of union organisation or the relative strength of these unions. It would be 'safer' to regard the figures as 'claimed' figures by the unions rather than depicting the actual strength and involvement of workers in union activities. As the Registrar of Trade Unions himself remarked, some unions after obtaining their certificates of registration made no efforts either to file their financial returns and other particulars as required by law, or even to hold annual conferences as required by their own rule books. In other cases, some of the unions existed only in the Registrar's records, and the frequent notices in the federal government's *Gazettes*, stating that the certificates of certain unions have been cancelled, confirm this view. Moreover, the four central trade unions that existed in the country until the end of 1977 jostled and canvassed for membership. In order to impress the federal government and perhaps to secure recognition, each tended to inflate the actual number of its members.[12] Accordingly, we treat the total number of unions and membership, as revealed by the figures above, with some caution.

3.1.2   The emergence of four central labour organisations

The development of trade unionism in the country was hampered by splits and crises in the labour movement, and the first major split occurred in 1948. There were two reasons for this division. The first was the problem of rivalry for leadership in the movement, and the second and most important was the difference of opinion among trade-union leaders over affiliation to one or the other of the national political parties. The split led to the emergence of another labour centre, the Nigerian National Federation of Labour (NNFL). The NNFL attracted some of the unions that hitherto were affiliated to the Nigerian Labour Congress. Meanwhile, the situation had become so confused fhat some unions were unsure which federation to support and many did not affiliate to any of the rival trade-union centres.

The Enugu tragedy of 1949 brought the unions together and efforts were again made to forge a single labour movement. These efforts were not successful, and by 1953 yet another central trade union, the All-Nigeria Trade Union Federation (ANTUF), had come into being. But like its predecessors, the ANTUF was not successful. The problem of ideology has always been and continues to be a major set-back for trade-union leaders in Nigeria. There were those trade-union leaders who were left-leaning – like Michael Imoudu, Wahab Goodluck and Samuel U. Bassy – and who favoured dealings with the communist bloc and affiliation to the World Federation of Trade Unions (WFTU) on the one hand; and those who favoured the mixed economy – such as H. P. Adebola and L. L. Borha – and who wanted affiliation to the International Confederation of Free Trade Unions (ICFTU), on the other. The differences appeared so fundamental that neither the unionists themselves, nor the government, were able to resolve them. The ideological differences led to a split within the ANTUF and the formation of the National Council of Trade Unions of Nigeria (NCTUN) in April 1957. The situation continued unchanged until 1959. In that year a conference was held at Enugu during which all parties agreed to work together irrespective of ideology and political leanings under a new Trade Union Congress of Nigeria, which was inaugurated. Thus, at the time of independence in 1960, there was only one central trade-union movement, the second Trade Union Congress.

Unfortunately, the life-span of the Congress was short. In 1961 the Congress, again beset by problems of ideological differences, split into two rival bodies. One faction, which was led by the left-leaning Michael Imoudu, and which resented the aid that the ICFTU was giving the TUC, broke away to form the Nigerian Trade Union Congress (NTUC). The other faction, which favoured continued association with the ICFTU, was led by H. P. Adebola and became known as the Trade Union Congress of Nigeria (TUCN).

In August 1961 the government of Nigeria sponsored an All-Nigeria Peoples Conference on the 'Role of Nigeria in African Affairs'. This Conference set up a number of committees, one of which was the Labour and World Economic Committee, headed by Dr S. A. Aluko, of the University of Ife. The Committee recommended that Nigeria should play an important and prominent role in African labour affairs but, to do so effectively, it needed to put its own house in order by first forging one central labour organisation. It further recommended that a small committee whose duty would be the reconciliation of the two warring factions in the central labour movement be set up. Following the recommendations of the Committee, a unity conference was held in Ibadan in May 1962 with a view to establishing a single trade-union centre. Unfortunately, the parties could not agree and the conference collapsed. The failure of the Ibadan Conference was the result mainly of the conference decision that the proposed congress should be affiliated to the International Confederation of Free Trade Unions (ICFTU). The NTUC leadership had opposed affiliation to any international body. Following the vote, they walked out of the meeting arguing that in keeping with Nigeria's policy of non-alignment in foreign affairs, no affiliation to an international trade-union organisation should be permitted.

In December 1962 an international seminar was organised by the Pan African Workers Congress (PAWC). The PAWC was then the African Regional Wing of the International Federation of Christian Trade Unions (IFCTU) based in Brussels. Its role in Nigeria was principally to organise a workers' education programme and its activities were wholly financed by the IFCTU. At the end of the seminar the Nigerian Workers Council (NWC) was launched – on 22 December 1962. At the inaugural conference attended by twenty-eight unions, the following principal officers were elected:

Mr N. Chukwurah	President
Mr E. N. Okongwu	General Secretary
Mr J. O. Enigbokan	Treasurer

Thus, at the end of 1962, the ULCN, NTUC and NWC were operating as the three central labour organisations. Meanwhile, the federal government, eager to deal with a single trade-union movement, had accorded recognition to the ULCN only. The government did not give any reasons for its action but observers had known for a long time that the fear of communist influence in the NTUC had made the government prefer the ULC. The Federal Ministry of Labour justified the action by insisting that 'the ULC was generally acknowledged as commanding the largest followership which seems to have made it eligible for Federal Government recognition'.[13]

The NTUC had all along suspected the hand of the government in the apparent success of the ULCN during conferences on reconciliation, and the overt act of recognition confirmed their fears. Indeed, it was a widely held belief that the government was secretly happy to see the labour movement divided. The government, accordingly to this view, feared a powerful single labour movement, which could be manipulated by either the opposition parties or external forces to their advantage. Even then, outward efforts continued to be made to bring all the trade-union centres under one umbrella. One such significant effort was undertaken by the leaders of some of the larger white-collar unions, including the Nigerian Union of Teachers and the Civil Service Union. These unions had refused to be involved in the struggle and were now in a good position to try and effect reconciliation between the warring centres and bring about labour unity in the country. The 'Peace Committee', later known as Labour Unity Front (LUF), held its first meeting in 1963 but, like all previous efforts at reconciliation, this one also failed. The LUF continued as a peace committee until 1966, when the federal government accorded it and the other three trade-union centres recognition as the four central labour organisations in the country. The following were the principal officers of LUF, elected in September 1963:

Mr A. A. Ishola	Chairman
Mr Gogo Chu Nzeribe	General Secretary
Mr F. N. Kanu	Treasurer

The four trade-union centres, the ULCN, NTUC, NWC and the LUF, existed until 1976 when they were all dissolved by statute to pave the way for the restructuring of the unions.

3.1.3   The General Strike of 1964

The existence of four national trade-union centres sealed the splits in the trade-union movement, but the General Strike of 1964 had a unifying effect. There were a number of causes of the strike, but broadly speaking those of class and status were most prominent.[14] Independence had brought hope and the possibility of a more equitable society than the colonial one; but the politicians retained the old institutions and privileges, including the salary structure which gave advantage to European civil servants at the top. Moreover, while the economic circumstances of the workers remained unchanged, politicians and top civil servants were seen to be living in affluence. The workers' frustration was articulated in a policy paper issued by one of the trade-union centres:

> Independence Day, October first 1960, freed us from colonial domination. It did not, unfortunately, free us automatically from colonial institutions. The edifice of privilege remains; only its proprietors are different. . . . This situation, in which a senior official may receive fifty times the salary of a junior official, or a daily labourer, is politically and economically intolerable. . . . The United Labour Congress of Nigeria will fight against the continuation of exploitation of class by class as fervently as it fought against imperialism.[15]

As the grievances were articulated in terms of economic class rather than international politics, all factions sank their differences and formed the Joint Action Committee (JAC) in September 1963. Earlier, in June 1962, the ULC, the NTUC and the staff side of the Federal

Industrial Whitley Council had separately made demands for increased pay and improved working conditions for the workers. All three organisations also demanded the abolition of the system of employment on a daily pay basis. The ULC and the NTUC went further to demand the introduction of a national minimum wage. These demands were vigorously pursued by the JAC and ultimately resulted in a strike action which began on 27 September 1963. The timing of the strike is significant. Nigeria had adopted a new constitution that would confer a republican status on the nation on 1 October 1963, and it would appear that the strike was deliberately planned to coincide with the period of celebrations. According to the Ministry of Labour, more than 34 513 workers participated and there was an aggregate of more than 76 006 man-days lost.[16] The federal government intervened and, following agreement to appoint a Commission of Inquiry to examine the demands, the strike ended on 3 October 1963. The six-man Commission was headed by Mr Justice Morgan. The Commission completed its work in April 1964; although the government was aware of the tense atmosphere in the country, it nevertheless procrastinated on the publication of the report. Eventually, when the government White Paper on the Commission's report was published, it did not satisfy the unions, because the government reduced the wage recommendations and rejected some of the other recommendations of the Commission. A nation-wide strike was started on 1 June 1964. The industrial and commercial life of the nation were completely paralysed. Following the Okotie-Eboh negotiations in which private employers were represented, the strike ended on 13 June 1964, with the workers receiving substantial awards.[17] The strike was very successful, because it received the blessing of many, including self-employed persons. It was seen as a disapproval of the excesses of politicians who flagrantly displayed their material wealth. However, in spite of that success, the strike did not heal the schism in the trade-union movement.

3.1.4 Unions attempt to form a national centre

The need for strong and responsible trade unions had been expressed at different times by trade unions themselves in the form of resolutions adopted at their conferences and seminars and via observations and recommendations by various government commissions and Tribunals of Inquiry. Thus, the Morgan Commission (1963–4) and the Adebo Commission (1970–1) both made similar recommendations to that effect. In the main all those bodies advocated the reform of trade unions, the establishment of collective-bargaining machinery, the strengthening of the financial base of trade unions through check-off, and trade union education.

Meanwhile, the lack of labour unity at the national level hampered the effectiveness of the trade unions in the country. By 1974, the last year of the Public Service Review Commission (the Udoji Commission), it had become clear to the trade-union leaders that a united front of labour leaders was necessary if the interests of labour were to be protected in the expected report; however, there was no common platform for dialogue. The opportunity came during the burial ceremony of J. A. Oduleye, a former treasurer of the ULC, at the Apena Cemetary in Lagos. Perhaps as a result of the seriousness of the occasion, the labour leaders were able to reflect on the futility of disagreements. One man who was moved by the solemnity of the gathering was Okon Eshiett, a veteran trade unionist and the then Director of the Trade Union Institute in Lagos. He wrote some notes on a piece of paper which he gave to the labour leaders present to sign. Representatives of the four central labour organisations in the country signed. In the document, later known as the Apena Cemetary Declaration, the unity of the labour movement was accepted by all the labour leaders present. They said that they felt ashamed of their split and stressed the urgent necessity for them to work together in the interest of the country. They declared:

> Conscious of the historic mission of labour movement, ... we solemnly declare that we are now resolved to form a single national centre which shall protect, defend and promote the interests of the workers and the community as a whole. By this declaration, we hereby recommend to the existing centres, the setting up of a working committee that shall arrange for the convening of a conference of all registered trade unions in Nigeria for the formation of a national centre.[18]

The declaration further mandated the working committee set up to act as spokesman for the workers until the formation of one central labour organisation.

The objective of labour unity was pursued with vigour and in December 1975 all four trade-union centres merged to form the Nigeria Labour Congress (NLC). This major breakthrough by the union leaders themselves was unfortunately not to yield results. A section of the labour movement did not accept the constitution adopted and neither did they accept the manner in which the first officers of the new federation were appointed. As a result of the receipt of several petitions, the federal government announced then that it would not recognise the NLC as constituted becasue it did not appear to have been democratically established. Thus ended the one major effort genuinely made by all unions in Nigeria to forge a single national labour centre.

3.1.5   The emergence of national unions and a new labour centre

As the military government was restructuring all institutions in the country, there had been various calls and suggestions for the same to be done with the trade-union movement. In 1976 the government appointed a Tribunal of Inquiry headed by a High Court Judge, Mr Justice D. Adebiyi, to inquire into the activities of trade unions in Nigeria. As a result of the findings of that tribunal, eleven prominent trade-union leaders were banned by law from holding future offices in the trade-union movement. The unions were furious and accused the government of unnecessary intervention in union affairs. In addition to banning certain trade unionists, the government had taken a series of actions that the top echelon of the labour movement considered inimical to themselves. However, in assessing the propriety of government action in banning certain trade-union leaders from future participation in trade unionism, one must remember that the government at the time was military and that one objective which the regime prosecuted openly was that of correcting the ills in society. The regime had probed political leaders and senior civil servants and had in appropriate cases recovered ill-gotten gains. In the case of the trade unions, the tribunal investigating their activities established beyond doubt that their leaders had fallen short of expectation. They had played on the ignorance of the rank and file and had used unions' resources in any way they wished. Moreover, the central labour organisations could not improve union administration because of ideological differences and rivalries for leadership. In the circumstances, affiliated unions contributed little or nothing to the upkeep of these unions. This therefore made the central unions rely exclusively on external aid. The ULCN, for example, relied almost exclusively upon foreign sources for both financial and material aid for the running of its affairs. Such aid came mainly from the USA, the UK and West Germany. Even the cost of running the Trade Union Institute for Economic and Social Development in Lagos, was paid for almost exclusively with American aid. The Adebiyi Tribunal also found that because of the dependence of the Congress for financial support on the ICFTU and the African-American Labour Centre (AALC) established by the American Federation of Labour and Congress of Industrial Organisations (AFL–CIO), the leadership of the Congress allowed the local representatives of these organisations to have a free hand in running the affairs of the Congress. They attended the conferences of the Congress and took part in the deliberations at meetings of some of the organs of the Congress, such as the Central Working Committee. Undoubtedly, he who paid the piper was calling the tune.

The NTUC, on the other hand, was affiliated to the WFTU. Like the ULC, it could not raise funds locally from its affiliated unions to run the affairs of the centre. Accordingly, it too had to rely heavily on foreign aid, which came from Eastern European countries, including the Soviet Union, China, Bulgaria and Rumania. The funds for the running of the Patrick Lumumba Academy, established by the NTUC in Lagos for the local training of both political and trade-union leaders, were exclusively from external sources.

The other two central labour organisations had more limited activities and in consequence did not seek for external aid. The NWC was originally concerned with the main objectives of furthering the PAWC assignment which was 'to educate the workers on their rights and obligations to their unions and their country'. The council decided to be ideologically neutral, a situation that would no doubt suit the objectives of the IFCTU to which the Council was subsequently affiliated. The LUF, emerging as it did as a peace committee, could not and did not affiliate to any international body. Its objectives until the time of the dissolution of all central trade-union organisations was to unite the labour movement.

Notwithstanding the findings of the Adebiyi Tribunal which are not subject to debate, it is still open to question whether it is justifiable, for a government of whatever origin, to ban a citizen for life from holding office in a trade union solely on the ground that such a citizen could not account properly for monies entrusted to his care or that he contributed to the careless running of a trade union of which he was an official. In our view, that judgement should properly and conveniently be left to union members to decide whether to retain or not to retain them. Accordingly, it is our submission that the ban placed on the eleven trade-union leaders should be lifted. After all, politicians who were found corrupt, and who have been proved to have enriched themselves at public expense, were not similarly banned from any future political activity.

Meanwhile, at the National Seminar on Workers' Education held in Kano in 1975, it was recommended that, 'the Federal Government should appoint a committee on Trade Union structure with appropriate terms of reference to make practical recommendations on the method and means of speedily creating industrial unions which would correspond to the Nigerian Standard of Industrial Classification'.

It was against this background that the government decided, since the unions themselves had tried in vain to improve their own organisation, that a proper framework must be established within which the unions will operate. Such a framework should ensure that the unions are made self-sufficient financially. This will avoid the ridiculous situation highlighted in the Adebiyi Report, whereby the trade-union centres relied exclusively on external aid for survival. As a result, the government passed the Trade Unions (Central Labour Organisations) Act 1976. This Act revoked the registration of all unions to pave the way for reorganisation. Mr M. O. Abiodun, formerly of the Ministry of Labour and who had been personnel manager of Mobil Oil Nigeria Limited, was appointed Administrator of Trade Unions. He was assisted by three other persons who had knowledge of industrial relations in Nigeria.[19] The Administrator was charged with the responsibility of effecting the formation, whether by amalgamation or federation of existing ones, of strong and effective trade unions. It was his duty also to draw up a constitution to govern the new central labour organisation to which all trade unions in Nigeria shall be affiliated, and to conduct the elections of the first officers of the new body.

The action of the federal government in dissolving the four trade-union centres was bitterly criticised by trade-union leaders. They argued that the government was getting involved in matters that did not concern it. The unions carried the matter a stage further by reporting to the ILO. But Major-General H. E. O. Adefope, who was federal Commissioner of Labour, made it clear in his speech at the ILO Conference in Geneva in 1976 that the federal government was determined to bring discipline into the Nigerian labour movement and would not tolerate any outside interference in that regard.[20]

Meanwhile, the Administrator and his team had commenced work on 16 September 1976 and had completed the assignment by the end of 1977. After extensive consultations, the Administrator grouped all unions into forty-two industrial unions, all affiliated to a new Nigerian Labour Congress.[21] All the new unions and the NLC were inaugurated during the first half of 1978.

The *Daily Times* in its editorial on the day the NLC was to be inaugurated commented on the problems that had beset labour unity in Nigeria and rejoiced: 'The successful inauguration of the NLC today will close an important phase in the new trade union structure and open a new era of responsible, disciplined and viable labour movement.'[22] However, there was a last-minute crisis concerning the provision in the NLC constitution that the President should be on full-time basis. This provision inserted by government to ensure that the president of the Congress devotes all his time to trade-union activities rather than combine that with a paid employment elsewhere, had invoked a lot of arguments among trade unionists. A committee of trade unionists headed by S. K. Babalola, the general secretary of the Nigerian Union of Teachers, had rejected the proposal and favoured a part-time president. At the inaugural conference of the NLC held at the Western Hall, Ibadan on 28 February and 1 March 1978, there was going to be a hitch. The Administrator who chaired the conference reported the incident as follows:

> Mr Etienam, the General Secretary of the Customs and Excise and Immigration Staff Union, told the Congress that his delegation was opposed to the idea of a full-time President as there might be a clash of interests between the President and the Secretary of the NLC. As Mr Etienam proceeded to read his address, he was shouted down by the delegates and could not continue with his speech. Before the commotion ceased, J. M. Jack, the General Secretary of the National Union of Road Transport Workers, moved the adoption of the constitution of the NLC and he was supported by Alhaji H. P. Adebola, the General Secretary of Nigerian Ports Authority Workers Union. There was general acclamation of support by the whole house and the motion for the adoption of the constitution was carried.[23]

Thus, a hitch that could have caused another delay of labour unity in the country was averted.

On the adoption of the constitution, the following were elected officers of the new NLC:

President	Hassan Sunmonu (Civil Service Technical Workers' Union)
Deputy President	D. C. Ojeli (Nigeria Civil Service Union)

National Treasurer   P. O. Ero-Phillips
                               (National Union of Electricity and
                               Gas Workers)
Deputy National Treasurer   M. E. Mpamugo
                               (Metal Products Workers' Union
                               of Nigeria)

In May 1978 Malam Aliyu Dangiwa, a former trade unionist who
studied at Ruskin College, Oxford, and Pittsburgh University, USA,
and who was a lecturer at Ahmadu Bello University, Zaria, was
appointed General Secretary of the NLC.

3.1.6   Trade-union organisation and government

(i)   Union structure

At the end of April 1977 there was a total of 896 registered unions in
Nigeria. Of these, details of membership were available in respect of
884 unions. Unions that had a membership of 250 and below totalled
503, representing 57 per cent of all registered unions. Yet in membership, this group of unions accounted for only 58 180, or 8 per cent of
the total membership. On the other hand unions with 1000 members
and above totalled 114 or 13 per cent, yet together they had a
membership of 533 922 or 74 per cent of the total union membership.
It is interesting to note too that only twenty-one unions or 2.3 per cent
had more than 5000 members and these accounted for 356 071
members or 49 per cent of the total membership. Table 3.2 shows the
membership by size of union.

TABLE 3.2   Distribution of trade unions by size

Range of membership	No. of unions	Membership
50 and under	107	3 509
51– 250	396	54 671
251–1000	267	130 595
1001–5000	93	179 851
Over–5000	21	356 071
Membership not available	12	—
Total	896	724 697

Source: Compiled from the *List of Registered Trade Unions at 30 April 1977*,
            Office of the Registrar of Trade Unions, Lagos.

It will be seen from Table 3.2 that the small unions predominated. The basis for union organisation was provided by the Trade Unions Act 1938 which stipulated that: 'Any five or more members of a Trade Union may, by subscribing their names to the rules of the Trade Union and by otherwise complying with the provisions of this Act with respect to registration, apply for registration of the Trade Union under this Act.'

This provision naturally led to the multiplicity of trade unions which characterised the labour movement in Nigeria. The problem of prolif- eration and leadership of unions has been of major concern in the country since the mid-1950s. The situation was not helped by the failure of the four trade-union centres to form one national labour movement. The rivalry at the national level and the instability it generated permeated the whole labour movement. Early in the 1960s, the Federal Ministry of Labour reported on the problem thus:

> The Workers' Organisations . . . are still facing tremendous difficul- ties caused by internal squabbles in the central labour union organ- isations. This disunity is often reflected in rivalry for leadership in individual trade unions resulting in ineffective organisations, lack of purpose and painful experience in working the system of labour– management relations.[24]

Apart from the legal provisions that encouraged proliferation of unions, other factors were also responsible. Nigerian workers seemed to realise the importance of unions only at time of union–management negotiations and during industrial crises. When these were over, they tended to forget about unions. Consequently, collection of union dues was always a big problem, and because there was competition among trade-union leaders for membership, they dared not threaten mem- bers who refused to contribute. In the circumstances, trade-union leaders and secretaries devised the strategy of encouraging the break- away union in the hope that the more unions they looked after, the better their chances of making ends meet. To this end, a number of secretaries were in charge of anything between two and six unions. It is, of course, not necessary to emphasise that in such circumstances union administration and leadership gradually degenerated and in some cases became non-existent. It is little wonder that having surveyed the pathetic situation, the Wages and Salaries Commission of 1971 lamented thus:

> The proliferation of trade unions in Nigeria is a crying scandal. Our

labour movement consists of an untidy assemblage of some 700 unions purporting to cater for the interests of under a million salary and wage earning population. It is hardly surprising that there is a lack of personnel with suitable background and experience to give them the right leadership.[25]

The Trade Unions Act 1973 tried to correct the situation by restricting the number of trade unions of which a person may be an official. Under the law, no person may hold office as general secretary in more than three trade unions. However, with the new industrial unions, that provision has now become irrelevant, as no one person can be an official in two national unions. In any event, the factors which encouraged that trend no longer exist.

As would be expected, there is a concentration of unions in the urban centres because that is where the industries are. Thus, there is a large concentration of unions in Lagos, Ibadan, Benin, Port Harcourt, Enugu, Jos, Kaduna and Kano. In these urban areas, the manufacturing industry tends to encourage the growth of unions more than the commercial sector. Hence, there is a large number of commercial organisations, including supermarkets, catering institutions and hotels, where trade unionism is relatively undeveloped. One interesting aspect of the union set-up, is the relatively unimportant role that women have played in unionism. Although, in relation to men, women employed are few, a large proportion of them are employed in the civil service, and process industries such as biscuits, cigarette and textile companies. A possible reason for the apathy is that most of the women employed are housewives who would not really want to be involved in the rigours of trade-union activities. Second, the societal norms in Nigeria do not exactly encourage a woman to be a leader of men in the struggle for improvements to the conditions of employment.

As we have seen, one major reason for restructuring the unions in Nigeria, was to bring some order into a chaotic situation. The question to ask at this stage is whether the new structure, among other things, provides for a better system of union government.

(ii)   Union government

At the end of 1980 the NLC claimed a total membership of 2 464 000. Of the forty-two industrial unions, five had a membership of over 100 000, as shown in Table 3.3.

TABLE 3.3   Industrial unions with a membership of over 100 000

	Union	Estimated membership
1.	Nigerian Union of Teachers	400 000
2.	Nigerian Union of Construction and Civil Engineering Workers	280 000
3.	Agricultural and Allied Workers Union of Nigeria	250 000
4.	National Union of Shops and Distributive Employees	180 000
5.	Civil Service Technical Workers' Union of Nigeria	120 000
	Total	1 230 000

Source: From data supplied by the Nigerian Labour Congress.

The five national unions in Table 3.3 account for 50 per cent of the total estimated union membership in Nigeria. The other national Unions, which are not as large as the five mentioned in the table, are strong enough financially to be self-sufficient.

The grouping of all unions into industrial unions and the establishment of one central labour organisation, the NLC, has brought significant changes into the industrial relations system and trade-union government in the country.

Figure 3.1 below illustrates the present organisation of unions in Nigeria.

FIGURE 3.1   Trade-union organisation

At the apex of the structure is the NLC, to which all forty-two national unions are affiliated. The branch or company unions are affiliated to the national unions, while the state councils act as supervisory agents of the national unions. We now discuss the government of the unions at each level.

The branch union. The basic unit of trade unionism is the branch or company union. Each company has its own branch union which caters for the interests of all workers employed in that organisation, irrespective of trade or discipline. Thus, the Guinness (Nigeria) Limited branch union, which is affiliated to the National Union of Food, Beverage and Tobacco Employees, covers messengers, cleaners, clerks, salesmen, fitters, electricians, mechanics, operators and other workers below the management level. Where the check-off system existed at all, it was negotiated and many employers were quick to withdraw the facility each time they felt the union had 'misbehaved'. In other cases, the employers left it entirely to the unions to collect dues directly from their members, and this made the financial position of many unions precarious. In some companies, many workers refused to pay their dues, which were only about 20K per month. For example, although Guinness (Nigeria) Limited employed about 3000 workers in 1977, and operated a voluntary check-off on behalf of the union, only about 60 per cent were paid-up members. The figure was much lower in many other companies. The figure for paid-up members was high in Guinness because the management through gentle persuasion encouraged new workers to join the union.

However, with the compulsory check-off now introduced into the system, that problem may have been solved. Under the Labour (Amendment) Act 1978, an employer is obliged to make deductions from the wages of all workers eligible to be members of the union for the purpose of paying contributions to the union. This means that a worker need not be a union member before he can be made to contribute to the union's fund. Although there is a proviso that a worker may contract out of the system in writing, it is unlikely that many workers will have the courage to do so. The new compulsory check-off system has had the effect of making the unions financially buoyant, but there is the apparently incurable problem of apathy among the rank and file members in respect of union activities. Meetings are rarely held and even when these are called to discuss important issues, they are poorly attended. Even the annual delegates conference – at which the activities of the union for the year are reviewed, policy for the future established, and officers elected – does not appeal to many members. As a result, many unions have resorted to holding these conferences once in every two or three years. All this has implications for trade-union government and democracy. It means that contrary to the democratic principles enshrined in the unions' constitutions, only a few activists are in control of the unions. The worker who is perceived to be able to 'give the management hell' is simply acclaimed to be union president. The author had an interesting experience in 1975, when a most troublesome operative in the company's brewery in Ikeja was elected union president to lead the workers' team to the negotiations to be held the next year. These negotiations, which were over increases in wages and salaries, were concluded after a week of arguments. But throughout the whole week, the 'troublesome' union president did not say anything; he left everything to the General Secretary. Apparently, he did not understand what was going on and neither could he comprehend the arguments. Just before signing the agreement, the author reminded him that, as president of the union, if he did not like what was agreed, he need not sign the agreement. In reply, he said that he did not know that such a difficult process had to be followed before arriving at a collective agreement. He was happy with what had been agreed and would go along with it. Of course, he was voted out of office at the next election and went into oblivion in the company.

In other cases where the activists are more resolute, they tend to equate themselves with the union. For example, there have been many instances where the local executive of a union took important decisions without the sanction of the rank and file. The spate of unofficial strikes common in Nigeria are the result of this fact. The local executive can decide on an action without consulting or contrary to the advice of the national executive and without getting the consent of the rank and file. Inevitably, all such strike actions fail, because after the first few days of euphoria when all workers join the strike, support tends to dwindle as the average member has not been briefed as to why he is on strike.

The state council. The state council is a creature whose role the unions themselves do not seem to understand. Rule 10 of the constitution of the National Union of Food, Beverage and Tobacco Employees, provides as follows: (i) There shall be a State Council in every State of the federation where the Branch of the Union is existing'. The duties of the council are supposed to be, 'to coordinate the activities of the Branches in its State's jurisdiction, ensure that Union's policy is widely known, understood, implemented and generally strengthen the Union in its jurisdiction'.

Unfortunately, however, many of the chairmen and state secretaries are confusing their role with that of the branch executives. Under the new industrial relations, collective agreements can only be concluded at the national level between the national union and the relevant employers' federation. Other items, not considered negotiable at that level, are left for in-house discussion between the particular company and the branch union. But the state councils now insist that they must be represented at such in-house discussions. This means that they are (perhaps without knowing it) introducing another layer of national negotiations at company level. This is clearly against the present set-up. What is envisaged at the enterprise level is discussions on matters peculiar to the organisation on which agreements may be reached between the particular enterprise and the branch or company union.

It would appear also that, because of lack of proper training and briefing, the state-council officials do not seem to know the boundaries of their responsibilities. Accordingly, at least in their minds, there is an overlap between their responsibilities and those of the branch unions. Instead of confining themselves to the 'co-ordination' of union activities, they want to deal direct with the different employers. This confusion may have arisen because in the procedural agreements concluded between employers' federations and national unions, there is no role mapped out for the state councils. They have been created by the unions for their own administrative convenience. Unless this is seen to be so, there will continue to be conflicts not only between the state councils and employers but also between the state councils and branch unions.

The national union. Under the model constitution adopted by all national unions, the objects of the national union can be grouped into two headings as follows:

(a) to secure improvement in wages and salaries and other conditions of employment; and
(b) to protect and advance the socioeconomic and cultural interest of the workers in the community.

In order to achieve these objectives, the government of the National Union of Food, Beverage and Tobacco Employees is vested in the following five bodies: (i) the Triennial Delegates Conference, (ii)

National Executive Council, (iii) administrative committee, (iv) state council, (v) Branch Executive Committee.

We have already discussed the last two bodies and we now deal with the remaining three.

The *administrative committee* is made up of the national president, the general secretary and other national officials of the union. Its role is to administer the day-to-day affairs of the union in between the meetings of the National Executive Council. The role also includes the filling of vacancies in the union and the imposition of disciplinary measures against an erring member. The committee is supervised by the National Executive Council and its actions are subject to approval by the Council.

The *National Executive Council* has a wider composition and is a more powerful body than the administrative committee. It is made up of all the members of the administrative committee and, in addition, the chairmen, secretaries of state councils and branch chairmen and general secretaries. The Council administers the union in between Triennial Delegates Conferences and in particular has the duty to:

> guard and further the interest of members of the Union, carry out policy determined by the conference, ensure proper and strict observance of the rules of the union by members both individually and collectively, safeguard the funds of the union, set up such departments or committees as it may deem necessary for the smooth and orderly conduct of the affairs of the union, issue directives for proper governance and administration of Union affairs, and perform such other functions as may promote the objects of the Union.

On paper at least, the composition of the Council is representative and democratic and the duties if carried out can make for an effective union. However, as we have already pointed out, there are problems in union government at the branch level. In the circumstances, those who represent the branches in the Council may not be of the right calibre. Even where they are of the right calibre, it is difficult for them to know how the rank and file feel on an issue since they do not attend meetings called to discuss such issues. This makes it difficult for meaningful communication to take place. Moreover, as check-off is now automatic, there is no longer any incentive on the part of the national officials to contact and consult other branch unions regularly. Similarly, the new system of industrial relations has made poaching of union members unnecessary. All this may well have the effect of making the national union officials complacent and completely remote from the realities of the workplace.

The supreme authority of the union is vested in the *Triennial Delegates Conference*. It is the policy-making body of the union. The Conference is composed of all national officers of the union, state chairmen and secretaries, and branch delegates which must include their chairmen and secretaries. The number of delegates representing a branch depends on the numerical strength of the branch. The business of the Conference includes the consideration and determination of internal questions of policy affecting the members of the union, reports from the National Executive Council, state councils and branch committees. Elections to offices are also held during these conferences. Elections are usually by secret ballot or where necessary by a show of hands. To be elected, a candidate must obtain a simple majority of the votes of members present and voting. The president of the union presides over the Conference.

The Nigerian Labour Congress. The aims and objectives of the Congress include, among other things, the general improvement of the economic and social conditions of Nigerian workers and all matters of workers' education at national level.[26] In order to carry out these objectives, the NLC has established a complicated structure which encompasses the following bodies:

(a) the Congress-in-Session;
(b) the National Executive Council;
(c) the national secretariat;
(d) the national departments;
(e) the State Executive Council of Congress;
(f)   the state secretariats of the Congress;
(g) the representatives of national department at states;
(h) the Local Executive Council of the Congress;
(i)   the local Congress secretariats, and
(j)   the advisory councils.

However, the three most important bodies of the Congress are the Congress-in-Session, the National Executive Council and the State Executive Council. The Congress-in-Session is made up of accredited delegates of affiliated unions, all members of the National Executive Council, and all heads of departments of the Congress. It has supreme authority over all matters concerning the labour movement. It can delegate powers and responsibilities to the National Executive Council, which in turn may delegate such powers to other bodies of the Congress or officers. The Congress meets only once in every three years, except in the case of emergency, that is, when three-quarters of its members vote for the declaration of such emergency. The principal officers of the Congress, including the president, the deputy president, the national treasurer and the deputy national treasurer, must submit to elections during these sessions. Only the general secretary is exempt from these elections. He is appointed to the post, not elected.

The National Executive Council is made up of the president, deputy president, the president and secretary of each affiliated national union, chairmen of State Executive Councils, national treasurer, heads of departments of the Congress, and assistant general secretaries. The NEC is the executive body of the NLC, and it conducts and directs the activities of the Congress.

The State Executive Council is made up of a chairman, assistant secretary, treasurer and a representative from each branch of the unions in the state. Members hold office for three years and are eligible for re-election. The function of the SEC includes transacting the business of the Congress at the state level and 'keeping watch on all industrial movements in the state'.

The restructuring of unions had the objective of establishing more viable unions. We shall now, therefore, examine the changes the new system has introduced with particular reference to union administration, union finance and union education.

(iii) Union administration

It is too early at this stage to assess the effectiveness of the new union organisation in respect of its government and adherence to democratic principles. It would appear, however, that as a result of the bureaucratic nature of the union set-up, the poor union government that had prevailed in the past might become worse. Apathy among the rank and file was exploited by union officials. The general secretaries, whose knowledge, experience and skills were better than those of the local union executives, virtually took over decision-making. Communication between the centre and rank and file members was anything but effective. These developments encouraged oligarchic tendencies in trade-union government. However, it was not the structure of the unions that was responsible for that poor state of affairs. Adrian Peace has argued that the old union organisation, apparently simple and straightforward as it was, did not particularly ensure the flow of communication and exchange of ideas between the central labour leaders and the local union executives of unions affiliated to the central organisations.[27] He illustrated this alienation by showing that during the Adebo Commission's awards crisis of 1970, initiative for industrial action came from the rank and file members in the various enterprises rather than from the central labour organisations. A similar thing occurred in 1975, during the Udoji Commission's awards of that year. Thus, the old union structure was not a guarantee against union oligarchy and bureaucracy and subsequent alienation of the rank and file members. These are probably matters that are connected with commitment to trade unionism on the part of the leaders and their ability to motivate their members to participate and be involved in union activities, including attendance at meetings and taking part in union elections.

Professor O. Oloko of the University of Lagos has also argued that the problems of industrial relations in Nigeria were contributed not by the structure, as it existed, but by the Nigerian socioeconomic system as a whole.[28] He believes that the form of organisation in any national industrial relations system is the product of various historical factors, such as the structure of productive activity and organisation, the nature of politics and ideology, its effects and the role workers have collective-ly played in it. Also relevant is the pattern of power relations as lodged within the state structure, the dominant socioeconomic groups, and the extent to which these possess any strong linkages with various areas of socioeconomic life including that of industrial relations. It is these aspects rather than the structure of unions that has influenced the pattern of industrial relations in Nigeria.

While we agree with the analyses of Peace and Oloko, it is our contention here that the new structure has created a bigger problem of bureaucratisation and oligarchy, and this does not make for effective union administration. The structure of any organisation does affect the morale of those who work within it, in one way or another. An organisation that is structured in such a way that there is no free flow of information, vertical and horizontal, is bound to develop bottlenecks, which in turn will hamper the effective performance of individuals. This is particularly important when it is remembered that apathy has been a problem in the trade-union movement in Nigeria. The structure itself must make it possible for trained union leaders to get to and encourage the rank and file members to take active interest in union activities. We can draw parallel lessons from other countries whose industrial relations systems we have studied on the danger of the remoteness of union officials from the rank and file workers. In Ghana, Dr Nkrumah had wanted the trade-union movement to be a mass movement and accordingly established a bureaucratic Trade Union Congress, the Ghana TUC. Unfortunately for Dr Nkrumah, he believed, erroneously as it turned out, that once he had talked to the leaders of the Ghana TUC and had secured their consent, then automatically he had secured the co-operation of all the workers in Ghana. He was proved wrong in 1961 when, to his dismay, a General Strike engulfed his nation. The events that followed led to his downfall in 1966. Similarly in Tanzania, the bureaucratic union set-up in 1964 under NUTA lost touch with the ordinary workers. The result was that NUTA became completely ineffective, and the ordinary workers had to take their problems direct to the government over NUTA.

It is only when the workers are fully involved in trade-union government, in practice and not in theory, that we are likely to reduce the incidence of 'wildcat' strikes called either by the workers contrary to the decision of the unions or by the branch union without the authorisation of, or even against the advice of, the national executive. It was in recognition of this problem that the government included a provision in the Code of Practice for Trade Unions on members' rights and responsibilities. The Code has been incorporated into every union's rule book. Article 4 of the Code provides that each member of a trade union should have the right to full and free participation in the government of his trade union. This right includes voting periodically as provided for in the union's constitution, the right to honest and democratically conducted elections, to stand for and hold office, and to express his views as to the method in which the union's affairs should be conducted. Moreover, each member of a union should have the right to fair treatment in the application of union rules and constitution. Disciplinary procedures must contain elements of equity and fairness and the principles of natural justice. The article also enjoins each member to exercise fully his rights of trade-union membership and loyally to support his union. To make certain that meetings are held and attended, a responsibility is placed on the unions to call such meetings and to ensure that all members attend and participate actively. Nevertheless, from past experience we know that what the constitution says may be completely different from what individuals do.[29] Therefore the fact that a democratic structure has been established, does not *per se* guarantee democratic unions. The union leaders themselves must be prepared to make the system work.

In the past, for the reasons we have already discussed in this study, trade unions did very little for their members outside wage negotiations. The time has now come for them to extend their services. They must, for example, be prepared to adapt workers to industrial life as the country is now on the threshold of industrialisation. They must also contribute, through consultation and co-operation with employers and the government, towards the development of social and economic policies, and to promote increased efficiency and productivity. The prosperity of the nation will effect the standard of living, not only of trade-union members, but other members of society. This will satisfy one of the objectives of the unions contained in their charter. The unions can only do this if they exercise firm and responsible leadership and if they ensure that their members are well informed. It is only when unions and employers' organisations exercise firm leadership in respect of their members, that the collective agreements reached can be meaningful, without the fear of flagrant breach.

Union finance. Under the new system of industrial relations, the financial base of unions has been strengthened. A situation has now been created that should enable trade unions to show interest in other positive activities such as the provision of welfare and educational facilities for their members. The unions should now be able to look after themselves, rather than look outside the country for aid as they did in the past.

While availablility of funds appears to have solved some of the unions' problems, it has created others. Many union officials have suddenly found themselves in charge of large sums of money. In the past, cases of fraud and misuse of union funds were common. With the accumulation of large sums through the 'check-off' system, there is no guarantee that the past events of history will not be repeated. Indeed, quite recently there have been problems in the National Union of Shop and Distributive Trades and the National Union of Food, Beverage and Tobacco Employees, in respect of mishandling of union funds. All this is happening in spite of the revelations made by the Adebiyi Tribunal in 1977 regarding misuse of union funds and property, which led to the banning of certain trade unionists from future participation in trade unionism. It becomes necessary therefore that both the Registrar of Trade Unions and the NLC should ensure that every union renders adequate and properly audited accounts each year as provided for by law. Those found guilty of misappropriation of funds, in breach of the union's code of practice, should be made liable and prosecuted in the normal way.

Trade-union education. Trade-union education involving both union officials and rank and file members was neglected in the past. In addition to the general educational background of trade-union leaders in Nigeria, they need specialised knowledge. They must, for instance, be able to read and understand the financial reports of companies, prepare and file claims on behalf of their members, and understand some aspects of economics and sociology, the relevant labour laws and the precepts of democracy. The deficiency of this knowledge in the past contributed to a lot of misunderstanding between trade-union leaders and employers, the latter having the advantage of better education and training. It meant that at the negotiating table the parties were not communicating effectively with each other. The government, for its part, has a role to play in trade-union education. In 1975 the federal government, in its National Labour Policy, announced that it would set up a National Institute of Labour Studies where trade unionists would be trained. Ilorin has now been chosen as the site. Employers of labour can also help in the over-all efforts in respect of training by encouraging liberal and vocational training and by pursuing liberal policies in respect of study leave for workers involved in labour education. The NLC and the national unions should constantly monitor and identify the training programmes for their members. They must give priority to the education and training of rank and file members to bring them up to the educational level of the leaders, or at least to a reasonable level. The unions themselves should ensure that only those with the relevant union training are voted into positions of responsibility. In this way the benefits of better education and training will be realised in the over-all administration and government of unions.

3.1.7 Union effectiveness

From the historical survey of the union development, it would appear that the unions were not in a position to cater adequately for their members. They were plagued by splits and leadership crises and there was no effective direction from the centre because the labour movement lacked cohesion. Each house union more or less fended for itself. This situation has led some to suggest that the trade unions in Nigeria have not been effective, at least in the area of improved wages. John Weeks, for example, has argued that as the unions were 'weak and precariously grafted onto the Nigerian industrial relations system', they had virtually no impact on wages.[30] These weak unions had developed in an unfavourable economic environment and had as a result developed a progressively less militant posture. The fact that the strike pattern was characterised by major work stoppages *after* and not *before* wage awards, confirms that the initiative for wage review was from the government rather than the unions. Elliot Berg supports Weeks's thesis. He disagrees with the view that the trade-union movement had had a critically important influence on government wage policies. Rather, what is significant is the ideological or intellectual environment which shapes the ideas of policy-makers, and the nature of decision-making in the public sector. Thus, wage behaviour must be explained in terms of 'the role of prevailing ideas of social justice and "fair" wages, and taking into account the administrative process by which wages are fixed'. As wage changes were generally initiated by government, the trade unions had little or no part to play in the process.[31]

Peter Kilby does not share that view. According to him, 'there is little doubt that trade unions [in Nigeria] have raised wages in the organized labour market appreciably higher than they otherwise would have been'. However, because the unions were weak and unable to organise properly, 'this has not been achieved through collective bargaining process; rather it has been achieved by bringing political pressure to bear on the government, which in turn has established independent wages tribunals'. In addition to the political pressure brought by the unions at the national level which resulted in the Wages and Salaries Commissions, private-sector collective bargaining also contributed to the maintenance of the real wage, the variable margin above the government rate.[32] W. M. Warren also reached the same conclusion in his study of urban real wages in Nigeria. He states:

> In Nigeria, between 1939 and 1960, the actual and potential strength of the wage-earning classes in the urban areas permitted the trade unions to mobilize political sources of strength and thus to counteract the handicaps under which they were operating the several internal weaknesses and unfavourable economic conditions, especially in the labour market. As a result, the trade unions have, in certain periods and over these years, generally been effective in raising real wages.[33]

While we do not consider it necessary to repeat the arguments that have been put forward to support the thesis that trade unions in Nigeria have been effective, there are two important points we must draw attention to. Those who argue that the unions have not been effective seem to think that the level of wages that are being paid and the introduction of such fringe benefits as housing and transport allowances (which the employers resisted for a long time) were granted out of the benevolence of the employers' hearts. This is not so, the pressure came from the unions. Moreover, the facts are there for everyone to see. In the unorganised private sector where unions do not exist, wages and fringe benefits are substantially lower than in the organised one. By unorganised private sector, we mean those small companies where no formal management structures exist and where no formal personnel policies and procedures have been established. In some of these companies wage and salary scales do not even exist, and these companies do not pay any monetary allowances apart from the basic wage. To illustrate the point, we will draw our examples from the Food, Beverage and Tobacco Industry. Until 1978, a number of companies in the unorganised private sector of the industry did not have unions and did not belong to an employers' association. However, in that year, and under the new industrial relations, most of these companies joined an employers' association. Changes to conditions of employment in these companies were therefore affected by two factors. First, as a result of belonging to an employers' association, the companies were influenced by what other companies did, and accordingly they made changes in conditions of service in 1979. Second, the Employers' Association concluded a collective agreement with its national union, as a result of which substantial monetary improvements that did not exist before were introduced into these companies. Table 3.4 compares two companies that had no unions until 1980 – namely, Lisabi Mills (Nigeria) Limited and the Biscuit Manufacturing Company of Nigeria Limited – with two that had had unions for a long time – namely, the Nigerian Tobacco Company Limited and Guinness (Nigeria) Limited.

While we accept that bigger companies in Nigeria on the whole appear to be more profitable and therefore could be said to be able to pay better wages and salaries even without the pressure of unions, this is not always true. Based on return on capital, there is a number of small companies that are more profitable than big ones, and yet do not pay good wages and salaries. While an enlightened employer, big or small, will be prepared to improve the conditions of work (including compensation) of his workers, our argument is that this process is accentuated by the presence of unions. Indeed one major area of NECA's activity has been concerned with trying to convince such

TABLE 3.4 Comparison of companies in the food, beverage and tobacco industry

Item	Companies without unions			Companies with unions								
	Lisabi Mills			Biscuit Manufacturing Co.			NTC			Guinness		
	1977	1979	1980	1977	1979	1980	1977	1979	1980	1977	1979	1980
Lowest wage scale	None published	None published	₦1200 p.a. to increase by 5%	₦770– ₦898 (p.a.)	₦850– ₦982 (p.a.)	₦1200– ₦1330 (p.a.)	₦790– ₦1090 (p.a.)	₦790– ₦1090 (p.a.)	₦1200– ₦1364 (p.a.)	₦783– ₦973 (p.a.)	₦862– ₦1070 (p.a.)	₦1200– ₦1350 (p.a.)
Selected benefits												
Housing allowance	₦72 p.a.	₦120 p.a.	₦180 p.a.	₦72 p.a.	₦96 p.a.	₦180 (p.a.)	₦96	₦96	₦180	₦180	₦180	₦180
Transport allowance	₦72 p.a.	₦120 p.a.	₦156 p.a.	Nil	Nil	₦156 (p.a.)	₦96 (p.a.)	₦96 (p.a.)	₦156 (p.a.)	₦156 (p.a.)	₦156 (p.a.)	₦156 (p.a.)

Notes: (i) The Employers' Association was formed in 1978 and the procedural agreement with the national union was signed in 1979. Note the effect of this agreement on the conditions of service of Lisabi Mills and the Biscuit Manufacturing Company with respect to the items listed above.

(ii) A collective agreement throughout the industry was signed in 1980 covering many items, including housing and transport allowances. Both Lisabi Mills and the Biscuit Manufacturing Company had to comply.

(iii) All companies had to pay a minimum wage of ₦1200 p.a. as a result of an executive order.

Source: From data supplied by the Secretariat of the Employers' Association.

employers to tolerate unions and to bargain with them collectively. This was to ensure that such employers paid reasonable wages.

It is true that the period 1939–60 was used in the assessment of the effectiveness or otherwise of the unions. Nevertheless, we think it is an exaggeration on the part of Berg to insist that the trade unions were 'a minor factor in wage determination'. In spite of their weakness and lack of cohesion, union agitation led to the several Wages and Salaries Commissions that were appointed in Nigeria between 1941 and 1960.

In any event, the trade-union leaders themselves realised their own weakness and after 1960 devised a strategy to overcome that weakness. In 1963 the unions formed the Joint Action Committee (JAC), already discussed. The success of the JAC in the General Strike of 1964 became an eye-opener to the unionists, demonstrating that if only they could come together they would achieve more.

Thus in 1970, when the government set up another Wages and Salaries Commission (the Adebo Commission), the unions again came together to form the United Committee of Central Labour Organisations (UCCLO), whose aim was to represent workers' interest before the Commission. The UCCLO presented a joint memorandum to the Commission on behalf of the unions and also followed it up with oral evidence to ensure that in spite of lack of cohesion in the movement, the workers were fairly treated.

Similarly, in 1974, when the Wages and Salaries Commission (the Udoji Commission) appointed two years earlier was being wound up, the labour leaders got together under the Apena Cemetary Declaration, to present a united front, which again resulted in substantial awards to the workers. Thus, in spite of their fundamental differences and weaknesses, when the interests of the workers were at stake and because they knew the main body of workers would support them, the central labour organisations were prepared to speak with one voice.

3.1.8 Unions and politics

While the unions have supported collective bargaining as a means of improving wages and salaries and other conditions of employment, they seem to have come to the conclusion that there are limitations to that system for achieving their social objectives. In the preamble to the Workers' Charter of Demands, presented to the government early in 1980, the NLC made it clear that it stood for the masses, including 'workers who live by wages and salaries, and its considerations extend to the labouring poor who, though not in paid employment or organized labour must reap directly from the fruits of their labour. Both groups combined constitute the bulwark of the nation's labour force.' In order to achieve the social objectives in the Charter, the NLC wants to be involved in the development of a new basic-needs strategy for the country. The Charter draws attention to rural development, problems of urban development, education, unemployment and old-age pensions, housing and a national minimum wage.[34] The Congress wants all these to be improved. On the last item, the unions resorted to legal enactment. The Congress insisted that there should be an enforceable legal minimum wage of ₦300.00 per month in Nigeria.

Yet, legal enactments and other statutory measures for securing unions' objectives have their limitations because legislators may not wish to go along with union demands. Indeed, the cold reception the NLC got in the National Assembly over its fight for a legal minimum wage is a pointer.[35] In these circumstances, in order to achieve their objectives, the unions may turn to political action, that is, either by forming a party or allying itself with a political party. But will such a development take place in Nigeria in the near future, having regard to the earlier efforts in this regard?

In spite of an occasional brush with party politics, the labour movement in Nigeria has not achieved its ends through party political action, although the colonial government was always frightened of that possibility.[36] The first TUC had come into existence in 1943 with the full support of the leading politicians.[37] However, there were two main political movements in the country at the time, namely, the National Council of Nigeria and the Camerouns (NCNC) led by Herbert Macaulay and later by Dr Nnamadi Azikiwe, and the Nigerian Youth Movement led by 'elitist Yoruba Lagosians'.[38] The NCNC was eager to work closely with the labour movement which had displayed its strategetic importance when it organised the General Strike of 1945. Accordingly, the TUC was formally affiliated to the NCNC and Michael Imoudu of the Railway Workers' Union, who had played a prominent part in the General Strike of 1945, became closely identified with that political movement. Indeed, Imoudu was one of the delegates sent to London in 1947 by the NCNC to discuss the shortcomings of the Richards Constitution of 1946 with the Colonial Secretary, Arthur Creech-Jones. In spite of the affiliation of the TUC to the NCNC and the apparent zeal and enthusiasm of Imoudu for labour to play an active role in the struggle for independence, labour's contribution as such was not significant. Although the movement was in its formative stage, membership was growing rapidly and was concentrated in the important centres of political activity. If it had been properly organised and if other external factors had not intervened, it might have played an important role in the struggle for independence.

The failure to use the labour movement platform to fight colonialism can be traced to ethnic considerations which had plagued Nigerian politics since the early 1940s. These considerations made it impossible to have a national movement and a charismatic leader with whom the rank and file could identify, as in the case of Dr Nkrumah and his Convention People's Party (CPP) in Ghana (see Chapter 1). Neither was the situation similar to that which prevailed in India, where the different political movements had their ideologies so clearly spelt out that the unions with different ideologies were able to decide on affiliation (see Chapter 1).

In Nigeria, in contrast, the affiliation of the TUC to the NCNC was shortlived because, as O. A. Fagbenro-Beyioku – himself a prominent trade unionist – saw it, 'politics and trade unionism could not go together'.[39] Obviously, external influences were at work and other considerations had come into play. At a meeting held in December 1948 in Lagos, the TUC was disaffiliated from the NCNC. The disaffiliation led to the first split in the labour movement, a phenomenon that continued to recur to the disadvantage of the movement. A statement put out later explained that the Congress felt that as an organisation grouping people with diverse political sympathies, it should maintain a stand independent of all political or tribal groups in order to avoid an obvious clash of interests. Plausible as the statement may sound, it belied the true reason for the disaffiliation. The truth of the matter was that there was rivalry between the NCNC and the NYM political movements which, at least after 1946, began to be associated with the Ibos and Yorubas respectively. An affiliation to one was therefore seen as an advantage to that ethnic group. In such circumstances, the labour movement could not operate on a single platform.

However, the influence of tribalism in the Nigerian trade-union movement should not be overemphasised. While political leaders may have tried to use the labour movement as a means of achieving their own objectives in matters that touched upon the welfare of the workers, the movement, as we have seen, spoke with one voice. Also, the appointment of union officials, especially general secretaries, seemed to have been based on the proven ability and commitment of the individuals rather than on ethnic considerations. This observation seems to hold good in other parts of Africa. In a study of an East

African trade union, Grillo emphasises that the tribal factor is just one means that individuals exploited. He observes:

> The tribal factor may play an important part as one, but only one, of the weapons that leaders use in the struggle for power. What is basic here is not 'tribal rivalry' so much as a system which provides a multiplicity of sources from which the competitors can draw support.[40]

Yet, we think it is too early to dismiss the influence of ethnicity on worker political behaviour in Nigeria. By and large, the worker still looks up to his own ethnic group for security, and faced with the choice between loyalty to his ethnic group and the union, he will choose the former. We therefore think that while the unions might make 'political' statements and do things that might have political undertones, they are unlikely in the near future either to ally themselves with a political party or to form a workers' party. This is not to say that the NLC officials who are favourably disposed to a certain party or parties will not manipulate the workers and the trade-union system against other parties. However, if the NLC were to openly ally itself with a political party, there would be a conflict between loyalty to a union and loyalty to an ethnic group (the latter forming the basis of present political parties) and we have no doubt that the latter would prevail and the Congress might collapse.

3.1.9 Management unions

A recent phenomenon in the industrial-relations scene in Nigeria is the rise of management unions. The management in any organisation has always been equated with the employer although not correctly so, at least in the majority of cases. For it is the management that negotiates with the workers' union on behalf of the company. What has happened suddenly to make managers in industry realise that their salvation lay in a formal association, the union? Of course, management unions are not new phenomena, as they exist in certain European countries including Denmark, France, Italy and the UK. The interesting aspect of the Nigerian situation is that under the Trade Unions (Amendment) Act 1978 employers are now obliged to recognise management unions, wherever they exist. Unlike workers' unions, management unions are not affiliated to the NLC: they exist as separate independent national unions.

It has been suggested that for a management association to emerge in any organisation, two factors must be responsible.[41]

1. There must be threats to the managers' status and prestige.
2. Such threats must be strong and persistent enough for the affected managers to perceive them as insurmountable through individual efforts.

We shall now analyse these two factors to see how they have influenced the growth of management unions in Nigeria.

(i)   Threat to status and prestige

For many years the Nigerian manager had relied on the goodwill of his employer in changing his conditions of service. During that period he had watched how the workers through their own organisations had been able to establish themselves as a force to be reckoned with. The managers, acting individually and being treated on an individual basis, had not been able to develop that front which would enable them to negotiate (rather than be told) their conditions of service. Thus, in the eyes of the manager, the system left him in a weak and helpless position. The situation was further aggravated when some employers introduced good fringe benefits, including housing and car-running allowances, while others refused to follow the lead of such employers. Those not privileged to have these facilities felt their salvation lay in combination.

The point must not be overlooked that Nigerian managers have been alive to developments elsewhere and might have been influenced by the fact that management unions have helped in influencing for the better conditions of service of managers in other countries. For example, Travernier reports that in Denmark, France, Italy, the UK and West Germany, management unions have in recent times won for their members collective agreements on detailed salary structures, greater job security and more consultation in the decision-making process.[42] Such developments elsewhere may have influenced action in Nigeria and made it possible for managers to discard any doubts that may have lurked in their minds about the wisdom of the approach.

One other factor that has led to management unionisation is the fact that in Nigeria, organisational control in the large, well-established companies has been firmly in the hands of Europeans. There has always been polarisation (for several reasons) in the conditions of service of Europeans and Nigerian managers, with the latter insisting on equality of treatment in all respects. Accordingly, the ground was fertile for managers' militancy which can only be demonstrated through combination.

(ii)   Were the threats perceived as persistent?

The trend in management unionism started early in the 1970s but since then the 'indigenisation' of the economy, capital and manpower has been pursued with some vigour by the government. Although complete control has not yet been passed to the Nigerian manager, it would appear that, possibly as a result of the measure, there has been no rush in recent years to form management unions. Indeed, the management unions now existing are those that were formed between 1970 and 1975. Since the Nigerian Enterprises Promotions Act of 1972 was amended in 1977 restricting certain economic activities to Nigerians, the urge to join a union seems to have subsided. However, the fact that management unions in certain industries are negotiating with employers' federations, under the new industrial relations system, may act as a motivating factor for other managers to want to do the same.

Moreover, the security that managers and senior officers enjoyed in their jobs (especially in the public service) prior to 1975, was shattered when the military government forcibly retired a large number of people on such grounds as inefficiency, incompetence and old age, the reason for each case being decided upon by the military. That action drove home to many managers and other senior officers that each and every one could be easily asked to leave by an employer. To combat that situation, combination became necessary. There was a need for collective action. That need was reinforced by the fact that the workers' unions seemed to have benefited from the collective bargaining process. This is shown by the relatively higher wages paid to junior workers in the private sector in comparison with their counterparts in the public service where there is no collective bargaining. It is possible therefore that the managers, having examined the role of collective bargaining, came to the conclusion that it has a lot of advantages to commend it. Accordingly, they geared themselves up for the establishment of unions.

3.2   EMPLOYERS' ASSOCIATIONS

Employers' associations in the modern sense are a new development in

Nigeria. In 1954 there existed eight employers' associations registered under the Trade Union Ordinance. With the exception of the Nigerian Mining Employers' Association, these were really local associations, some restricted to one town such as the Abakaliki Contractors' Union or to a province – as in the case of the Ondo Provincial Timber Contractors' Union. Furthermore, these bodies were not concerned with labour matters as such; instead they concerned themselves with the regulation of trade practices and in providing friendly service in order to minimise the risks of competition.[43] Thus, while house unions and trade-union centres were active by the middle of the 1950s, there were no organised employers' associations to deal specifically with industrial relations at national level. Instead, each company dealt with its own union (where it existed) as best it could without the benefit of the views of other employers, especially those in the same type of business.

The slow development of employers' associations in the country could be attributed to three factors. First, the government had always been and continues to be the largest single employer and had tended to set the pace in the change of wages and other conditions of service which other employers had to follow. Accordingly, it was easy for an employer to convince his workers that he had done what the government had asked him to do. In such circumstances the need to seek protection from and agree a common front with other employers could not and did not arise. Second, until the mid 1950s, the organised private sector was made up of essentially commercial houses, as we have seen, and these were generally scattered throughout the country in small groups. The unions, with the exception of a few cases, did not constitute any real threat from within as they were loosely organised and very weak. Once an employer was in a position to contain the internal situation, he did not see the need to worry about the activities of the unions (mainly those in government establishments) at the national level. Third, individualism was encouraged by the fact that the personnel management function as we know it today is of relatively recent origin in Nigeria.

The function was generally performed by a general manager of a company in addition to his general management duties. Usually, there were no personnel specialists to lay down personnel policy and to consult other employers on their policies and practices. It was much later that labour and staff managers were appointed and even these were not always people with a personnel-training background. Consequently, each individual company tackled its industrial relations problems as best as it could, without having regard to the probable consequences for other employers, and indeed for itself. The failure to appoint qualified persons to man the personnel function had certain important consequences. The relatively unimportant matters that experienced practitioners could have dispensed with were allowed to fester and degenerate into industrial actions and, in some cases such as the Enugu coal mines shooting of 1949, into tragedy. Furthermore, the parties looked upon the labour officer as their saviour in all cases of dispute, because he was the only one who knew how to solve their problems. So long as he was around, there was no need for the employers to form their own association.

The lack of established personnel policies in organisations in Nigeria had important implications for industrial relations. It meant that little attention was paid to good industrial relations and even where efforts were made, they were made by those who had not received the right training or who did not have the necessary background. Such persons were, predictably, anti-union and during the decade 1950–60, the general attitude towards the development of trade unionism was that of rejection. As a result, organised unions could only be found in the traditional government corporations such as the railways, the ports and the coal mines, and in some of the large industrial organisations, some of which had come into existence during the period. The unions were in no position to assert themselves effectively not only because they were weak at the national level but also because of the proliferation of small unions at the enterprise level. There were constant problems of refusal to recognise unions and frequent strikes which lasted for a few days. There was no discernible pattern of industrial action because it was mainly *ad hoc*, directed at a particular move or non-action by the employer.

While the government was disposed towards the development of trade unions, it did relatively little to encourage collective bargaining in industry. Indeed, formal collective bargaining did not take place until 1957 when the Nigerian Tobacco Company Limited and its house union established a joint industrial council. The United Africa Company followed in 1959 with the establishment of collective bargaining machinery at their African Timber and Plywood factory at Sapele. Other companies soon followed. Thus, left on their own, the employers dictated the pattern of industrial relations in the country. In many cases, conditions of service, including wages, were changed unilaterally and protests were quickly muffled by the termination of employment of those concerned. The annual reports of the Department of Labour (later Ministry of Labour) are full of details of industrial disputes during the period 1950–60. The causes of such disputes were the result of a spontaneous demand by workers for a particular thing, followed by refusal on the part of the employers. One dispute recorded in the 1950–1 annual report concerned the one-day strike action by 150 workers in the Electricity Corporation of Nigeria (now NEPA) in Ibadan. The demand by the workers was for the reinstatement of a fitter and the matter was 'amicably settled' when a labour officer intervened. Another action by the same workers reported in the 1952–3 annual reports concerned a six-point demand covering claims for increases in salary, provision of uniforms and other service conditions. On the advice of a labour officer, the union withdrew the notice of the trade dispute. In these examples and many more in the reports, it can be seen that the demand of the workers were *ad hoc* and sporadic, because in all the cases there were no recognised unions to promote their demands, and there were no established procedures to follow.

3.2.1 The growth of employers' associations

The growth of economic activities in Nigeria and, in particular, the shift by many employers to industrialisation by the middle of the 1950s, helped greatly in the development of employers' associations. The Manufacturers' Association of Nigeria (MAN) is an association concerned purely with production and manufacturing problems including energy, water and other poor infrastructural facilities which constitute constraint to production. The Nigerian Association of Chambers of Commerce, Industry, Mines and Agriculture (NACCIMA) is concerned mainly with trade and commercial matters and issues directly associated with them. Such matters include overseas trade policy, tariffs, government regulations on imports and exports, port congestion, etc. While both associations inevitably play some role in industrial relations, the association concerned solely with industrial relations, and to which members of both MAN and NACCIMA belong, is the Nigeria Employers' Consultative Association (NECA). We shall therefore now trace the development of the NECA and examine its role in the development of industrial relations in Nigeria.

3.2.2 The development of NECA

The NECA was formed in 1957 at the initiative of the Federal Ministry of Labour. The initial membership was made up of twenty-eight employers including such well-established companies as the UAC of Nigeria Limited, Shell–BP and the Nigerian Tobacco Company Limited. The Association came into existence as a result of the need for a separate central body of employers to deal with labour and labour-related matters both nationally and internationally. The government wanted a representative body of employers, a counterpart to the trade-union movement, to liaise with on matters concerned with labour. The time was also ripe for the emergence of an employers' association. As the country moved closer to independence, the trade unions began to assert themselves more and more. The unions were so active at the national level (in spite of their disagreements) that there were speculations of a workers' party emerging. There was therefore the fear in the employers' minds that the trade unions might be in a better position to influence government policy to the detriment of the employers. In the circumstances, the old practice of each employer going it alone could no longer hold and employers sought strength and security in association instead of the informal consultations that had taken place. Thus, it became necessary to have a platform to ensure uniformity of actions on all matters of common interest to employers and for making representations to the government on all major industrial relations issues that might affect the interest of employers.

The development of NECA was fostered by the Overseas Employers' Federation (OEF) which provided the initial assistance and guidance to the Association on its formation. The OEF provided NECA with a model constitution and the Association has continued its special relationship with the Federation ever since.

The main objects of NECA relating to industrial relations may be grouped under four categories as follows:

1. To ensure the orderly development of a good industrial relations system, and in particular to encourage the payment of equitable rates of wages and salaries and to assist members with advice on the settlement of disputes.
2. To encourage employers, as far as is practical, to establish uniform points of custom and to adopt reasonable standardised forms of employment contracts.
3. To liaise with the government on all issues relating to labour, such as labour legislation and other topics that may affect the interest of employers.
4. To promote or encourage any technical or other form of education

and research for the development of efficient employees in all or any branches of industry and commerce in Nigeria.

The Association pursues these objectives by ensuring that it presents a common front on all matters concerned with the employment of labour. It also plays an active part on bodies concerned with labour legislation and ensures that those charged with responsibility for labour matters in member-companies are conversant with industrial-relations principles and practices through participation on its courses and committees on industrial relations.

3.2.3   The structure of NECA

The highest policy-making body of the Association is the Co-ordinating Committee. This Committee is made up of representatives of each of the employers' federations affiliated to the Association. It meets once a month to review and make general policy decisions. There are three specialist committees whose duty is to do the research and groundwork to enable the Co-ordinating Committee to lay down policy for all employers. These are the Industrial Relations Committee, the Training and Education Committee, and the Finance Committee.

In 1963 the Association was structured into trade groups. These trade groups were companies that had operations or activities that were similar, such as the Brewing and Mineral Waters Group, which covered all the brewing companies and the bottlers of soft drinks in the country, and the Tobacco Manufacturers which covered the two main tobacco companies in the country. These companies with similar interests met regularly to discuss and examine problems that were common to their industry and to adopt a united front in their approach.

However, the old trade groups have now given way to employers' federations following a further restructuring exercise carried out by NECA in 1979. The Association had felt that following the restructuring of all unions into national industrial unions, with classification not exactly corresponding to NECA's trade groups, it had to regroup its members. Moreover, while under the new industrial relations system the national unions are free to negotiate with individual companies in an industrial sector, NECA felt this would lead to 'leapfrogging' of wages. Thus, the Association favoured an arrangement whereby a national union would negotiate with an employers' federation representing all the organisations in the industrial sector. The Association has therefore regrouped its members into employers' federations, corresponding to the national industrial unions in the private sector of the economy.[44]

The geographical group is another of the NECA's approach for employers in a locality to get together regularly to discuss their common problems. The criterion for belonging to a group is geographical location, so that all the employers in the Ikeja Industrial Estate near Lagos, for example, belong to the Ikeja Geographical Group of NECA. This is so irrespective of the type of business or service the particular company carries on. The creation of these groups is particularly important because of their relevance to common industrial relations problems, such as transport, medical facilities and housing. Indeed in 1977, when the federal government directed that all employers should arrange to provide their workers with housing, all the employers in the Ikeja Geographical Group commissioned Knight, Frank & Rutley, with experience in housing, to advise them on a low-cost housing scheme. By thus acting as a group, companies that otherwise would have acted or refused to act, without regard to events happening around them, are obliged to consult and co-operate with other employers in a forum to find solutions to their common industrial relations problems. In this way NECA ensures that all its members not only obey the law of the land, but also improve general conditions of employment in consonance with its aims.

3.2.4 The functions of NECA

The main functions of NECA can be grouped under the following five headings:

(a) labour–management relations;
(b) training and education;
(c) advisory service;
(d) membership of tripartite bodies;
(e) representation to government on specific labour matters.

The NECA has adopted different methods to achieve its objectives. First, through its several committees that meet regularly, the Association is able to establish a common front for employers to follow, and in this regard brings into line recalcitrant employers who otherwise would have gone ahead to do something different, generally not in the interests of the workers.

Second, the Association has played a major role in the education of employers in industrial relations. It has issued a series of guides, *Memorandum of Advice and Guidance*, to employers to cover such matters as collective bargaining, recognition of trade unions, redundancy, strikes, time-off for union officials, training, safety, end-of-service benefits, disciplinary procedures, unionisation of supervisory and management staff, etc. Over forty of these guides have been issued by the Association since its inception. Moreover, the Association runs an advanced course on industrial relations which is very popular and is over-subscribed each year. In all these attempts, the Association is aiming at raising the level of knowledge of those charged with industrial relations matters.

Third, as the employers' voice in all government tripartite bodies on labour matters, the Association has been able to influence government thinking on labour policy. This has been reflected in new labour legislation and the constant involvement of the three parties – the government, employers and trade unions – in matters affecting labour in the country. Thus, NECA has been represented on many bodies, including the following: (i) the National Manpower Board, (ii) the national Provident Fund Advisory Council, (iii) the National Board of Technical Education, (iv) the West African Examinations Council, (v) the National Industrial Safety Council, (vi) the Council for Management Training and Education, and (vii) the Industrial Training Fund.

In addition, NECA represents the Nigerian Employers at ILO Conferences. In this regard, it is pertinent to note that whenever the government ratifies any ILO convention or recommendation and it thereby becomes part of the laws of Nigeria, the Association ensures that its members are fully briefed to ensure compliance.

Fourth, the government consults the Association on its views on a number of issues. The NECA has produced papers for the government covering such matters as housing for workers, transportation, collective bargaining, national minimum wages, etc. For its part, the Association makes representations to the government on all sensitive issues on industrial relations so that employers' views may be heard before a policy is formulated. Thus, in recent years the Association has made representations on such issues as housing for workers, reintroduction of car loans and the sale of company shares to workers.

It is true to say that since the mid-1960s, employers' attitudes towards unions have improved considerably. Employers now accept unions as institutions that have come to stay and which have a stake in the business, and with which they must deal. The non-recognition of unions which was a common feature of some employers' policy is now a thing of the past. Furthermore, employers have now accepted the concept of employing personnel specialists to deal with industrial relations matters. That change in attitudes on the part of employers can be attributed largely to the activities of the Nigeria Employers' Consultative Association.

As an association of employers' federations, NECA's role among its members is purely consultative and it does not enforce its rules or advice on its members. Part of the work of the officials of the Association is to assist its members in the resolution of their internal labour problems. More significantly, members are warned about impending government legislation that may be of general application to industrial relations and that may have particular bearing on their employer–employee relationships.

One functional area of NECA that has been of significance to industrial relations is the encouragement the association gives to its members, especially the smaller employers, to pay equitable rates of wages and salaries and to improve working conditions generally. It is today an accepted fact that any employer whose conditions of service for its workers can be considered bad is more likely to be outside the Association than inside it. Thus, NECA has been able to influence industrial relations practices in this country for the better. The usefulness of the Association to its members is demonstrated by its growth between the years 1965 and 1980, as shown in Table 3.5.

However, the unions have always been suspicious of NECA. They argue that but for NECA, many employers would be prepared to improve the lot of workers to a much higher level than it is at present. There are some grounds for the unions' suspicions. As an association of employers, NECA's loyalty has naturally been to the employers. To that end, it has on occasions taken actions and decisions that were clearly not in the interest of the unions. For example, during periods of Wages and Salaries Commissions, NECA's stand has always been to ensure that the recommendations are not automatically applied to all workers in the private sector. That stand cannot in itself be faulted, as such extensions would tend to stifle collective bargaining which NECA has always upheld. However, the relevant point here is that the Association did not seem to learn from the experience of the past. In 1964, for example, the Association opposed the recommended increases of the Morgan Wages and Salaries Commission. In the end, after a lot of strikes, the government forced the employers to pay. In spite of that experience, NECA again opposed automatic extension of the Adebo Commission's recommendations in 1971 to the private sector. Again the Association lost the battle. Yet, it fought a similar thing in 1975 during the Udoji Commission's awards and yet again in 1980 over the question of ₦100 per month minimum wage.

TABLE 3.5   NECA membership, 1965–80

Year	Individual companies	Employers' federations	Associate members	Total
1965	293	4	3	300
1966	320	4	4	328
1967	338	5	5	348
1968	346	5	5	357
1969	363	5	7	375
1970	367	5	7	379
1971	383	6	7	396
1972	410	5	6	421
1973	436	5	6	448
1974	467	5	7	475
1975	466	5	7	478
1976	480	5	7	492
1977	498	5	7	510
1978	513	5	7	525
1979	532	5	7	544
1980	641	19	5	665

Article 6 of the NECA Rules and Constitution defines Associate Members as 'Any Corporation established by statute [whose] activities are carried on in a manner similar to that of an industry, trade or business and [which] maintains separate accounts not forming part of the General Budget of the country.' Such public corporations would include the National Electric Power Authority, the Nigerian Railway Corporation and the Nigeria Airways.

Source: NECA, Annual Reports, 1965–80.

NECA has also been opposed to the introduction of new fringe benefits on the ground that they would increase the wage bill for employers. Thus for years the Association fought to prevent the introduction of a housing allowance and transport allowance for workers. It preferred a 'clean wage'. In this, the Association has lost because, once again apart from a few employers breaking the 'ban' – as in the case of Total Nigeria Limited which went ahead and introduced a housing allowance for junior workers early in the 1970s – the government forced all these fringe benefits on the unwilling employers, following union pressure.

It must be remembered also that NECA as an association is distinct from the individual members. It is a consultative association and although its advice to Members is persuasive, it has no mechanism for enforcing a breach. The Michelin Company's case is a good example. This company is based in Port Harcourt and manufactures rubber products. Early in 1980 the National Union of Footwear, Leather and Rubber Products Workers Union of Nigeria, to which the workers in Michelin belong, concluded a collective agreement with the relevant employers' federation. Michelin refused to implement the agreement, arguing that it did not recognise the national union. The NECA appealed to the company pointing out the illegality of its action. The company remained adamant and this led to a serious strike in which much of the Michelin factory was damaged. The matter was later reffered to the Industrial Arbitration Panel for settlement. NECA could not help.

In the light of the above, and to ensure that NECA retains its credibility with the other parties in the industrial relations system, perhaps the time has come for the Association to adopt completely new approaches. It should now be prepared to represent the employers more forcefully at the national level. That may entail the expulsion of a non-co-operating member from the Association. It should also engage in vigorous research on movement of wages and fringe benefits and the effect of these on inflation. The results of all such findings should be made available to the other bodies either at the meeting of the National Labour Advisory Council or at the Wages Advisory Council, in order to guide policy-making in these matters.

3.3 THE GOVERNMENT AND ITS AGENCIES

Although the employer–employee relationship in Nigeria is generally stated to be based on the free voluntary ethic, that 'freedom' is exercised within a tight framework established by the third actor in the system, the government. In Nigeria, the government has in recent times been playing an active role in industrial relations. Originally, because the system of industrial relations in Nigeria was imported from Britain, it followed the pattern there. The colonial administration was concerned mainly with the establishment of voluntary systems to guide unions and employers in their relationships. After independence, a shift occurred that made government an active party in the industrial relations system. We shall now trace and examine that development from the colonial times to the present day.

3.3.1   Colonial philosophy and labour policy

Although the initiative to establish trade unions in Nigeria did not emanate from the British government, it did encourage and actively promote the development of trade unions as part of its general policy in the colonies. The Colonial Development and Welfare Act 1940, for example, was part of that encouragement. The purpose of the Act was to make available in the colonies, over a period of years, subventions from the UK for approved schemes of economic and social development. The Act had provisions that stipulated that no territory might receive aid unless it had in force legislation protecting the rights of trade unions, and unless the projects for which the aid has to be used were carried out under a contract that embodied a 'fair wages clause' and that forbade the employment of children under 14 years.

The colonial government's policy on trade-union development in Nigeria was spelt out in 1950 by the country's governor, Sir John S. Macpherson. While commenting on the Fitzgerald Report into the disorders in the then Eastern Provinces of Nigeria in 1949, he said:

> First of all, I must make a brief reference to the general policy of the Government in relation to trade unions. The Government had repeatedly made it plain that it wishes to see strong and responsible unions built and in spite of many set-backs ... a great deal of practical evidence has been given of Government's determination to carry out that policy. The difficulties to be overcome have been and still are great and it would be over-optimistic to hope for very quick and spectacular progress, but the Government policy of encouraging the establishment of strong and responsible unions will be pursued with increased energy and with a renewed determination to succeed.[45]

Two aims are discernible in the British government pressure on the colonial governments. First, trade unions must not only be allowed to develop, they must be channelled in the right direction, presumably as unions concerned with the economic well-being of their members only. This view is confirmed by the fact that all the 'guides' prepared for trade unions in the colonial era and the trade unions ordinances passed lay emphasis on how trade unions can keep their house in order. Nothing on trade-union philosophy and its role in society was ever touched upon. This is understandable. The colonial administration was not prepared to have political agitations that would disrupt the economy of the country with economic consequences for the metropolitan country.

Second, based on the experience in the UK, the government wanted to ensure that workers in Nigeria were protected by legislation. It was with this background that the colonial administration in Nigeria passed a number of labour legislations, the important ones being the Labour Ordinance 1929, the forerunner of the Labour Code; the Trade Union Ordinance 1938, which provided for unions to register in order to have legal existence; and the Trade Disputes (Arbitration and Inquiry) Ordinance 1941. Thus, by the end of 1941 the legal framework for the regulation of employer–employee relationships had been established.

Meanwhile, a labour inspectorate was set up in Lagos in 1939 and this was converted into a separate Department of Labour in 1942. The Department was charged with the responsibility of enforcing labour legislation in the country and of reporting to, and advising the administration on, trade-union development, the state of industrial relations, the operation of employment exchanges, the supervision of recruitment of labour to the Spanish colonies of Fernando Po, Rio Muni and Equatorial Guinea, and at the end of the Second World War with the resettlement of ex-service men. In 1959 the Department of Labour was absorbed by the new Federal Ministry of Labour and Social Welfare.

It is interesting to note that the anxiety of the British government to ensure the development of viable trade unions and machinery for industrial relations was not, generally speaking, translated into practical terms by the colonial administration in Nigeria. It would appear that the Department of Labour, having come to the conclusion that 'the unions were immature, unstable and badly led and that the employers on their part were as ignorant as the unions', resisted the development of effective unionism and did not encourage attempts at collective bargaining.[46] It seems also that the administration deliberately wanted a weak trade-union movement, for purely political reasons. That inference is confirmed by the views of the Department of Labour itself. In its 1951 report, the Department said: 'Equally, or perhaps even more important were the frequent absence of means of consultation between employers and workers, poor trade union organization and, particularly the activities of demagogic trade union leaders with political ambitions'.[47] What is interesting about that opinion is that it came from British nationals, whose country, at the time of the report, had produced Labour Prime Ministers and Ministers. Yet in

Nigeria, they considered it 'demagogic' for trade-union leaders to have political ambitions.

The depth of frustration with union activity is revealed in S.130 of the 1950–1 report, where the Department of Labour said:

> So much has been said about the 'right to strike', that the general public, no less than the trade unionists, have exaggerated ideas concerning the degree of departure from the ordinary canons of decent behaviour that can be tolerated in the exercise of the right . . . It is distressing, for example, that most sections of the local press could print, during the course of a strike, accounts of brutal assault, upon some defenceless worker, without a hint of condemnation.

Evidence of resistance to trade-union development was certainly available to the Fitzgerald Commission which inquired into the strike at the Enugu coal mines culminating in the shooting down of twenty-one miners in 1949. In its report, the Commission found it necessary to remind the colonial administration thus: 'Trade unionism is part and parcel of the law of Nigeria, it cannot be ignored; it must be made to work as it has worked in Britain to the advantage of the workers and the advantage of the state.'[48]

With regard to collective bargaining, the efforts made were minimal. Instead of encouraging viable institutions for the purpose, the administration merely set up Labour Advisory Boards that were concerned with establishing minimum wages in various organisations. The Department of Labour was more inclined to the promotion of joint consultation rather than collective bargaining. 'It is gratifying to note', said the Department in 1947, 'that Government establishments are leading in joint consultation and discussion with trade unions. . . . It is hoped that the establishment of Joint Negotiation Machinery, on the lines of those adopted in more advanced countries, will be found in Nigeria, before long.'[49] It is clear from this that Nigeria, being a *developing* and not an *advanced* country, did not qualify to have joint-negotiating machinery for the regulation of industrial relations at the time. Yet it was precisely the absence of such machinery that led to the tragedy at the Enugu coal mines. As late as 1957, the Department of Labour was still pushing the idea of *consultation* to the detriment of *negotiation*. In that year the Department reported: 'Consultative Committees are finding favour in many establishments, and private enterprise seems to have recognised the need for a machinery whereby contact can become routine and current information and viewpoints exchanged at frequent intervals.'[50]

Thus joint consultation was encouraged in the tin-mining industry on the plateau, in the collieries at Enugu and in the Electricity Corporation of Nigeria (now NEPA). Whitley Councils, which were supposed to be bodies for consultations, were established for government employees. However, as everyone in Nigeria knows, these bodies did not work as their objectives were unclear and never fully understood. Only a minimal role was assigned to the workers whose interests were at stake in the discussions. Moreover, the government had a dual role as mediator and employer. This created a conflict of interest that rendered the experiment as a failure.[51]

The irony of the situation is that the records are full of the efforts made by the colonial administration to train labour leaders in modern trade unionism. Trade-union experts were sent from the UK and the USA to Nigeria to conduct seminars and courses, and Nigerian labour leaders were given scholarships to visit or study in both the UK and the USA. Furthermore, relevant books were made available and the unions were given generous help to stand on their own feet. Beneath these efforts lay the underlying philosophy of developing 'constitutional' unions capable only of keeping books and being concerned with discussing wages and conditions of employment. They must not be unions with any political orientation and neither must they push things beyond the stage of discussions. The Fitzgerald Commission reflecting this philosophy had the courage to say:

> We would now be failing in our duty if we did not speak to the members of the trade unions of Nigeria with brutal frankness. We should first remind them that most of the things which are now regarded as inalienable rights of the workers are only being gained after a century of struggle by their fellow workers in the UK. The Nigerian worker should therefore consider himself fortunate that he is not faced with a similar struggle and that those hard-won rights are available to him today if he chooses to act with reason.[52]

It followed from this reasoning that if the Nigerian unions did not act with reason, then they forfeited rights that had taken 100 years to acquire and that were imported into Nigeria by the goodwill of the colonial administration. This philosophy permeated the private sector where the employers for flimsy reasons refused to tolerate the emergence of unions. Consequently, at the time of Nigeria's indepen-

dence in 1960, only a few organisations had had experience in collective bargaining.

3.3.2   Government labour policy after independence

Just before independence, the federal government in a policy statement in 1955 confirmed its adherence to the voluntary ethic in
industrial relations when it said: 'Government re-affirms its confidence in the effectiveness of voluntary negotiation and collective
bargaining for the determination of wages. The long term interest of
the Government, employer and trade unions alike would seem to rest
on the process of consultation and discussion which is the foundation
of democracy in industry'.[53] And in the first year following independence, the Federal Ministry of Labour in its annual report was able to
state: 'The principle of collective bargaining between employers'
associations and the trade unions has been widely accepted in this
country as the normal way of settling wages and other conditions of
employment'.[54]

However, the government, though committed to the principle of
free voluntary collective bargaining and had stated that policy publicly
times without number, did nothing to practicalise the policy either in
the civil service or in the companies and corporations owned by the
government. The rather cavalier attitude of the government to the
growth of effective unionism and the failure to encourage machinery
for joint negotiations was exploited by a number of employers. Thus,
in spite of NECA's efforts in encouraging the collective bargaining
process, many employers refused to recognise the development of
unionism in their organisations and this in turn discouraged the
development of collective bargaining as a process of regulating the
employment relationship. It is significant to note also that throughout
the period before the military take-over of the country (1960–5), no
significant new legislation on labour matters was passed. The government appeared content to operate the labour laws it had inherited from
the colonial administration.

The first major shift in government policy from the voluntary ethic
in industrial relations occurred in 1968. In that year there was a lot of
industrial unrest occasioned by the economic hardships of the civil war.
The military administration promulgated the Trade Disputes
(Emergency Provisions) Decree 1968. That Decree, together with the
amendment of 1969, introduced some radical changes into the
industrial relations system. The voluntary statutory machinery for the

settlement of disputes was replaced by another which banned strikes and lockouts and made arbitration compulsory. The new law also provided that no collective agreement may be implemented unless with the prior approval of the government. Thus, by the end of 1969, the government had started to regulate the main components of the collective bargaining process.

Although the 1968 Decree has been repealed, its essential provisions have been retained in new laws. With regard to the settlement of trade disputes, the Trade Disputes Act 1976 (discussed in Chapter 5) has an elaborate statutory machinery for the settlement of disputes. Arbitration is still made compulsory and the awards of conciliation and the Industrial Arbitration Panel (IAP) where confirmed and those of the National Industrial Court (NIC) are binding on the employers and workers concerned. While strikes and lockouts are no longer banned, they are so hedged round that the effect, at least on paper, is the same.

Since 1976 government incomes policy guidelines have been a persistent feature of Nigerian industrial relations. The introduction of a policy for prices, productivity and incomes was one of the commitments of the military government that the civilian administration inherited and has decided to continue with. A percentage norm for pay increases is specified to be exceeded only in a defined range of exceptional circumstances. An obvious implication of the policy is that the exercise of free collective bargaining remains circumscribed by limits and restrictions.

Meanwhile, union activity is not allowed by law to take place in organisations classified as *essential services*. The assumption behind the ban is that unions are disruptive and once trade-union activity is permitted, it will encourage the breakdown of collective bargaining which in turn will result in industrial actions. As such industries are considered strategic, the thinking is that the nation cannot afford strike actions in them. In all these industries, therefore, the freedom of the workers to negotiate collectively with their management for the improvement of conditions of service has been taken away by the state.

We have already discussed government's intervention in restructuring the trade unions. That exercise included the drafting of a new constitution and a code of practice for the unions to operate. Like other institutions in the society, the trade unions were probed and those found guilty of fraud, maladministration or any other act of misconduct were disciplined by being banned from future trade-union activity.

In spite of the great dent made in the collective bargaining process, the government was still able to state in the Third National Development Plan 1975–80 that 'the government continues to pursue its policy of industrial self-government, whereby it encourages employers and workers to try to settle questions of wages and conditions of employment by collective bargaining and only intervenes in the last resort or in the public interest, as an impartial conciliator or arbiter' (p. 283). Yet, the government continued to be an active participant in industrial relations through new labour legislation, policy statements and other administrative measures. In December 1975 the government published its National Labour Policy,[56] in which it admitted to direct intervention. The government emphasised that it was merely 'pursuing the policy of guided democracy in labour matters', and that it was still committed to the 'promotion of labour/management cooperation and of consultation at appropriate levels'. The government stated its intention, 'which will involve limited government intervention in certain areas of labour activity in order to ensure industrial peace, progress and harmony'. It was further made clear that in matters of industrial relations, the government was not satisfied with being an umpire, and instead it would assume the role of an active participant. Thus government policy on labour matters during the military regime clearly shifted from 'absentionist' to an 'interventionist' one. The rationale for the shift was spelt out by the Federal Commissioner for Labour when he said:

> Economic development always entails a complex set of policies and action programmes which emanate in the great part from the political machinery of the State. To participate in economic development the trade unions cannot isolate themselves and act in a social vacuum, as it were. They should participate actively in the country's development efforts and ensure that plans and programmes which serve the interest of the trade unions are introduced. Any institution, if it is to be effective, should be able to cope with additional or different responsibilities. Trade unions are no exception to this rule. On the contrary they have been confronted and are being called upon to reconsider their role in a rapidly changing society and to define their position in relation to other institutions which at present are helping to shape the future destiny of our country.[56]

The civilian administration that took over from the military in October 1979 was quick to reassure that it was dedicated to the principles of collective bargaining between employers and trade unions. The President, Alhaji Shehu Shagari, in his first budget speech to the National Assembly on 18 March 1980, stated his commitment to return the country once more to free collective bargaining; but in the same budget speech the President went ahead to announce that the minimum wage to be paid in the country would be ₦100.00 per month. This made further negotiations on the matter between employers and unions unnecessary. In fact, although belated efforts were made to explain that employers and unions were still expected to negotiate this figure, the harm had been done. The figure of ₦100.00 per month was simply adopted by all employers and trade unions without further bargaining. Once again, the government rather than the employers and the unions had decided an issue concerning the other two parties.

Meanwhile, the government had made it clear that it would continue to be actively involved in industrial relations. According to the Minister of Labour, an active role for government is necessary because, among other things, the growing interdependence of modern industry means that the strike weapon in certain circumstances can inflict disproportionate harm on the rest of the society. Moreover, the organised system of collective bargaining does not appear to have got to grips with a number of economic and social issues. It is in the light of this unsettled industrial relations atmosphere that the government decided to be an active participant.[57]

The government's decision to continue its active participation in industrial relations poses the question: to what extent should a government of a developing country that is industrialising rapidly, be involved in industrial relations? It is now well established that industrialisation has in its wake labour discontent. Professor Kindleberger, for example, considers that 'the social change which is inevitably associated with economic development, whether as prelude or result, seems, more often than not, to be convulsive'.[58] Kerr, Harbison, Dunlop and Myers also believe that discontent is a phenomenon of industrialisation but wonder whether the discontent and protest would become so 'radicalised' as to threaten the success of economic growth.[59] Agitation or discontent is to be expected during the period of industrialisation because accelerated growth is likely to depend on the postponement of the gratification of the many wants it creates. Other problems include the incidence of unemployment among industrial workers, which may be accentuated by rural–urban migration. These are some of the problems that distinguish developed from developing countries. Perhaps it was the recognition of this difference that led Asoka Mehta

to suggest a completely different role for unions in developing countries, rather than imitating those in developed countries.[60] Mehta
argues that it is in the interest of the unions and the developing country
that the unions render active co-operation in the development plans
that aim at the prosperity of the country. As the major problem in
these countries is economic growth, the major question for the unions
is the subordination of immediate wage gains and similar considerations to the development of the country. Fundamentally, unions favour
consumption but economic development requires keeping aggregate
consumption down and accordingly the unions must play a major role
in ensuring that resources are freed for investment. Moreover, unlike
the unions in the West, the scope of the activities of unions in
developing countries should be limited. Thus, 'fighting the elections on
specific issues, forming the government or the opposition, agitation
and propaganda on political problems and similar issues should be left
outside the trade union field'. While these aspects could be tolerated in
a colonial economy for political reasons, trade unions in a free democratic country on its path of economic development can hardly afford
such activities. Therefore one of the functions of unions in these
countries should be 'to mitigate the feeling of distrust by the workers of
the legally constituted Government and to assist it in implementing the
development plans'.

Some authorities doubt the viability of Mehta's thesis. They believe
that its scope, even in relation to developing countries, is too narrow.
Adolf Sturmthal, for example, doubts whether unions can exist 'for
long periods of time, as social welfare agencies ... and even less as
instruments of wage restraint'. He argues that:

> the suggestion that unions delay for a whole period – the 'take-off' –
> their mission of raising their members' standard of living can only
> result in these unions ceasing to exist as genuine unions – whatever
> their name – and, if circumstances permit, new organizations will
> come into being to perform the function which the original unions no
> longer fulfil. In a divided world, this prospect can hardly be enter-
> tained with equanimity.[61]

Others see the role of trade unions not simply in the context of
economic models, but primarily as issues of political economy. They
believe that the developing countries, and particularly their labour
movements, are the main target of communist organising and propaganda activities. Labour unions that can be convincingly accused of

being ineffective in the struggle for improved conditions and standards will have little chance to survive in the highly competitive struggle.

> Free trade unions in a democratic society must ordinarily appeal to the worker on an all out consumptionist platform. No matter how much 'responsibility' the union leader exhibits in his understanding of the limited consumption possibilities existing at the outset of industrialisation, he cannot afford to' moderate his demands. To do so would mean abdication to the irresponsible demagogue or to the communist machine, neither of which has any compunction about outbidding him in promises.[62]

The objections to Mehta's thesis are based on the Western concept of the trade-union role. That role covers social, economic and political aspects. The democratic principles that prevail in the institutions of the West are also extended to trade-union activities. Therefore, since the development of democracy and unionism must and should take the same path, any deviation towards control and curtailment of democratic principles as known in the West is totalitarian. However, it must be remembered that the nature, form and role of any organisation must be influenced by the environment in which it operates. As Friedland has correctly remarked, 'the form of any institutional structure can be expected to reflect both the functions of the institution and the social, cultural, economic and political organization of the society within which it develops. No institution can develop along pre-conceived lines without some adaptation taking place'.[63]

As a result of changes in the Nigerian environment, social, economic and political, and especially the upheavals brought about by the civil war, many Nigerian institutions have changed. These changes also affected the industrial relations system. Government intervention in industrial relations in Nigeria must be seen in the wider context of the government's efforts to develop the whole economy as the country industrialises. Tom Burns has argued that as industry is the characteristic institution of modern advanced societies, newly independent nations of whatever political complexion have adopted industrialisation as a major political goal. In consequence, socioeconomic and political changes that were once conceived of as being consequences of industrialisation are today thought of as a necessary precondition for creating or revitalising the component factors of industrialism. The intervention of governments to regulate the economy, overcome 'bottlenecks' and stimulate technological and economic change –

interventions that are primarily oriented to the needs of the national economy – are a major factor in the intensifications of the subordination of society to the economy. As a result, the role of governments in countries entering upon industrialisation may be expected to be greater than before.[64] Similarly, Albert Tevoedjre has remarked that, learning from the experience of the industrialised countries, African governments have accepted and are applying the policy that workers and employers cannot be left entirely on their own to regulate all aspects of the work situation since instability of economic activities directly or indirectly affect the welfare of the whole nation.[65]

In many respects, the rigid adherence to the principle of non-intervention in industrial relations in Nigeria hampered the development of the system for a long time. The government had believed that, as in the UK, the system should be allowed to develop naturally. Yet the UK had a long history of industrialisation, and its institutions – including the industrial relations system – had developed in circumstances peculiar to itself. What Nigeria needs at this early stage of its development is to associate all interest-groups in the society with its economic efforts. In so doing, the country will be better placed to cater for the interests of all citizens whether they are on paid employment or whether they exist on the land as peasant farmers.

4 The Machinery of Collective Relations

We have already seen that the environment plays an important part in the type of industrial-relations system that emerges in any country (see Chapter 1). Changes that have been taking place in the Nigerian environment have invariably affected the country's institutions, and industrial relations has in consequence been affected. Thus, although the British model of industrial relations was imported into Nigeria, the environment has affected it to such an extent that what has now emerged and continues to develop, is completely different from both the original model and what obtains today in the UK. In the UK, national policy is still predicated on *laissez-faire* doctrine with both sides of industry left largely to determine the scope of relations between them. The role of government is to ensure that facilities are provided that will enhance collective bargaining. The law intervenes only when both parties have exhausted their own internal procedures and when the presence of a third party may be necessary to break the impasse. Even then, the statutory procedures are voluntary and there is generally no obligation on either party to submit to the statutory machinery.

Yet there are countries where the law or government plays an active role in the industrial relations system. As we have seen, in the USA and most of Europe the law positively encourages collective bargaining. In the case of the USA, the National Labour Relations Act 1935 conferred on employees freedom to bargain collectively with their employers. In France and Italy, a written constitutional right to strike exists. In all these cases, collective agreements can be enforced as legal contracts whose breach can lead to orders for damages or injunctions. By implication, therefore, a 'no strike, no lockout' obligation is imposed on unions and employers for the duration of the agreement.

In Nigeria, on the other hand, the law and government agencies play a prominent role in the industrial relations system. Accordingly, a system that started as a voluntary one is today hedged about with legal restrictions and government orders. It is within that framework of law that the employers' associations and workers' unions interact. We therefore start our analysis by examining the legal framework.

4.1 THE LEGAL FRAMEWORK

We saw in Chapter 1 that by and large in the Western countries social sanctions are more significant than legal sanctions in industrial relations, and that the function of the latter is of an auxiliary or ancillary character. The law intervenes only to strengthen those social and moral obligations on which the relation between management and labour rests. It is in this respect that the strike and lockout are accepted as the ultimate sanctions in the collective bargaining process. Yet even in these countries, the law has placed certain limitations on the use of economic pressure in industrial relations. This has become so because it is desirable that the society protects the individual. Such an individual may even be an employer against whom a strike action is threatened, or has already been taken. It could also be the ordinary citizen, the consumer of goods or services who is liable to suffer as a result of any stoppage of work in a particular organisation. The law therefore plays a mediating role between those individuals or groups who wield economic power and the interest of those likely to suffer by its exercise.

There is no doubt that the development of labour law in the Western countries has been controlled by the history of those countries and is today also based upon, and related to, other prevailing democratic institutions. In assessing the role of law in the Nigerian system, this distinction must be borne in mind, because Nigeria is a developing country with a completely different history where 'social sanctions' alone may not be enough for the effective operation of the industrial relations system. Among the factors to consider here are the low level of income per capita; the fact that over 70 per cent of the population is engaged in peasant agriculture, most of whom are illiterate; the reliance of the government on development plans based on objectives; therefore economic disruptions tend to postpone the achievement of these objectives; the fact that the small wage-earning proportion of the population is also the most literate and most vociferous sector in the society and unless their demands are properly channelled they may focus on themselves while disregarding others in the society, etc. In addition, the Nigerian economy exists in an international context.

During the past decade or so there have been major problems of increasing energy costs, inflation and recession, etc. In the midst of all this, if the economy of the country is to grow, then there is a need for increased investment, increased productivity and, most importantly, a stable political and industrial-relations climate.

4.1.1 Trade unions

A trade union is defined in the Trade Union's Act 1973 as

> any combination of workers or employers, whether temporary or permanent, the purpose of which is to regulate the terms and conditions of employment of workers, whether the combination in question would or would not, apart from this Act, be an unlawful combination by reason of any of its purposes being in restraint of trade, and whether its purposes do or do not include the provision of benefits for its members.

A trade union, therefore, at least in law, is essentially concerned with the regulation of the terms and conditions of employment. However, as in many other contries, the trade unions in Nigeria have widened the scope of their functions and are also concerned not only with the worker at work but his place in the society.

The right to form or belong to a trade union is contained in s.37 of the Constitution of the Federal Republic of Nigeria, which came into force on 1 October 1979. The section provides as follows: 'Every person shall be entitled to assemble freely and associate with other persons, and in particular he may form or belong to any political party, trade union or other association for the protection of his interests.'

At common law, certain inpediments were placed in the way of trade unions because they were regarded as conspiracies. However, most of these impediments have now been removed by statute. Unions are no longer liable either at criminal law, in tort or in contract for any acts done in contemplation or furtherance of unions' interests. Under the Trade Unions Act 1973, the courts in Nigeria will not entertain any action against a trade union in respect of any tortious act alleged to have been committed by or on behalf of the trade union in contemplation of or in furtherance of trade dispute. Similarly, the Act recognises peaceful picketing as a method to be employed by unions to further their objectives. Presumably, however, the situation might be different where such picketing is not peaceful. Non-peaceful picketing would probably amount to intimidation or assault which may constitute a criminal offence under s.367 of the Criminal Code.[1]

Where one person knowingly induces a third party to break his contract to the damage of the other contracting party without reasonable justification or cause, this will amount to a tort and is actionable. This means that each time a trade-union official asks the members of his union to go on strike and thereby break their contracts of employment, the union official becomes liable for damages. This general liability clearly puts trade-union leaders at a great disadvantage and could have a profound effect on the conduct of industrial relations. Fortunately, trade-union officials in Nigeria have nothing to fear in this regard as a statute has come to their aid. Under the Trade Unions Act 1973, an act done by a person in contemplation or furtherance of a trade dispute shall not be actionable in tort. It is immaterial whether such an act induced some other person to break a contract of employment or whether it interfered with the trade or business of some other person.

No association may operate as a trade union unless it has first been registered. Once registered, recognition by employer of the union is automatic. Thus, one frustration of the unions in the past over non-recognition by some employers has now been removed by law. In the past, the unions had difficulty in collecting union dues from their members. This made union administration difficult and, as we observed elsewhere in this study, led the unions to rely almost exclusively on external financial aid. In order to strengthen the finances of the unions and to ensure that they do not look outside the country for survival, the law has now made check-off compulsory. Each employer is obliged to deduct the approved union dues from each worker's wages. This means also that each worker is automatically a member of a union. Again the old problem of union officials trying hard to persuade workers to join the union and to pay their dues regularly has been removed. Although a right exists for the individual to join or not to join a union or having joined a union, to contract out in writing, we think it is most unlikely that under the present union organisation a worker would be prepared to be outside the union.

4.1.2 The contract of employment

A worker may enter into a contract of employment with an employer on agreed terms. Such a contract will, however, be subject to the general law of contract. In law, the employment contract, like other contracts, is regarded as one that is arrived at after hard bargaining. While it is true that there is some bargaining, especially as regards wages, in the main the accepted rights of the parties are in practice found in the conditions already existing in the company – established by the employer alone where a trade union does not exist, or through collective agreements between the employer and the trade union. In most cases, what is agreed between the employer and the employee is within the framework already in existence in the company.

The law has always regulated and varied the common-law position specified above. Before 1945 a number of laws were passed whose aim was to protect workers against serious abuses. These laws were consolidated into the Labour Code Ordinance in 1945, which has since been amended culminating in the enactment of the Labour Act 1974. The relevant provisions of the law stipulate which contracts of employment shall be oral and which written and the manner in which those contracts shall be terminated. The law also regulates the hours of work, annual holidays and the payment of wages. It makes the grant of maternity leave for female workers compulsory and lays down certain conditions for the employment of women and young persons. With the exception of wages and salaries, this legislation has provisions covering almost all aspects of employer–employee relationships. Both the Labour Act 1974 and the Trade Unions Act 1973 constitute the basis of collective bargaining in Nigeria.

The health, safety and welfare of workers are provided for in the Factories Act 1958. The health provisions cover cleanliness, overcrowding, ventilation, lighting, drainage of floors, sanitary conveniences and protective clothing and appliances. The safety provisions are concerned, among other things, with fencing of all prime movers and transmission machinery and the provision of a safe means of access to every place at which any person has at any time to work. Precaution must be taken in all places where dangerous fumes are liable to be present; suitable breathing and reviving apparatus, belts and ropes must be provided and maintained so as to be readily available. For the prevention of fire, the Act provides that every factory must be provided with readily accessible means for extinguishing fire which must be adequate and suitable having regard to the circumstances of the case. Goggles or effective screens must be provided for the use of workers engaged in certain specified processes. The welfare provisions required an adequate supply of drinking water, positioned and maintained at suitable points conveniently accessible to all employees. Adequate washing facilities should also be provided and, where there is no clinic attached to the factory, a first-aid box or cupboard must be provided for the treatment of the workers.

With regard to industrial injuries, a worker would normally be entitled to claim damages from his employer if it is established that the accident which caused the injury happened while the worker was at work. An alternative course of action is also open to the worker: to claim damages under a statute. Under the Workmen's Compensation Act 1958, a worker will be entitled to damages for injuries, according to a formula provided for in the Act, if he is able to establish that he suffered a personal injury that had been caused by an accident arising out of and in the course of his employment.

The law has thus established *minimum* standards in respect of certain conditions of employment of workers, including the nature of the contract, the health, safety and welfare at work and compensation for injuries at work. It must be stressed that with the passage of time the provisions contained in some of the laws are completely inadequate, while others are out of date. Although some of the laws appear recent, they are all in fact modifications of old English legislation that have since been changed in the UK. For example, the compensation provided for under the Workmen's Compensation Act is so insignificant that an injured worker cannot survive on it. All the laws need drastic revision.

4.1.3 Collective bargaining and the law

There is no statutory provision to the effect that there shall be collective bargaining machinery in a company or industry. But its existence would seem to be implied in many of the provisions of current labour legislation. The process is also recognised at common law. Thus, in a case where a union member complained that he had been wrongly expelled by his union because of a break of discipline in his employment, the court in dismissing the action said:

> The great benefit of a trade union is that you have collective bargaining between employers and employed, and, if the union come to an agreement or come to a decision regarding any man or body of men, and then that man or body of men refuse to be bound, it destroys the confidence that should exist between the employers and the unions, and it is to the detriment of collective bargaining.[2]

However, the collective agreements that result from collective bargaining are not enforceable contracts between the collective parties, as they are regarded as binding in honour only, and to be enforced through social sanctions.

In spite of the view now generally accepted that collective agreements are not enforceable at law, the fact of the matter is that they do vary the individual contract of employment. This can happen in two ways. First, there may be an express clause in the contract of employment incorporating the terms of such collective agreements. Many employers do this by referring the new worker in his letter of employment to another document—generally the *Employee Handbook*, which contains the collective agreements. The terms of the handbook may change from time to time without further obligation of notifying such changes to the worker. In one case,[3] a group of safety deputies in the coal mines had refused to work Saturday shifts. Before then, in 1952, a collective agreement had been concluded determining wages, among other terms and conditions of employment, and committing deputies to work such days 'as may reasonably be required by the management in order to promote the safety and efficient working of the pit'. This clause became a term in Galley's contract of employment, if only by reason of his original contractual acceptance of collectively agreed terms relating to wages and kindred matters. As a result of the damage suffered by the management, Galley was sued for damages and the Board was successful, although actual damages awarded were small. But the case did underline the principle that collective agreements can be incorporated into individual contracts of employment.

Many companies in Nigeria have clauses in their employment contract incorporating the already agreed collective agreements. In one of the companies surveyed, the letter of employment has this relevant clause: 'You should signify your agreement to the above terms and the other conditions of employment in the *Employee Handbook*, a copy of which has been given to you, by signing at the foot of the copy which should be returned to us for retention.'

Where the employment contract says nothing about the collective terms, in which case there is no express incorporation, such terms can be incorporated only if they can be regarded as customary or implied terms of the contract. Thus, although the collective bargaining process itself has not received any statutory backing, and the collective agreements are not legally enforceable, yet such collective agreements concluded by employers and workers have legal consequences for the individual contract of employment.

4.1.4 Minimum-wage legislation

Collective bargaining presupposes the existence of strong and effective unions whose leaders are knowledgeable in industrial relations. The process therefore can only be effective where both parties have full knowledge of the problems of the undertaking and of the country in which they operate and accept that agreements between them are likely to be appropriate and workable. In some companies trade unions are not sufficiently developed, and there may be no unions at all in some, to conclude effective wage agreements, and in consequence wages in such organisations may be unduly low and involve privation for the workers. It is in such circumstances that the law has intervened in the form of statutory regulation of wages. The Wages Boards and Industrial Councils Act 1973 provides for the establishment of Industrial Wages Boards, National Wages Boards, and Area Minimum Wages Committees for the states and for Joint Industrial Councils for particular industries. The Minister of Labour is empowered under the Act, if he is of the opinion that wages are unreasonably low or that no adequate machinery exists for effective regulation of wages or other conditions of employment of any worker, to refer to a commission of inquiry the question whether an Industrial Wages Board should be established with respect to any of those workers and their employers. On the recommendations of the commission, the Minister may, if he thinks fit, make an order thereby giving effect to the recommendation. Wages and other conditions of employment fixed by the Board become statutory minimum wages or conditions. No employer covered by such an order should apply to his workers wages or conditions of employment that are less favourable than the statutory minimum provisions.

However, although unions had been weak in a number of companies including the catering industry and some other commercial organisations, such as supermarkets, this regulatory machinery has hardly been used during the past twenty years. As a result of the new industrial relations systems in the country, this law will become even less important as the failings that it sought to remove have been taken care of by the new developments.

4.1.5 Industrial disputes

An elaborate statutory machinery exists for the settlement of trade disputes. We shall discuss the provisions of that machinery in more detail in Chapter 5.

There is no statutory provision expressly recognising the right to strike. However, the right to strike is by implication recognised by statutory provisions, and the right is also recognised at common law.

A strike is defined in the Trade Disputes Act 1976 as

> the cessation of work by a body of persons employed acting in combination, or a concerted refusal or a refusal under a common understanding of any number of persons employed to continue to work for an employer in consequence of a dispute, done as a means of compelling their employer or any person or body of persons employed, or to aid other workers in compelling their employer or any other person or body of persons employed, to accept or not to accept terms of employment and physical conditions of work.

Under the Trade Unions Act 1973 it is provided that one of the matters to be provided for in the rules of a trade union is the condition that no member of the trade union shall take part in a strike unless a majority of the members have in a secret ballot voted in favour of the strike. The right would seem to derive also from the language of the Act which protects a trade union acting in contemplation of or in furtherance of a trade dispute, from liabilities for any tortious act alleged to have been committed for or on behalf of the trade union. Thus, strike action as a legitimate weapon to be used by the union in appropriate cases is indirectly endorsed by statute.

Furthermore, English common law on which Nigerian law is based recognises the workers' right to strike. In a leading case, the judge summarised the position thus: 'When the rights of labour are concerned, the rights of the employer are conditioned by the rights of the workmen to give or withhold their services. The right of the worker to strike is an essential element in the principle of collective bargaining.'[4]

At common law, the strike still represents a unilateral breach of the employment contract on the part of the workers concerned. This would tend to create an anomalous situation because it is an established principle of industrial relations that collective bargaining cannot work without the ultimate sanction of the strike and lockout. To treat the cessation of work for a period as a breach of the employment contract, therefore, appears a contradiction of that principle. However, judicial pronouncements seem to have clarified the position. The strike will be legal and will not constitute a breach of the employment contract if due notice as required by the terms of the contract is given. Thus, in the words of a leading English judge: 'Workmen have a right to strike ... provided that they give notice beforehand; a notice is sufficient if it is at least as long as the notice required to terminate the contract. ... Each side is, therefore, content to accept a strike notice of proper length as lawful. It is an implication read into the contract by the modern law as to trade disputes.'[5]

The view that a strike merely suspends all or some of the mutual contractual obligations for the duration of the period of such a strike, was confirmed by the Supreme Court of Nigeria, when it said: 'A servant who deliberately absents himself from work ... does not merely by absenting himself terminate the contract of service unless there is something to show an intention no longer to be bound by it. *Prima facie* a striker intends to return to work once the objects of the strike have been attained.'[6]

The strike therefore is a temporary stoppage of work as the workers intend that, at its conclusion, they will return to their jobs and the employers themselves view the strike in the same light.

At common law an employer is not under any obligation to pay his workers during the period of a strike. Both the awards of the Industrial Arbitration Panel and court judgements in Nigeria confirm this.[7] To this established common-law position has been added a statutory confirmation. The Trade Disputes (Amendment) Act 1977 provides that 'where any worker takes part in a strike he shall not be entitled to any wages or other remuneration for the period of the strike'. The anxiety of the government in ensuring that strikes are contained in such a way as not to disrupt the economy of the country is clearly brought out by the necessity to promulgate the law at all, as employers were already observing the principle of 'no work, no pay'.

While the right to strike is recognised in the Nigerian legal system, it is nevertheless hedged around with provisos. The use of a strike is acceptable to the extent only that it is properly used for the furtherance of legitimate union objectives. Where a strike fails to satisfy this test, it is considered to have lost more of its legitimate nature in the following circumstances:

1. When it is diverted from its proper objective of settling a trade dispute between employers and workers.
2. When the methods adopted for the conduct of the strike are contrary to public order, for example where there has been arson or assault. Those involved may be charged under the Criminal Code.

3. When the means for the peaceful settlement of disputes have been established by agreement or legislation, and the union fails to use this or embarks on a strike action without first exhausting those procedures.

Moreover, the Trade Unions Act 1973 provides that every union rule-book must contain a provision to the effect that no member of the union shall take part in a strike unless a majority of the members have in a secret ballot voted in favour of the strike. The aim of the provision evidently is to ensure that union activists do not 'drag' all union members into strike action without their agreement. Generally, the decision of the executive committee of a union authorising a strike action is enough. At most, an emergency meeting of a union could also authorise a strike action. In all these, it is possible for a few union officials to manoeuvre the workers in an organisation into a strike action without securing their consent. This is what the provision purports to prevent. However, the provision has not and it is unlikely to achieve the objective. The union rule-book constitutes a contract among its members, and it is only a member that can sue for the breach of any provision. We think it is most unlikely that a union member in Nigeria will go to court to challenge the validity of a union executive's decision to embark upon strike action. As the Government is concerned about union democracy, a better approach would be to have the provision in the law, so that failure on the part of a union executive to follow the procedure would constitute a breach of the law.

In many countries there is a group or groups of persons who are not allowed to go on strike because they are considered to be an essential service of the state. What is essential, however, depends on the particular country. Although membership of trade unions is voluntary and open to all workers, employees in the following bodies are forbidden by law to belong to a trade union and by implication to go on strike:

(a) members of all armed forces and the police;
(b) employees in: (i) the Prisons Department, (ii) Customs Preventive Service, (iii) Nigerian Security Printing and Minting Company Limited, (iv) the Central Bank of Nigeria, (v) the Nigerian External Telecommunications Limited, (vi) employees in every federal or state government establishment where such employees are authorised to bear arms.

In addition to the above, the Minister of Labour may from time to time by order specify any other establishment which, in his view, should not entertain union activities. The problem is, of course, that having banned these bodies from trade unionism, they are left without machinery for collective relations, as they cannot negotiate collectively with their employers. However, all the bodies concerned are exclusively state bodies in which collective bargaining (excepting perhaps the Central Bank and the Mint) had not taken root. Also, there is a provision in the law that if the employees and management of the bodies concerned so wish, they may set up joint-consultative committees to discuss, and not negotiate, their problems.

In the case of other essential services where trade unionism is permitted, the workers are not allowed to go on strike until they have exhausted the statutory machinery for the settlement of disputes. These services include:

(a) the Public service of the federation or of the state;
(b) any public authority connected with: electricity, power or water, or fuel of any kind, sound broadcasting or postal, telegraphic, cable, wireless or telephone communications, ports, harbours, docks or airports; transportation of persons, goods, livestock by road, rail, sea, river or air; hospital and other health matters; outbreaks of fire.

In all these bodies, it is illegal for a union wilfully to fail to comply with the procedure specified in the Trade Disputes Act 1976 in relation to the reporting and settlement of trade disputes. Any failure on the part of a union to comply will be regarded as a calculated act to disrupt the economy of the country, and will attract penalties including the proscription of the unions concerned. Thus, a number of unions were proscribed in 1977. These included the Barclays (now Union) Bank Workers' Union, the Pan Ocean Branch of the Consolidated Petroleum, Chemical and General Workers' Union of Nigeria, and the Shell–BP and Allied Workers' Union and the Shell–BP Senior Staff Association.

It is thus clear from the above discussion that although the right to strike exists in the Nigerian industrial relations system, in effect the law does not expect strikes to take place, or at least makes it difficult for them to take place.

4.2   THE COLLECTIVE BARGAINING PROCESS

Much of the interaction that goes on in the workplace is informal. All such informal relationships, which are not structured, form part of the industrial relations situation in any particular organisation. However, we are concerned with the formal group relationships at work, that is, the machinery established to regulate the relations between management and workers. To understand the workings of these relationships, therefore, we shall examine the type of procedures established for the purpose, to determine whether a definite pattern exists that will represent the industrial relations system in Nigeria. We shall also examine such procedures to see whether the system of industrial relations thus created is viable, having regard to the developing nature of Nigeria.

The collective bargaining process is based on the principle that workers have a right to contract with their employers as to wages and conditions of work and that the employers recognise that right. It is in effect a system of wage and conditions of service determination in which the employer shares administrative decision-making responsibilities with the union. The federal ministry of Employment, Labour and Productivity has defined collective bargaining in the traditional sense, as 'negotiations about working conditions and terms of employment between an employer, a group of employers and one or more employers' organisations, on the one hand, and one or more representative workers' organisations, on the other, with a view to reaching agreement.'[8]

In the view of the Nigeria Employers' Consultative Association, any definition of collective bargaining that tends to emphasise the determination of wages and conditions of employment is narrowly conceived and inadequate. In the light of this, the Association's definition is as follows: 'Collective bargaining is a process of decision-making. Its overriding purpose is the negotiation of an agreed set of rules to govern the substantive and procedural terms of the employment relationship, as well as the relationship between the bargaining parties themselves.'[9]

In this study we have adopted NECA's definition of collective bargaining because we see negotiations, especially those now carried out at national level, as going beyond changes to wages and fringe benefits. They cover such intangibles which may not be on the agenda – such as status and the dignity of man, fairness and the equitable distribution of income. Thus while there will always be debate as to the extent of the effectiveness of collective bargaining as an instrument for equitable income distribution, mainly because there will always be a margin for alternative interpretation of statistical results, collective bargaining does act as a marginal corrective of the conflicting interests of workers and employers. The essence of collective bargaining therefore is that its results should reflect the respective strength, economic positions, organising ability and bargaining skill of the parties and their capacities to make effective agreements, not just agreements to be observed in breach. Therefore the relative positions of the parties is important in a viable collective bargaining system.

4.2.1 Preconditions for collective bargaining

We recognise the following prerequisites in any collective bargaining process:

1. The parties must attain a sufficient degree of organisation.
2. They must possess the necessary skills to manage the intricacies of the bargaining process. Thus a sufficient degree of literacy is essential.
3. They must be ready to enter into agreement with each other within the framework of the machinery established for the purpose.
4. Collective agreements concluded must be observed by those to whom they apply.

In assessing the viability or otherwise of the collective bargaining process in Nigeria, we must use the four criteria stated above. On the basis of these, our judgement is that collective bargaining seems to have a viable future in Nigeria. The changes that have occurred in labour laws and the system of industrial relations since 1973 have, by and large, resulted in these conditions being satisfied. First, the trade unions have been restructured along industrial lines with vastly improved strength and status and have attained a reasonable degree of parity of bargaining power with the employers. Second, there has been a remarkable growth of counterpart employers' associations willing and able to negotiate in good faith and who have in fact entered into procedural agreements with the trade unions as the framework for voluntary collective bargaining. Third, under the Trade Disputes Act 1976, collective bargaining is made a prerequisite for the settlement of trade disputes. Finally, with the improvement of the primary and secondary school system during the last twenty years, most workers are literate and therefore able to have a better appreciation of the issues at stake in collective bargaining.

4.2.2 Forms of collective bargaining

We can identify five different forms of collective bargaining in Nigeria. First, discussions that take place between the government and the employers and workers within an established machinery with a view to devising policies to combat inflation and unemployment and to advise on relevent labour legislation, etc. Such bodies established include the Prices, Productivity and Incomes Board (PPIB) and the National Labour Advisory Council (NLAC). The agreement reached in these bodies are sent to the government in the form of recommendations.

Second, government discussions and consultations, independently of any established institution, with employers and trade unions on certain topical social and economic problems such as the provisions of proposed labour legislation or the introduction of an incomes policy. No formal agreements are reached but views expressed are noted by the government.

Third, discussions held as part of works-level consultation. In practice these discussions often result in agreements that may or may not be in written form but are normally implemented.

Fourth, agreements on procedures for settling labour disputes. The main purpose of these procedures is not to call in an independent third party to settle the disputes but to get talks between the parties going again, with the help of a conciliator or mediator, so that the solutions eventually reached will, as far as possible, have been achieved by the parties involved themselves.

Fifth, the actual bargaining process with the obligation to negotiate in good faith; to ban certain practices that might impede the bargaining process; to provide various other measures whose purpose is to ensure that the parties have relevant information which would enable them to negotiate in full knowledge of the facts.

However, while all the five approaches may constitute collective bargaining, it is important for us to emphasise that in Nigeria a *collective agreement* can only result from an item (or items) that has been collectively negotiated. Thus matters discussed and agreed may be implemented but may not be regarded as flowing from a collective agreement. This subtle distinction is important in the Nigerian system because of its psychological effect on the parties. Both parties, the employers and the unions, believe that in normal circumstances a breach or a refusal to implement immediately matters agreed during discussions, will not, in contrast to the case of negotiations, lead to a serious disagreement resulting in industrial action. However, the truth that has dawned on many employers in recent years is that the mode of securing the agreement is irrelevant. What is relevant and what causes an industrial action is the breach or refusal to implement an agreement of whatever origin.

Until 1978, when the new industrial-relations system was established, all formal relationships between the unions and the employers were at the enterprise level only. The house union concluded a procedural agreement with the employer, and conducted collective bargaining on the basis of that agreement. Although such house unions were affiliated to national trade-union centres, the officials of these centres had relatively little to do directly with the rank and file members of the unions. All matters that were not covered by the collective agreement were discussed at joint-consultative committees, also at the enterprise level. Thus there was only one level of collective relations.

Under the new industrial relations system, collective bargaining is now at two levels: the enterprise and the national levels. At the enterprise level the formal interaction is between the employer and the branch union. Also at this level are the joint-consultative committees, which are made up of representatives of management and workers. Relations at the national level can be subdivided into two. The first sub-division covers the machinery for collective bargaining between each employers' federation and the relevant industrial union. The second sub-division that has emerged recently in the Nigerian industrial relations system involves dialogue on certain key labour matters between the Nigerian Labour Congress, the government and the Nigeria Employers' Consultative Association. Represented diagrammatically, the framework for collective relations in Nigeria is as shown in Table 4.1.

TABLE 4.1   The levels of collective relations

Level	The parties	Nature of relations
1. Enterprise	Branch union Employer	Collective bargaining
	Workers' representatives Management representatives	Joint consultation
2. National	Industrial union Employers' federation	Collective bargaining
	Nigerian Labour Congress The federal government Nigeria Employers' Consultative Association	Discussion

In the pages following, we examine the machinery for collective relations at enterprise and national levels, and in the public service.

4.3   RELATIONS AT ENTERPRISE LEVEL

Relations at the enterprise level are made up of the collective bargaining process and the joint-consultative machinery. According to the procedural agreements concluded between employers' federations and industrial unions in 1979, all those things that affect working relationships are grouped into two. The first group, which the unions consider more important because it includes wages and other monetary fringe benefits, is negotiated at the national level between the national union and the employers' federation.[10] The second group, which is mainly items peculiar to the particular organisation and the bulk of which is welfare in nature, is negotiated at the enterprise level between the individual employer and the branch union. Yet other items that are of interest to the various sections or departments of the organisation are discussed at the joint-consultative committees.

In the procedural agreement between the Precision, Electrical and Related Equipment Employers' Association and the Precision, Electrical and Related Workers' Union, for example, the items for negotiation at the two levels are agreed as follows:

1. *Matters for negotiation at national level*
   Wages and salaries
   Overtime rates (ordinary, Sundays, public holidays and rest days)
   Hours of work
   Annual leave
   Leave allowance
   Sick benefits
   Out-of-station allowance
   Redundancy benefits
   Acting allowance
   Transfer/disturbance allowance
   Maternity leave
   Housing allowance.
2. *Matters for discussion at enterprise level*
   Method of production
   Increased efficiency
   Safety
   Welfare
   Training of workers
   Disciplinary procedures
   Christmas bonus
   Scholarship awards

Long-service award
Compassionate/casual leave
Medical facilities
Death benefits.

It will be seen from the above that there is a sharp distinction between monetary benefits and non-monetary benefits in the Precision agreement. The agreement stipulates the object of negotiation at the enterprise level to be: 'To provide a regular method of consultation between the management and the employees on mattters of common interest, in order to prevent friction and misunderstanding, and to secure the fullest cooperation for the prosecution of measures undertaken in the common interest of both parties.'

4.3.1 Collective bargaining

Under the Precision arrangement, the parties are not allowed to discuss any question that is covered by a collective agreement between the employers' federation (to which the employer belongs) and the national industrial union (to which the branch union belongs). Meetings are held at least once every six months during working hours. Special meetings may be called at any time to discuss pressing issues. The chairman of all meetings is appointed by management. Although minutes are taken and agreements recorded, no formal collective agreements are signed. Yet all collectively agreed matters must be implemented by the parties.

However, because written collective agreements are concluded only at the national level, and because the procedural agreements do not refer specifically to collective bargaining at the enterprise level but to consultations or discussions, many employers are misled into believing that what they agree with their union is not through collective bargaining. They still regard the meetings at this level as joint consultations where management prerogative prevails. This lack of appreciation of the fact that it is not the *name* given to the process but the *nature* of the process that matters, has resulted in a lot of misunderstanding, and in some cases strikes. As one trade unionist put it to the author: 'We do not care what name you call these meetings: discussions, negotiations or consultations, so long as we achieve our objectives.' That of course is the important point, and the employers must appreciate it if they are to avoid unpleasant incidents at work. The discussions with the branch union on specified matters must not be confused with consultations that are carried out in the joint-consultative committees discussed below.

One characteristic of union bargaining at enterprise level is the large initial demand that the union knows will not be met by management. But that approach does represent the Nigerian way of bargaining. A seller of goods in the local market does not ask for the *actual* price he (or she) wants for the goods. Instead he mentions a figure to the prospective buyer – sometimes three or more times what he will eventually accept. The figure he has in mind will only be reached after haggling. We had an interesting experience of this recently. A woman was selling fresh fish near a local market. We were interested in the big sea bream that she had. On inquiry she put the price (after looking at us and the cars we had: two Mercedes Benz 200 saloons) at ₦30.00. But after a lot of bargaining we paid ₦10.00, a third of what she originally asked for. There are examples of this every day when one wants to buy plantains, yams, vegetables, meat and other items of foodstuffs in the local market. In the same way, the unions would present inflated demands in the hope that after much bargaining they would secure a good deal for their members. In 1975, for example, the Nigerian Tobacco Company General Workers' Union presented their employer, the Nigerian Tobacco Company, with demands. One of these demands was an increase in the level of extra duty allowance, paid to such employees as salesmen whose overtime hours could not be controlled because of the nature of their jobs. The demand was an annual allowance as follows:

Grade	Current allowance (₦)	Proposed by union (₦)	Proposed % change
1	84.00	350.00	317
2	112.00	370.00	230
3	140.00	400.00	186

After a lot of bargaining, agreement was eventually reached as follows:

Grade	Current allowance (₦)	Proposed by union (₦)	Agreed by the parties (₦)	Actual % change
1	84.00	350.00	144.00	71
2	112.00	370.00	180.00	61
3	140.00	400.00	210.00	50

Similarly, the demand for increase in redundancy payments by the same union was enough to frighten the 'uninitiated' in the subtleties of the Nigerian bargaining system. The union's demand was as follows:

Number of years of service	Current rate per year of service	Union proposed rate per year of service
Up to 5 years'	10 days' pay	3 weeks' pay
5 years' but with less than 10 years'	2 weeks' pay	6 weeks' pay
Over 10 years'	3 weeks' pay	8 weeks' pay

Agreement was eventually reached as follows:

Up to 5 years'	10 days' pay
5 years' but with less than 10 years'	18 days' pay
Over 10 years'	25 days' pay

The other reason for the union presenting inflated demands is the way these demands are collected from members or branches of the union. These demands are submitted to the union executive and are merely passed on in the form in which they are collected. It is surprising to note that even management unions have fallen into this 'trap'. They too present items submitted by their members to the company even where the executive is convinced that there is neither merit nor substance in the demand. In cases where the union executive has a firm grip on the rank and file members, they feel free to prune down these demands. When one trade-union leader was asked why his union presented demands to the company knowing full well that some of the demands lacked substance, he replied that they did so because 'that is what the workers want'. It may be what the workers want, but it is our view that the average worker is not in a position to consider the full implications of his demand. While there is some advantage in inflated demands helping the unions to secure their objectives, the rank and file members not party to the formulation of the union strategy often feel that the union has not done well enough. Consequently, there have been instances in recent times of the workers rejecting, or accepting reluctantly, an agreement concluded between the employer and the union. It is our view, therefore, that it is the union leaders' obligation to make certain that their members are fully aware of the situation and to ensure that expectations are not raised unduly high.

Another characteristic of bargaining at the enterprise level is the large number of demands submitted to management at any one time. It is not inconceivable to see a list of demands running between twenty and thirty. Whether this is a deliberate strategy 'to present everything' is difficult to establish. But it has certain advantages for the union. Personnel managers confirm that it makes it difficult for them to ascertain the union's real position on the various issues. As the demands cover up the real and important issues on which the union would not want to give way, the management then finds it difficult to establish a meaningful strategy. What the unions do in such cases is, after hard bargaining, drop or reduce the relatively unimportant demands and by so doing insist that they have made concessions and that in the spirit of harmony and good industrial relations atmosphere, the management should follow their example by making concessions too. Thus a large number of demands afford the union plenty of room in which to manoeuvre.

The unions also introduce some demands to facilitate future bargaining. The union, aware of management attitudes to certain matters, may know that a certain item introduced for the first time will not be entertained by the management. Yet such an item is deliberately introduced and withdrawn as soon as management shows opposition. However, at a future meeting, the item is again presented and because the matter has been on the agenda before, management may have had the time to think about it and perhaps agree to the demand as represented or in its modified form.

The employers' strategy has always been different from that of the unions. As managements in Nigeria have been in a stronger position than the unions, they do not delay before coming on to their final position. Generally, after hearing the unions' demands, the management state an intermediate position and by the third time round they state their settlement position and stick to it, even though such an action may result in a strike. But the employer knows that the union members could not withstand a protracted strike as no union has yet established a strike fund. Many union officials are able to tell from experience when the management side has reached what it regards as a settlement position. The author had the experience of this during his period as the leader of the management negotiating team. The general secretary of the union would ask for an adjournment and call him aside saying that since the management appeared to have nothing more to offer, he would like to have a compromise on other items on the agenda so that discussions on the particular matter under negotiation could be closed. In this way we were able to ensure that, although in principle we stuck to our positions, we were nevertheless able to make concessions to the union so that its members did not feel that they had failed on every issue. This face-saving strategy worked to the advantage of all parties concerned as it led to a speedy settlement of agreements. In every negotiation, therefore, we had certain items in which we just had to give way to 'soften the atmosphere'.

An important development in the new industrial relations is that collective bargaining involving the conclusion of written collective agreements has moved from the enterprise level to the national level. The collective bargaining that takes place at the former level is concerned essentially with non-monetary matters. This has certain implications for the industrial relations situation in each enterprise. First, the workers' representatives on the NJICs are drawn from among the paid officials of the national union. Some of these officials may not even be familiar with the conditions prevailing in the companies they are representing. Consequently, they may not be in a strong position to push a particular item or items, which workers in one or more enterprises may consider important to themselves. Moreover, the local (or branch) union president and general secretary, who wielded power until now, are suddenly left without power – at least on paper. They now discover that they cannot give any instructions to the workers in their branch union on matters nationally negotiated without first checking with the paid general secretary or some national officials of the national industrial union. This apparent loss of power, coupled with the alienation of the branch union officials, may cause resentment in the workplace, and possibly lead to a show of power resulting in industrial actions. However, the power could also be exercised in other ways. For example, when all national unions, on the instructions of the NLC, ordered all their affiliated unions to start a nation-wide strike on 11 May 1981 over national minimum wage, some branch executives simply ignored the order. In order to forestall any possible difficulties that may arise, it will be necessary to define more specifically the role of the workers' representatives at the enterprise level and to ensure that this is well understood. Both the NLC and NECA have a role to play here as, up to now, workers (including their local officials) have not been quite sure of the full ramifications of the new industrial relations and their place in it.

Secondly, there is the new situation created whereby some personnel managers who have been negotiating and concluding collective agreements with their house unions are left out of the negotiating team at the national level. Not only does the personnel manager affected lose the opportunity of acquiring skills of negotiation as a result of the new developments, but a unionist in his company who is active in the industry context, might have advantage over him especially in interpreting the intention behind certain provisions of the collective agreement. This may result in status problems, for all such managers who do not feature at the industrial level. As industry-wide collective agreements are now likely to determine the broad parameters of industrial relations practice, with each enterprise only possessing limited freedom based on its specific traditions and personnel practices, the significance of the diminished role of the personnel manager becomes obvious. However, as Professor Oloko has observed, we must not equate the status dissonance highlighted with the erosion of positive relations at work.[11] We are here concerned with matters of union–management relations rather than the basis of authority and status which is located in the authority structures of each enterprise. Moreover, the loss of enterprise autonomy in the specific area of collective agreements should be weighed in terms of the stability and progress that the new system seems to have introduced.

4.3.2   Joint consultation

The joint consultation machinery was the very first to be encouraged in both the public and private sectors. As unions grew and union leaders acquired more and more experience, it became necessary to have some formal machinery for dealing with the workers as a group instead of dealing with them individually, as failure to do so would encourage petitions and demonstrations. It was in these circumstances that joint consultation became established with the following purposes:[12]

1. To set up a scheme for regular contact between management and workers, as a means of improving communication and productivity.
2. To meet the workers' demand for better insight into the management of the organisation for which they work.

These purposes were based on the recognition of the desirability of the workers' understanding of their own jobs against the background of the organisation as a whole. At the early stage of its introduction, therefore, the system was popular for the workers were allowed to have a forum on which to raise their problems. According to the Ministry of Labour, the employers in the private sector did not look upon joint consultation with favour. They claimed that the machinery did more harm than good in that it 'contributed to the aggrandisement of leaders at the expense of the workers' welfare, that they waste time in handling complaints and that they form nuclei from which further dangerous combinations of workers may evolve'.[13] However, the joint-consultative machinery has survived, and in most companies today exists some form of joint-consultative machinery designed as a forum in which the management and workers' (not union's) representatives may discuss matters that are not normally covered by the joint-negotiating machinery. Two systems of joint-consultative committees are in operation. In the first type the company establishes a committee for each of its main departments. In the second type one single committee is established for the whole company and no separate role is envisaged for the branch union.

Among the companies that operate the first type is Guinness (Nigeria) Limited. In each of the company's breweries there is a joint-consultative committee for each of the main departments. Thus the production, engineering, accounting, marketing and personnel departments each have a joint-consultative committee. Membership is open to all workers, but actual representation is through elections that are held annually. Each committee is made up of about ten members, both management and workers. Meetings are held every month and during working hours. Unlike in the case of collective bargaining where only the union demands are negotiated, in these committees items are submitted by both management and workers. As the committees represent either a department or a section of a department, matters discussed are localised and relate to the operations in the department only. Such matters include production targets, safety at work, medical and canteen facilities, shift arrangements, uniforms, etc. The matters reserved for the branch union in the procedural agreement are not discussed in these committees.

The second type of joint-consultative committee, that is, the one big committee for the whole company, assigns no place to the local union and this has created problems. Membership may be by election, or partly by election and partly by nomination. Yet these committees discuss all matters that are reserved for discussions at the enterprise level without formal union participation. Companies that operate this system have been led to believe that as formal negotiations take place only at the national level, the branch union as union has no defined role to play in these discussions at the enterprise level. However, the intention of the various procedural agreements is that all local discussions must be with the branch unions on the matters so specified in the agreements. For a company to discuss these matters with a consultative committee that does not represent the union, is a negation of the intention of the system.

The joint-consultation system as currently practised in Nigeria has certain drawbacks. First of all, the representatives on the committees are expected to report back to their constituents what has been discussed. But generally, time for reporting back is not arranged for, with the result that the representatives rely on the minutes pasted on the boards as their means of communication. Of course many workers do not read them. Consequently, much of what is discussed in the committees is not effectively passed on. There is also a communication problem with regard to the type of worker elected into the committee. As the elections are an annual event, it seems that the workers elect any of their colleagues who show some interest. Whether someone has shown some leadership qualities or not, and whether they can communicate effectively on the work of the committee to constituents or not, do not seem to come into consideration in deciding who to send.

Another weakness of the system is that the union sees it as a rival body and as such does not accept fully its jurisdiction over certain matters which they consider to belong in the area of collective bargaining. The recent procedural agreements concluded between employers' federations and national unions that have provisions to the effect that certain matters are to be *negotiated* at the national level, while others are to be *discussed* at the enterprise level between the employer and the branch union, do not clarify the role of the joint-consultative machinery. Thus if the branch union feels so inclined, it may insist upon *discussing* a matter that has already been *consulted* upon in the workplace. There is a grey area here. Moreover, the matters that are generally discussed at joint-consultative committees are not those that are dear to the workers' hearts – such as wages and salaries and other monetary fringe benefits. Consequently, workers in general are not particularly enthusiastic about these committees. It is not surprising therefore that the joint-consultative committee as a machinery of collective relations in the workplace occupies a secondary position to the joint-negotiating machinery. That is not to say the joint-consultative committees do not serve any useful purpose. Indeed, they have been found particularly useful in connection with shift-work arrangements, planning the menu for the workers' canteen and in organising other workers' activities – including competitive activities between one department and another.

4.4 RELATIONS AT NATIONAL LEVEL

4.4.1 Industrial unions and employers' federations

Since 1978 collective agreements can only be concluded at the national level between employers' federations and national industrial unions. The machinery for the interaction at this level is the National Joint Industrial Council. There is one for each industry. Early in 1978 the Nigeria Employers' Consultative Association prepared a draft of the constitution of the National Joint Industrial Councils which was eventually adopted with slight amendments in the procedural agreements of the different industries. Consequently, the constitutions of the NJICs are similar in many respects. We shall therefore examine the constitution of the NJIC of the Food, Beverage and Tobacco industry to illustrate our point.

The objects of the Council are stated to be:

1. To secure the largest possible measure of agreement and co-operation between the Association and the national union in all matters listed under Part 1 of this agreement (i.e. matters for negotiation), with a view to increasing efficiency and productivity combined with the well-being of those employed.
2. To review and amend from time to time, agreements, decisions or findings reached by the Council.
3. To secure the speedy, impartial and amicable settlement of real and alleged disputes and grievances on negotiable and non-negotiable matters as covered by this agreement.
4. To consider the adequacy or otherwise of the machinery for settlement of grievances between parties in the industry and hence to use their best endeavours to ensure that no strikes, lockouts or any other action likely to aggravate the situation shall take place until such a time as the machinery provided by law for the settlement of industrial disputes has been exhausted.

The Council is made up of sixteen members, eight each from the employers' federation and the national union. However, where necessary, the Council is empowered to invite an expert on any subject to offer expert advice to the Council. Such advice would probably include the scope and extent of incomes policy guidelines, what they preclude and what they do not preclude, and the interpretation of certain provisions of various labour laws. There are two types of meetings, ordinary and extra-ordinary. An ordinary meeting may be called by either party provided at least twenty-one days' notice is given. Such notice must be accompanied by copies of the proposed agenda for the meeting. On receipt of the notice and the agenda, the general secretary of the union and the executive secretary of the employers' federation meet together to agree on a final agenda, date and place of meeting. Extra-ordinary meetings may be called by either party by giving at least fourteen days' notice to members, to consider any matters that may require urgent attention. An industrial action in a member-company, for instance, may necessitate an extra-ordinary meeting.

In the case of disagreement in the Council on any matter or matters, the disagreement is reduced to writing and signed by the general secretary of the national union and the executive secretary of the employers' federation. Thereafter, the disagreement is dealt with in accordance with the provisions of the Trade Disputes Act 1976. While the procedure for the resolution of the disagreement is being followed, both parties agree that normal work in member-companies will continue. It is also agreed, in the event of any industrial action, that workers in the medical, safety and security sections of the company shall not take part in any such action.

The parties have concluded two types of collective agreements, the procedural agreement and the substantive agreement.

(i)   The procedural agreement

The procedural agreement signed in August 1979 specifies the principles and procedures that regulate the relationship between the parties from time to time. The main provisions of the agreement are:

1. *The parties:* The names of the parties to the agreement are stated and also the date on which the agreement signed comes into operation, in this case 1 August 1979.
2. *Preamble:* This is an introduction showing the desire of the parties to establish cordial and formal relations. The principles on which the relations rest are spelt out as follows:

   (a) that the Association accepts the national union as the sole representative and negotiating body for all established non-management employees who are members of the union or who become members during the life time of this agreement, with the exception of those excluded by section 3(3) of the Trade Unions (Amendment) Act 1978;

(b) that the Association and the national union shall enter into collective bargaining and/or discussion on behalf of their respective members on all matters relating to wages, hours of work and other terms and conditions of employment as specified in the Appendix, and such other matters relating to terms of employment that may be agreed from time to time;

(c) all negotiations between the national union and the Association shall be effected by the National Joint Industrial Council under the terms of the constitution set out in Part II of this agreement. The parties agree that until the procedure for formal negotiations set out in Part II hereof has been fully exhausted the union shall undertake to prevent any form of industrial action, and similarly the Association shall guarantee employment while negotiations are in progress;

(d) that the national union undertakes not to interfere with the normal functions of management which gives member-companies of the Association the sole right and responsibility to conduct their business in such a manner as they consider fit and to engage, promote, demote, transfer and terminate any employees. Even so, it is agreed that the national union is free to intervene, under just and reasonable cause, in matters affecting the welfare and employment of its members;

(e) that the Association and the national union undertake that their officers and/or representatives shall accept responsibility for compliance by their members with the conditions and procedures laid down in this agreement and agree to take all possible steps to prevent or bring to an end as speedily as possible, any action taken by their members which is at variance with this agreement or the provisions of any other negotiated agreement, subsidiary to it.

3. *Negotiating machinery:* Provision is made for a constitution establishing the National Joint Industrial Council. Among items included in the constitution of the Council are:

(a) the title;
(b) objects;
(c) membership;
(d) officers, i.e. chairman, vice-chairman and secretary to the Council;
(e) matters for negotiation and consultation;
(f) meetings;

    (g)   quorum;
    (h)   records of proceedings of meetings;
    (i)   duration of agreements;
    (j)   disagreement;
    (k)   appointment of *ad hoc* or standing committees;
    (l)   grievance procedures;
    (m) amendment of constitution.

(ii)   The substantive agreement

The substantive agreement, unlike the procedural agreement, changes from time to time. Items listed for negotiation in the procedural agreement form the contents of this agreement. In the case of the Food, Beverage and Tobacco Industry, the agreement covers the following:

    (a)   wages and salaries;
    (b)   overtime and overtime rates;
    (c)   weekly hours of work;
    (d)   annual leave;
    (e)   leave allowance;
    (f)   sick-leave benefits;
    (g)   out-of-station allowance;
    (h)   overnight travelling allowance;
    (i)   acting allowance;
    (j)   redundancy benefits;
    (k)   shift allowance;
    (l)   extra duty allowance;
    (m) heat allowance;
    (n)   housing allowance;
    (o)   maternity leave;
    (p)   transport allowance;
    (q)   transfer allowance.

As in the case of the procedural agreement, there are certain essentials that have to be fulfilled with regard to the substantive agreement. These are:

1. *The signatories:* At the conclusion of the negotiations, decisions arrived at are embodied in a memorandum of agreement and signed by the representatives of the unions and employers.
2. *Effective date:* The effective date is the day the agreement is signed,

and all improvements take effect from that date, unless otherwise stated.

3. *The duration of the agreement:* The agreements include a duration clause stipulating a period of time, generally two to three years, when either party may reopen negotiations on any of the items already negotiated upon. The Food, Beverage and Tobacco Industry's agreement provides for two years, while the agreement between the Employers' Association of Leather, Footwear and Rubber Industries of Nigeria and its national union provides for three years. In some cases a wage reopener clause is included in the duration clause to the effect that if the cost of living were to rise substantially during the period, the question of wages might be reviewed after, say, the first twelve or eighteen months of the life of the agreement.

The importance of the duration clause lies in the fact that it enables the member-companies to make their plans on the understanding that unless an emergency occurs, they will not face union negotiations until the expiry of the life of the agreement. However, there are two objections to the duration clause. First, in the past the clause was observed more in the breach than in observance. In a number of cases, union rank-and-file members simply disregard the clause whenever they believed things had changed and insisted on fresh negotiations. Second, there was the tendency on the part of many unions to hold negotiations on all the items at the end of the period. This has led some employers to suggest that the duration clause is really not necessary and that where there are responsible trade-union leaders, it need not be added. It is our view, however, that a collective agreement should be made for a specific period, with the intention of reviewing only those items that need be reviewed at the expiry of the period.

There is no doubt that under the new industrial relations a trend has started that will eventually lead to more even power between employers and unions at the bargaining table. The unions are now very strong and are prepared to push for the best terms they can get. This has already created problems for certain companies. Collective agreements are reached in some cases without regard to the problems of either the smaller enterprises or those companies with financial problems. In 1980 the Food, Beverage and Tobacco Industry's NJIC concluded a collective agreement in which the lowest wage to be paid in the industry was but at ₦100 per month. A member-company, Philip Morris, a tobacco manufacturer, could not pay. Consequently, it had to enter into a separate agreement with its branch union for the lesser sum of ₦84.50, thereby varying the national agreement. That brought on them the anger of the national union. Crisis was only averted after much persuasion. It was in order to overcome the sort of problem highlighted above that the Chemical and Non-Metallic Industry grouped all companies in the sector into three categories, A, B and C. The idea is that different rates of pay would be negotiated for the three categories. In this way they hope to accommodate the problems that may arise for each employer. The approach adopted by the Chemical and Non-Metallic Industry would seem to be a good solution to a problem that otherwise could threaten industrial peace in many of the industrial sectors.

### 4.4.2	Interaction between the NLC, the employers' association and the government

In most industrial relations systems there is informal interaction between the parties at the national level. Such parties would be the national labour movement, the national employers' association and the government. In Nigeria these parties are the NLC, NECA and the federal government. The government consults the NLC and the NECA formally and informally on matters pertaining to labour and receives representations from both on the same matters. Indeed, legislation on labour matters generally provides for representatives of all three parties in certain tripartite bodies. Such bodies include the National Labour Advisory Council (NLAC), the National Provident Fund Advisory Council (NPFAC), the National Industrial Safety Council (NISC), the Industrial Arbitration Panel (IAP), the Prices, Productivity and Incomes Board (PPIB), to name but a few. These tripartite bodies advise the government on the relevant issues and it is the aim that the views of all parties concerned will at least be reflected in the advice given to enable the government to decide on the right course of action.

It must be stressed that the tripartite bodies deliberate and offer advice that may or may not be accepted. Accordingly, the recommendations of these bodies to the government are not agreements that the government is bound to implement. However, under pressure from the Nigerian Labour Congress, a new element has entered into the industrial relations system. In addition to informal and formal consultations with the government, the Nigerian Labour Congress now negotiates with the federal government and actually concludes signed agreements. Thus the NLC signed an agreement with the federal government on fringe benefits for workers in July 1979. Again in April 1980 the NLC concluded an agreement with the federal government covering car loans and basic allowances, rent subsidy and transport allowances. It is interesting to note that although, in the main, the unions who concluded these agreements with the government represented workers in the private sector, the employers were not party to these agreements. Nevertheless, the employers were expected to be bound by these agreements.

A further attempt was made in April 1980 to include the employers in one such negotiation. A tripartite meeting had been called by the government at the instance of the NLC which had demanded ₦300.00 per month national minimum wage. At the meeting the NLC suggested that since the meeting was made up of representatives of labour, the employers, all the state governments and the federal government, any decisions arrived at must be final and considered binding. In other words, the NLC expected a collective agreement to be signed at the conclusion of the discussions. As a result of these developments which the NECA considers detrimental to collective bargaining, the Association protested. It did not want to be goaded into collective bargaining by default, and the Association's spokesman made the following statement concerning the competence of NECA:

> NECA sincerely hopes that this tripartite body has not been set up to function as a negotiating council for the purpose of determining what should be the national minimum wage. NECA is a consultative and not a negotiating body. It will be ultra vires the Association's Constitution to undertake such a function. Besides, such a function is reserved, under the Trade Unions Act, for registered trade unions. NECA is not a registered trade union. The Association cannot therefore undertake to negotiate a national minimum wage on behalf of its members. This is quite apart from its conception of the preconditions, methods and procedures for determining such a minimum. NECA, however, feels itself competent to discuss the principles and concepts of determining a national minimum wage and of contributing to discussions aimed at arriving at an agreed method and procedure for doing so.[14]

As a result of NECA's protests, the meeting agreed that the outcome of the discussions would not be an agreement to be signed by the parties, but would be presented in the form of recommendations to the

government to enable them to consider the matter further. Thus, at
NECA's insistence, the meeting was able to recognise and accept that
it had no authority whatsoever to conclude an agreement on such a
national issue as the minimum wage, a matter which under the
Constitution can only be handled by the National Assembly.

The new trend towards formal collective bargaining between the
NLC and the federal government has brought some confusion into the
industrial relations system. Not only has the NLC no powers under the
law to formally bargain collectively, their doing so with the federal
government has created problems. A situation where collective bargaining is removed from those that are directly involved or their
representatives will only help to kill the collective bargaining process.
The other significant aspect of the problem is that, once the government concludes an agreement with the NLC, the general secretaries of
the industrial unions simply advise the employers in their industrial
sectors to pay up. Indeed, at the co-ordinating committee meeting of
the NECA, held in June 1980, some employers (apparently out of
frustration) wondered aloud whether it would not be more advantage-
ous to abandon collective bargaining altogether and wait for government directives before changing conditions of employment. In our
view, what the NLC should do is to reach an informal understanding
with the government on certain national issues. Where appropriate,
such issues as agreed should form the basis of collective bargaining
between unions and employers. In this way both parties will contribute
to the survival of the collective-bargaining process.

4.5   RELATIONS IN THE PUBLIC SERVICE

We saw in Chapter 3 that the government has always reiterated its
commitment to the encouragement of free collective bargaining between employers and workers. Not only has this policy been stated
publicly, it has manifested itself in the labour legislation passed before
1968. However, words alone do not constitute action, and in this
regard government rhetoric was certainly far from action. The government has not followed up this policy with the establishment, or even
the encouragement of, a collective bargaining machinery in the civil
service. Yet the government has not discouraged the existence of trade
unions in the civil service, and the civil service unions have been in
existence since the turn of the century. Under the new industrial
relations, the following unions exist in the civil service: the Nigerian

Civil Service Union made up of all workers of the federal and state governments but excluding those on the customs, immigration, technical, typists and stenographic staff; the Civil Service Technical Workers' Union of Nigeria covers all workers classified as technical employees; and the Nigerian Union of Civil Service Typists, Stenographic and Allied Staff is made up of workers in these professions. In addition, there is the Association of Senior Civil Servants of Nigeria, which covers senior officers in the civil service, both at the federal and state level. Government corporations, departments and companies – for example, the Customs, the Nigerian Ports Authority, the Nigerian Electricity Power Authority and the Nigerian Airways – all have unions.

Instead of collective bargaining machinery, the government has favoured and encouraged Whitley Councils, whose main objective was to discuss labour problems in the civil service. This, however, did not include the negotiation of wages and salaries. The unions on their part, being essentially those of white-collar workers, have been unable to insist upon or persuade the government to accept a machinery for collective bargaining. In the event, fringe benefits have always been changed in the civil service through administrative circulars issued by the federal ministry of Establishments. In the case of wages and salaries, the government has always relied on Commissions of Inquiry to advise it. Since 1941 the following Commissions have reported to the government:

Bridges Committee	1941
Tudor Davies Commission	1945
Harragin Commission	1946
Miller Committee	1947
Gorsuch Commission	1955
Mbanefo Commission	1959
Morgan Commission	1959
Morgan Commission	1964
Adebo Commission	1971
Udoji Commission	1974

Thus, with regularity over the years, the government has appointed Wages and Salaries Commissions and has altered wages and salaries as a result of their recommendations. The intention of the government in appointing the Commissions is to make up for the non-existence of collective bargaining in the public sector. Therefore the awards of the Commissions are supposed to be for employees in the public sector only, as changes are made through collective bargaining in the private sector. However, the experience in Nigeria since the Bridges Committee of 1941 is that as soon as the awards are announced for employees in the public sector, workers in the private sector all over the country clamour for the implementation of such awards by their employers. Thus, the unions have come to accept that in addition to changes that may be made to wages and salaries through collective bargaining, the state also has a responsibility to increase wages every few years for all workers, whether in the public service or not. Consequently, the workers have become psychologically attuned to this approach and any delay on the part of an employer to implement any government awards generally resulted in disaster for the employer.

In the recent past there have been cases when private employers and their unions have concluded collective agreements and implemented them only to be forced again to implement government awards on top of what has already been granted to their workers. In February 1964, for example, the Nigerian Tobacco Company Limited concluded a wages agreement with its union, the Nigerian Tobacco General Workers' Union. Following the Morgan Commission and the General Strike in June of that year, the government – which had earlier stated that the awards were meant for the public sector only – caved in, and NTC had to implement the awards four months later on top of what had been collectively agreed in February. The same thing happened to many employers in 1971, during the Adebo Commission and again in 1975 following the Udoji Commission. Indeed, in respect of the latter commission, the government anticipated the same type of agitation by workers in the private sector and in s.131 of the White Paper on the Commission's report, the government said:

The Public Service Review Commission was appointed to advise, among other things, on the appropriate level of remuneration in the Public Service as well as to examine the possibility of harmonising remuneration in the Public Service with those of comparable positions in the private sector. The Government, therefore, does not expect a general *pro rata* increase in the levels of remuneration in the private sector because such general increases would only serve to widen the existing gap between the private and the public sector. Employers may negotiate with their respective employees appropriate increase in salaries and wages to compensate for increases in the cost of living since the wage freeze.

In spite of the good intentions, evident in the white paper, when the pressures came from workers all over the country, and one strike after another followed, the government simply advised the employers to pay up. This uncertainty surrounding the effect of government action in the public sector on relations in the private sector has tended to diminish the role of collective bargaining and stultify its development. In fact, many employers have found the situation so frustrating that once the government appoints a Wages Commission, negotiations on wages and salaries would be suspended to await the outcome of the commission and to avoid paying twice. In general, the pattern of government determination of wages and salaries for a large section of the paid employees in the country detracts from the declared national policy of free collective bargaining. By its nature, scope and consequences, it has raised doubts as to the usefulness of collective bargaining in the Nigerian situation. What is needed in our view is a standing machinery, similar to that which obtains in the private sector, and which should have representatives of government and the various civil-service unions. The government, no doubt, is aware of the problem, and some half-hearted efforts have been made in the past to tackle the difficulty. The government in 1964 gave as one of the terms of reference to the Morgan Commission the following: 'to make recommendations concerning a suitable structure, as well as an adequate machinery for a wage review on continuing basis.[15] Here was the one opportunity for machinery to be established to save the country from the constant embarrassment of Wages Commissions. Unfortunately the Commission dodged this all-important issue. In its report the Commission said:

But the evidence before us convinces us that it will be unrealistic and inadvisable to fashion out a machinery of such limited application, because of the close inter-relationship between wages and other conditions of employment. We have, accordingly, come to the conclusion as already stated, that the whole machinery of industrial relations in Nigeria for the settlement of the levels and structure of remuneration and conditions of service, as well as for the settlement of labour grievances and trade disputes in general should be thoroughly reviewed in the light of the prevailing circumstances of the country.[16]

Although the terms of reference narrowed the scope to machinery for reviewing wages only as opposed to the total industrial relations situation, it is our view that the Commission, having regard to the circumstances surrounding the perennial appointment of commissions, could have come up with some recommendation in that regard. As it turned out, no recommendation was made and no formal machinery for collective bargaining was established.

The failure of the Morgan Commission to recommend a standing negotiating machinery led the government in 1970 to include the following in the terms of reference of the Adebo Commission: 'to consider the need to establish a system of ensuring that remuneration in the Public Services, the Statutory Public Corporations and State-owned Companies is periodically reviewed and kept in proper national balance'.[17]

The Commission in its report merely recommended that the Whitley Councils be revitalised for the various categories of employees in the public service and be renamed 'Public Service Negotiating Council, A,B,C'. But no new machinery was established and it took another Commission of Inquiry to change the wages and salaries of employees in the public service in 1975.[18] The failure of the Whitley Councils led to the search for a better standing negotiating machinery. In consequence, the Councils were replaced by the Public Service Negotiating Council recommended earlier by the Adebo Commission. The aims and objects of the Council include the following:

1. To secure the greatest measure of co-operation between the government of the federation in their respective roles as employer and the general body of civil servants in all the public services of the federation.
2. To deal with grievances of civil servants.
3. To promote industrial peace and efficiency in the public services of the federation.

With regard to the functions of the Council, the constitution provides that the Council shall:

(a) have general responsibility for negotiating all matters affecting the conditions of service of civil servants;
(b) advise the government where necessary of the best means of utilising the ideas and experience of civil servants with a view to improving productivity;
(c) review the general conditions of civil servants, e.g. recruitment, hours of work, promotion, discipline, salary, fringe benefits and superannuation, provided that in matters relating to recruitment,

discipline and promotion the Council shall restrict itself to general principles; and

(d) refer all disputes of differences whatsoever to the Federal Ministry of Labour for settlement in accordance with the Trade Disputes Act 1976 or any statutory modification or re-enactment thereof for the time being in force.

However, in spite of the stated objectives of the Council, actual negotiations do not take place. Conditions of service are still reviewed arbitrarily and fringe benefits are either curtailed or abolished without regard to the opinion of those employed in the civil service and quite often without reference to the Council. The recent curtailment of leave period, the unilateral changing of the qualifying period for pensions and the abolition of car loans and car-running allowances are but a few examples of government's arbitrary action. It is not surprising, therefore, that most employees in government employment would favour a situation where they share decision-making with regard to their conditions of service through the collective bargaining process.[19]

The fear that Wages Commissions will become concretised as the only means of changing conditions of service led the NECA to recommend to the federal government a move away from the practice of introducing wage and salary changes through the appointment of commissions.[20] The Association contended that the current practice was fraught with the potential danger of the government assuming and asserting that it knows best what is good for employers, trade unions, society and everyone in it. The Association pointed out that as the single largest employer, government's behavior as an employer, quite independently of its policy objectives in the labour field, exerts a powerful influence on industrial relations throughout the economy. Therefore, the government must ensure that it does nothing to upset the pattern that the employers and the unions have set for themselves.

The reason for the failure of the government to establish or encourage collective bargaining in the public service is given by the Public Service Review Commission 1974, in paragraph 196 of its Main Report:

The second factor militating against proper management/staff relations is the proliferation of staff associations or unions. The result is that however well educated and trained the staff relations officers are, they cannot be sure who represents whom, and in fact are often confronted with seriously overlapping jurisdictions and inter-union conflicts .... Obviously, it is impossible for government to give serious consideration to negotiating or consulting with this massive and heterogeneous collection of employee representatives.

If the Commission's reason is really the true reason for the lack of collective bargaining machinery in the civil service, then the problem no longer exists. With the restructuring of unions throughout the economy, we can no longer talk of a 'massive and heterogeneous collection of employee representatives'. Consequently, it is our hope that with the developments now going on in the private sector, and armed with the experience gained in the statutory corporations, the government will now see its way clear to establish formally collective bargaining machinery in the public service. In Chapter 5 we shall discuss the procedures for resolving conflicts that the parties in the industrial relations system have established.

5 Labour Disputes and their Settlement

In this chapter we shall examine the various causes of labour disputes; the effect of disputes and strikes on the Nigerian economy; and the procedures established for the resolution of these disputes.

5.1 TYPOLOGY OF LABOUR DISPUTES

Labour disputes may be grouped into two types, namely: disputes concerning an individual and disputes concerning the group, the union. In some cases a dispute that begins as an individual dispute can develop into a collective dispute. Generally, disputes involving an individual are over his rights, what he thinks he is entitled to as a workman in his workplace. These are regarded as *legal rights* because the claims are based on the contractual relations between the parties. However, the situation is not so clear-cut. There is a grey area in the management of people at work that is not controlled by law and where equity and fairness only can come into play. Thus it is difficult for a workman to claim the right that he should have been promoted to the next higher vacancy because he has been longest in the lower position. There are other considerations to be taken into account, and the question of 'right', whether legal or moral, does not arise. Having said that, it must be understood also that there are, or should be, laid-down procedures and rules that govern workmen; and if a company does not follow these in the management of the workmen, then those who feel the deviation has worked to their disadvantage will in that case have the legal right to complain about the breach.

The second category of disputes, that is, collective disputes, are concerned mainly with economic matters, except in cases where individual disputes develop into collective disputes. The economic matters that cause collective disputes are those that relate to collective bargaining. The disputes may arise either because of a breakdown in collective bargaining or may be the result of the interpretation of the collective agreement or, in yet other cases, the non-implementation of the whole or parts of the agreement. We now discuss examples of both individual and collective grievances.

5.1.1   Individual grievances

As we have observed above, individual grievances are those that emanate from what the individual considers a denial or breach of his rights. They may include promotions, awards of annual increments or the implementation of individual conditions of employment. But unlike collective grievances, it is not always easy to establish the real cause of a worker's grievance. This is so because it is not always that workers who have grievances know the exact causes of such grievances. It is true that they may give their reasons, but in many cases patient examination and discussion will reveal that these grievances arise out of frustration which may in turn be the result of extraneous factors not related to the employment situation. In the Nigerian situation, it is important to remember that most of the workers in industry today are the first generation of industrial workers. Some of them may have come straight from the village after primary-school education to the urban centres, where they suddenly find themselves working on machines and on shift systems. This initial dislocation of the rural-life routine (discussed in Chapter 2) leads to psychological problems as the worker struggles to adapt to his new environment.

Moreover, while dealing with individual grievances, it is important to recognise that when a worker has a personal problem, which he tries to suppress, it may surface in another direction without the worker himself realising it. The worker's complaint, therefore, may be merely an overt basis for the grievance, while the real problem may be a health problem, a domestic problem, or an organisational one. The author had an experience concerning a worker who wanted to be paid during the period of his casual leave when he went for a land case. According to the rules of employment in the company only casual leave granted on compassionate grounds, such as the illness or death of a relation, will qualify for pay. The worker was aware of the rules but insisted that he was entitled to be paid for his period of absence. A patient and prolonged discussion with him revealed that he was his mother's only child, his father was dead, and their land was being taken away by an apparently stronger man. He was so frustrated over his helplessness that he thought it was his employer who was denying him his legitimate rights.

There was another case of a worker who wanted to buy spectacles and asked his company to pay for them. The company's free medical facilities for workers did not cover the provision of glasses. The relevant section of the Employee's Handbook provided as follows: 'The company will not pay for expenses in respect of dental or optical treatment, nor will it pay for such things as false teeth ... or spectacles'. The particular employee, a chargehand, had his attention drawn to this as he was holding a copy of the Handbook, yet he insisted on his 'rights'. During the discussions he queried the company's procedures for promotions, discipline, etc., and stated how he was earmarked for promotion as foreman but was later passed over. Thus the grievance interview that started with the non-provision of spectacles for the employee ended with discussions of the company's procedures for the appraisal of employees and the basis of promotion.

It is not being suggested here that each time an employee comes up with a complaint it must be assumed that something other than the thing he complained about is the cause of the problem. What we are suggesting is that in the case of individual grievances involving 'rights', it is always very difficult to pin down the real cause of the grievance. This can only be achieved if, during the period of interviewing the aggrieved employee, the manager is patient enough to unravel the real cause. Where this approach is adopted, most individual grievances are settled through the internal grievance procedure.

5.1.2 Collective grievances

By far the most common cause of collective disputes in Nigeria is the management's refusal to grant a demand made by the union. A variation of this is the breakdown of collective bargaining as a result of inability of the parties to reach agreement on an issue or issues that the union considers important to their members. Such issues will normally include wages and salaries, housing allowance and other fringe benefits. The breakdown of negotiations is quite frequent because the parties approach the negotiation table with very different views and mandates and it is not always possible to reconcile such opposing views.

Until the promulgation of the Trade Unions Act 1973 which gives the Minister of Labour powers to compel an employer to recognise a union, recognition and refusal to bargain were a major source of conflict. But the failure to recognise a union was much more common among smaller employers, who were suspicious of union power and who wanted to avoid unions at all costs. There was quite a large number of such employers during the 1960s. Also, a number of large employers used non-recognition as a weapon to force recalcitrant trade-union leaders to behave. Most of the procedural agreements in existence then had the provision that the employer had the right to withdraw recognition of the union if the union breached the agreement. One common way of breaching the agreement was to call a strike without first exhausting the grievance procedure. However, non-recognition is now a thing of the past as an employer is obliged to recognise a union once it is registered.

A common complaint by workers was in regard victimisation or anti-union discrimination. Again, there were many cases where workers who took active part in trade unionism were allegedly discriminated against either in the award of increments or in promotion. Unfortunately, these charges are always difficult to prove because in each case it is the manager who reports on performance and it is he who decides who should get what increment or who should be promoted. However, in a number of cases where disputes developed, it was established beyond any doubt that workers who had been active in trade-union affairs were discriminated against. Many were dismissed. The cases that we investigated, following allegations of discrimination against certain workers for union activities, showed that such workers – including some local union officials – had acted in breach of the collective agreement and without the authority of their unions. Such actions tended to irritate the employer and led him to regard the workers concerned as having a disruptive influence on his operations.

Disputes may arise also as a result of the claimed violation of legislation or rule of conditions of work. In one particular case that we came across, the management had to recruit temporary employees in order to help out during a peak period in their sales operations. When the emergency was over, after about six months, and in accordance with the contract of employment, the management terminated the services of these temporary employees with due notice. But the union insisted that it should have been consulted over the matter. The management argued that as these employees were recruited specifically for a period, the collective agreement did not cover them nor could they be regarded as members of the union. The union did not accept this interpretation of the situation and an industrial action took place. The dispute was eventually resolved through arbitration.

The application or interpretation of provisions of collective agreements are also a constant source of conflict at work. In the case of lengthy agreements, there may be a conflict between one section and the other. Each party to the agreement may point to the section that favours its case. In some cases, too, the agreement may be silent on a particular issue, in which case each party puts forward its understanding of the situation. An example of this is the recent case involving the Federated Motors Industries and its workers' union, the Associated Companies African Workers' Union, now part of Automobile, Boatyard and Transport Equipment and Allied Workers Union.[1] On 3 February 1978 the union, through their leaders, approached the company to demand the removal of the works manager who was then on leave. The company did not accede to the request and made it clear to the union that it could not dictate to the company which manager to employ and which not to employ. The union's argument was that the works manager's managerial style and behaviour was against the interest of their members. Therefore, they had a legitimate right to ask for his removal. When the works manager resumed work on 8 February 1978, the workers embarked on a 'go-slow' action, a dispute arose that led to the dismissal of a large number of workers, and legal proceedings ensued with the final settlement by the National Industrial Court in January 1979.[2]

Disputes that arise from collective grievances may also be the result of non-observance of conditions of individual contract of employment or of work rules including disciplinary rules. Finally, a large number of grievances that occur in the workplace may be those concerning situations not governed by rules. Such grievances emanate essentially from individual workers and may be because of an alleged ill-treatment of the worker by his supervisor or manager or the result of some claimed right. In our survey for this study, we tried to determine which factors cause disputes often or very often. We found that wages and other matters concerned with the collective agreement and management's interpretation or implementation of such matters are the main causes of labour disputes.

5.2 STRIKES

There appears to be a general feeling among workers that an employer will not recognise their power unless and until they have gone on strike with consequences of economic damage to the employer. Therefore, in some cases, behind the apparently simple issues that cause strikes, such as the dismissal of a worker or the refusal to provide free meals in the canteen, lies the much more deep-rooted problem of a power struggle between the employers and the workers. A good example of this is the dispute between *Grizi (Nigeria) Limited* and *Grizi (Nigeria) Limited Group of Companies Workers' Union*.[3] In that case, one Joseph Njoku, a cleaner in the company who was also a union member, was dismissed for failing to obey the lawful instruction of his manager. As a result of this, the workers started a work-to-rule action designed to force the company to reinstate the dismissed worker. The company refused to change its decision and a chain of events followed that led to the dismissal of another 100 employees who were also union members. The matter went to the Arbitration Panel (IAP) and eventually to the National Industrial Court. The dismissed workers were not reinstated but received redundancy benefits. The significant aspect of this case is that it was simple enough to have been settled through the grievance procedure but, as the workers wanted to show their power by engaging in a strike action, the company on its part did not want to be seen to be weak. A similar situation arose in the Federated Motor Industries case when the workers, believing that the works manager was working against their interest, embarked on a go-slow to force the company to remove him.[4] That action led to the dismissal of 403 employees and eventually resulted in redundancy claims.

An interesting feature of strikes in Nigeria is that they are most common among factory manual workers and tend to be particularly prevalent in industries where unionism is strong. The examples of the Nigerian Railways Corporation and the Nigerian Ports Authority, each of which has a long history of unionism, are well known. The fact that strikes are more common among manual workers tends to suggest that other factors are at work. While clerks who work in offices are relatively docile, the manual worker on the factory floor, in uniform and surrounded by machines and unending noise, is usually glad to have some days off that he can justify as being the result of collective action.

The great majority of the strikes fall into the category which, in the words of Knowles, are 'demonstrations in force'.[5] Generally, the decision to stop work is spontaneous, though the dispute will probably reflect long-standing grievances that peaceful application has failed to remedy. In the main, groups of workers who believe that progress on a matter has been too slow organise the other workers to embark upon strike action without the authority of the union leaders. The spontaneous or demonstration strike is usually of short duration and quickly settled. Thus many strikes last for only a few hours or a few days. Very rarely do these strikes last for a week or more. There are several reasons for this. First, most of the workers are not properly briefed before they join a strike action. After a day or two of euphoria, they discover the true reason of the strike and the action tends to die down. Second, most of the workers cannot afford a prolonged strike. The unions have no strike funds, and workers are therefore exposed to severe privation during strikes. Finally, as the purpose of such strikes is to draw attention to the urgency of workers' feelings about their demands, the strikers are usually willing to return to work to enable negotiations to take place even when the employer has not offered any concrete concessions. The demonstration strike has suddenly acquired a new image and importance in Nigeria following the creation of industrial unions. The power base has moved to the national-union executives and in order to prove that power still lies with the local-union officials, many spontaneous strike actions – without the approval of the national unions – have taken place.

In other cases, conflicts may involve what has been termed, 'perishable disputes'.[6] These are issues that management would win by default if workers did not act immediately. Thus, in a case of a dismissed worker, his colleagues may feel that the only way to secure his reinstatement is to stop work. This type of strike action, which also comes without notice, is common. In spite of the progress made so far in industrialisation, the Nigerian society does not appear ready for strikes. Strikes are not looked upon with favour in the country, however strong the case of the workers may be. When a major strike is in progress, the public guided by the news media expresses its disgust and the government is forced to enter into the dispute. This is one reason strikes do not last long in Nigeria. In addition to the inconvenience that the society as a whole suffers, there are two other reasons for this. First, as in other developing countries, unions in Nigeria have been susceptible to the external influences of the West and East (Chapter 3). As the Adebiyi Report of 1977 revealed, a cold war was being fought in Nigeria between the Western countries led by the USA, on the one hand, and the countries of Eastern Europe led by the Soviet Union on the other. Therefore, strikes have been traditionally associated with sabotage of government efforts engineered by external forces. Moreover, the country has always relied on development plans as a means of effecting economic development, and strikes in such circumstances cease to be private matters between the employers and the workers. In the circumstances, any strike action is regarded as a negation of the economic objectives of the country. It is in the light of this underlying philosophy that the role of government in regulating strikes as discussed below must be evaluated.

5.2.1   The cost of strikes

Strikes, especially major ones, in a developing country like Nigeria always have a dramatic effect on the public. This is particularly so in the case of certain essential industries. In 1975 a single strike action by tanker drivers who deliver fuel and diesel oil from the ports and the only refinery at Port Harcourt to all parts of the country virtually paralysed the whole nation. Passenger transport was grounded and industries could not function.

Similar strikes by a large section of the banking industry and by the electricity workers have in the past paralysed the nation's economic activities. The greatest impact of such strikes is the chain reaction that is produced throughout all sectors of the economy. It was in an attempt to prevent strikes in certain key sectors of the economy that the government classified certain organisations as essential services and where trade unionism is not allowed.

Some hold the view that the effects of strikes are not all that devastating. Indeed, one view holds that participation in strike action may have some salutory effect on productivity. Hyman, for example, believes that such participation can raise workers' morale, resulting in a spontaneous rise in productivity – especially where the strike is successful.[7] There appears to be some truth in that view; the only difficulty is to determine what really causes the high morale: the strike or the achievement of the objective. Would the situation be different if the management conceded the demand, thereby preventing the strike? The Donovan Report has noted that it is possible for some of the working days lost to be made good after a strike, either by overtime or by greater effort under incentive schemes.[8] But that argument may not hold true in Nigeria for two reasons.

First, it has been difficult to consider seriously incentive schemes in Nigeria. As most of the industries are essentially process industries in which the product is fashioned by machines, the measurement of individual or even group effort becomes a very difficult task. Second, with the expansion of the domestic market, these process industries generally work a three-shift system, with the overtime element already built into the system. Therefore any hours lost as a result of strike action cannot be made good through overtime.

Yet there are those who argue that to speak of 'working days lost' in a strike in computing the cost of strikes is misleading, as that implies that days spent striking would otherwise have been spent working. Kornhauser believes that 'some strikes are merely substitutes for curtailments of work which would otherwise take the form of lay-offs'.[9] In other words, employers may welcome and even encourage a strike in their own organisations in a period of recession. This view seems to have been confirmed by a detailed analysis of strikes in Britain's car industry. The days lost owing to strikes tend to be highest in periods of recession, when the production lost could not have been sold anyway.[10] Therefore, 'the strike becomes almost a form of "work-spreading". To have a strike is not perhaps the most rational way to fill in a slump, but it is more interesting and sociable than some other forms of idleness, and helps to keep workers from drifting away to other jobs'.[11] In the light of the above, some authorities are led to believe that one cannot draw up an exact account of strike losses.[12]

To do so would require knowledge of what would have occurred in the absence of each stoppage and the ability to calculate and weigh the difference, an impossible enterprise.[13] In the circumstances, 'the judgement of most specialists is that the economic consequences of strikes are over-rated'.[14] They may well be over-rated in developed economies, but in Nigeria a major strike, as we have shown above, has a great impact on the economy. This is so because the base of the economy is 'hollow'. The nation relies almost exclusively on oil and, while industrial development is on the rise, the bulk of the population survives on subsistence agriculture. The infrastructure is poor and there are no alternatives to turn to in times of crises. Consequently a strike, even of a few days' duration, in one key industry would paralyse the whole economy.

5.2.2 Government regulation of strikes

Unfortunately there are no reliable strike statistics in the country. Not all the strikes that take place are reported and, in recent years, the Ministry of Labour has not been of much use in respect of such data.

However, with the scanty information available, it is clear that strike action is on the increase. This increase must, however, be related to the size of the labour force which has been increasing in recent years, and the total number of 'man-days lost' as a result of strikes must also be read accordingly. Moreover, strikes in themselves are only a partial indication of industrial conflict and must not therefore be used without other factors to assess the general industrial relations climate in the country. But there is no doubt that well-kept statistics on strikes can provide a useful indication of trends in industrial disputes.

The damage to the economy that strikes can bring about made the government take drastic action in 1968. In that year the government enacted the Trade Disputes (Emergency Provisions) Decree which introduced compulsory arbitration. The following year, the law was amended and strikes were banned completely. That approach was necessitated by the consequences of the civil war. The federal government had been directing all its efforts to fighting the war and was not prepared for any disruptive tendencies on the part of any interest-group. While the leader of the United Labour Congress, Mr H. P. Adebola, had indicated that all unions affiliated to the Congress would refrain from strike action during the civil war,[15] the leader of the NTUC held contrary views. The President, Mr Wahab Goodluck, had praised the 'sacrifices' that the workers had made in respect of the war effort, and urged a review of wage and salaries as failure to do so would be to 'sit on a keg of industrial gunpowder'.[16] In addition to these threatening statements there was a wave of strikes in 1968, and in the face of these the government brought out the measure, the aim being 'to prevent strikes and lockouts through early intervention by the Ministry of Labour'.[17]

However, the law did not have the effect that was intended, as can be seen from Table 5.1.

As can be seen from Table 5.1, when the law came into force in the middle of 1968 (1968–9 year) there was a drop in the number of strikes during the year. Again when the amendment banning strikes was introduced in 1969, disputes and strikes were low in that year, but by 1970 an increase in strike action was recorded. The strikes in 1970 necessitated the appointment of the Adebo Wages and Salaries Commission.[18] Although the law, but most especially the constant warnings of the Federal Commissioner for Labour and the Inspector-General of Police, had some restraining influence on the propensity to strike, the significant point to note is that the law as such did not act as a deterrent. The law appeared to have had some effect during the first few months on the number of disputes and strikes. Thereafter, once the workers were sure that the government was not really prepared to prosecute workers for a breach of the law, they went on strike whenever they felt they had a grievance against their employers.

It is clear, therefore, that on the basis of our experience in Nigeria, statutory prohibition of strikes does not necessarily prevent workers from going on strike. The workers are, of course, aware that sanctions in the country's labour laws are generally not enforced.

TABLE 5.1   Recorded strikes, 1960–77

Year	No of strikes	Workers involved	Man-days lost
1960–1	65	36 667	157 373
1961–2	58	18 673	57 303
1962–3	45	n.a	53 039
1963–4	62	45 409	96 621
1964–5	195	73 447	253 460*
1965–6	126	n.a.	238 679
1966–7	89	41 344	100 000
1967–8	63	11 767	70 955
1968–9	29	11 551	35 028
1969–70	46	18 357	71 895
1970–1	124	78 474	224 470
1971–2	85	31 915	63 254
1972–3	71	43 676	105 415
1973–4	105	41 527	148 130
1974–5	354	126 818	357 028
1975–6	264	122 546	439 296
1976–7	130	83 126	225 710

* These figures cannot be correct. Almost all wage earners in the country were involved in the General Strike of June 1964. As wage earners were estimated at about 1 million (see the Melson 1970 reference in the Bibliography p. 771), total man-days lost must be anything up to 13 million, as the strike lasted for thirteen days.

Source: Federal Ministry of Labour, Annual Reports. See also T. Fashoyin, 'The Impact of the Trade Disputes Decrees of 1968 and 1969 on Strike Activity'. *Quarterly Journal of Administration* (October 1978) p.59.

5.3   VOLUNTARY PROCEDURES FOR THE RESOLUTION OF DISPUTES

The machinery for the settlement of labour disputes in Nigeria is twofold: the *internal* machinery that is collectively negotiated and an *external* machinery that is statutory and established by the state. The statutory machinery takes over where the internal machinery fails. It is now an established practice in industry that whenever a dispute arises, an attempt must be made to settle it internally by the parties through

the grievance procedure. The aim is to ensure that the parties themselves resolve their differences through the collective-bargaining
process.

5.3.1   Grievance procedures

In an essay, Professor Diejomaoh has lamented the absence of proper
grievance procedures in many firms, which he believed 'will cause poor
bargaining (reflected in strikes, working to rule, lockouts, dismissal,
etc) and will lower worker morale, perhaps higher labour turnover
rates, and malaise at the peremptory nature of decisions'.[19] However,
the learned professor need lament no longer because the situation has
improved considerably. Almost all the industrial concerns in Nigeria
today have one type of grievance procedure or another.[20] The grievance procedure may be used for the settlement of both individual and
collective grievances, although it is used mainly for the former.

In the case of an individual grievance, the worker is expected to take
his grievance directly to his supervisor and if there is no satisfaction,
the worker can take the matter further to his manager. At the stage of
the manager, the matter is still personal and no other people are
involved. However, if the worker does not receive satisfaction from his
manager, the matter is referred to the personnel manager and at this
stage the local union secretary will be involved. Therefore a grievance
that started as an individual grievance now becomes a union matter. If
badly handled it may become a collective grievance involving all the
workers in the organisation and may result in a strike. Most grievances
are generally settled at the level of the personnel manager and local
union secretary. If, however, a satisfactory solution is not found, the
matter becomes a national issue involving the whole company and
national officials of the union. At this stage, the joint machinery starts
to function and should efforts at settlement fail, the matter is referred
to the Ministry of Labour and the statutory machinery takes over.

With regard to collective disputes, attempts are also made to settle
the matter at the local level by the two parties. If the situation becomes
difficult, the parties may call in a mediator.[21] The mediator is anybody
considered to have experience of industrial relations matters and who
is acceptable to both parties. Should there be a breakdown of these
negotiations, the matter would be referred to the Minister of Labour
who may apply any of the steps of the statutory machinery. It will be
seen from the above that in the case of Nigeria, once there is a failure to

resolve the dispute under the internal procedure, *the parties are obliged* to invoke the provisions of the statutory machinery.

An important aspect of the settlement process is that when a dispute is being dealt with or negotiations are under way, the parties must not resort to strikes or lockouts. To do so would be to break the law.

There appears to be general satisfaction with the grievance procedures in many companies. Many disputes, especially those concerned with individuals, are generally solved through these procedures. The disputes that are eventually settled through conciliation and arbitration are those that involve the group, and especially external union officials. The workers surveyed had at least one good thing to say about the grievance procedures in their company. For example: 'The system has been able to help us maintain industrial peace and harmony over the years. Many grievances which should have exploded into disputes have been settled amicably at the lower echelon of the organisation.' Another commented thus: 'The worker is given the opportunity to air his grievance. He can get redress where he has been found to be in the right.'

Yet others considered that the importance of the procedure lies in the fact that in most cases, when the union steps into a matter, management normally reconsider their stand and this leads to a settlement of the issue.

In the case of collective disputes that are mainly economic in origin, the union generally feels that the intervention of a third party, an outsider, will be to their advantage and only a very few cases are settled through the grievance procedures. They invariably reach either the conciliation or arbitration stage of the statutory machinery. On the employers' side, the pattern has been to want to settle the dispute internally, without the aid of the statutory machinery. However, where the dispute involves a point of principle, for example the payment of redundancy to workers dismissed during a strike action, or the payment for a strike period, the employers do all they can to ensure that the matter reaches arbitration. Consequently many disputes that could easily have been settled between the parties at the local level are brought to the Industrial Arbitration Panel for settlement. Dr A. A. Adeogun, who himself was a member of the Industrial Arbitration Panel, has stated that there have been many occasions when the IAP found that the parties had made no attempts at real negotiations and hearings have been suspended to enable them to do this. In most cases, the parties had returned to the IAP with a concluded agreement and pressed the IAP to put its stamp of authority and approval on such agreement.[22]

5.4 STATUTORY PROCEDURES FOR THE RESOLUTION OF DISPUTES

The statutory procedures for the resolution of industrial disputes are contained in the Trade Disputes Act 1976. Under the law, if the parties to the dispute state in writing that they have exhausted the procedures of the voluntary machinery established by themselves and further state the points on which they disagree, the Minister for Labour may take the following steps:

1. He may appoint a fit person to act as conciliator for the purpose of effecting a settlement of the dispute.
2. He may constitute a board of inquiry if, exceptionally, there are difficulties in the way of conciliation or arbitration and if he considers that the public interest is involved.
3. Where conciliation fails, he will refer the matter to the Industrial Arbitration Panel.
4. The Minister may also refer certain disputes directly to the National Industrial Court, otherwise that court acts as the final court of appeal for all industrial disputes.

There are therefore four stages in the statutory machinery for the resolution of disputes, namely: conciliation, arbitration, inquiry and the National Industrial Court. However, a dispute need not go through all four stages, as we shall see below.

5.4.1 Conciliation

The law assumes that before a dispute is referred to the Minister of Labour, the parties must have exhausted the voluntary machinery for dispute settlement, that is, the grievance procedure, which exists or should exist in the organisation. However, if the attempt to settle the dispute under the voluntary machinery fails or if no such machinery exists in the particular organisation, the parties shall within seven days of the failure to agree meet together by themselves under the chairmanship of a mediator, mutually agreed upon and appointed by or on behalf of the parties, with a view to the amicable settlement of the dispute.

The concept of the mediator being agreed upon by the parties as distinct from a conciliator is an innovation in the settlement of industrial disputes in Nigeria. The concept was first introduced into the Nigerian legal system in the Matrimonial Causes Act 1970. Under that law, if parties to a matrimonial cause – such as divorce – appear before a high court judge, he will advise the parties to consult some elders closely related to both parties with a view to settling the problem. It is only when all attempts at reconciliation have failed that the judge will proceed with the case. The concept itself had been so introduced because it reflects the Nigerian approach to dispute settlement. If two people are fighting in the street, for example, the passers-by do not look for a policeman, but instead they constitute themselves into mediators, apportioning blame after listening to both parties and ensuring that they do not fight again.

Similarly, in the case of industrial disputes, the parties are expected to agree on any individual acceptable to both sides as mediator. The practice has so far been that those who have retired from the Ministry of Labour, or well-known personnel practitioners from other companies, have been invited as mediators. Thus in 1976 Van Leer and its house union invited the Director of Personnel of BP Nigeria Limited (now African Petroleum) to mediate in their dispute. Many disputes have been resolved at this stage of the procedure. However, the unionists interviewed all argue that it would be better to carry the dispute to conciliation and arbitration, where the panels are made up of different individuals including those with sympathies for the unions. Furthermore, they argue that at a time when tempers are high, it is unreasonable to expect the parties to sit down within seven days to agree on an individual as mediator. In the view of the unionists, an external body is best suited to come in at that stage. Whatever the argument against mediation may be, the truth is that it has the important advantage of confining the dispute to the workplace and between the parties. Second, it helps to reduce the work-load on the few senior labour officers who are normally appointed conciliators.

If within fourteen days of the appointment of a mediator the dispute is not settled, the dispute shall be reported to the Minister of Labour by or on behalf of either of the parties within fourteen days of the end of the fourteen days. The report must be in writing and should indicate the points on which the parties disagree and describe steps already taken by the parties to reach a settlement. Where the Minister is not satisfied that all reasonable steps have been taken to exhaust the internal voluntary dispute settlement procedure, he may refer the matter back to the parties. If the Minister is satisfied that the parties have taken all reasonable steps to settle the matter but have failed, he may either refer the matter to conciliation, or in appropriate cases to arbitration.

In the case of conciliation, the law empowers the Minister of Labour to appoint a fit person to act as a conciliator for the purpose of effecting a settlement of the dispute. The Act does not define 'fit', but presumably it means somebody who is knowledgeable in industrial relations. This interpretation is reinforced by the fact that those appointed conciliators are normally from the Ministry of Labour and generally not below the rank of senior labour officer.

The duties of the conciliator are to inquire into the causes and circumstances of the dispute and by negotiation with the parties to the dispute endeavour to bring about a settlement. In order to ensure that conciliators achieve the objective, the Ministry of Labour sent out a guide to all professional officers in the Labour Division of the Ministry giving hints on the role of the conciliator.[23] The guide is divided into three parts, covering basic attitude and approach, meetings and the search for agreement. With regard to basic attitude, the conciliator is advised to maintain always a strictly impartial and neutral attitude towards the parties to the dispute. He is reminded that his intervention has simply been accepted because he offers his services on behalf of, or under the authority of, the government. Accordingly, he must not automatically assume that they regard him as a conciliator capable of helping the parties to resolve their dispute. He will have to establish his acceptability to the parties. The conciliator as chairman must not criticise a party at a joint meeting or in the presence of the other party. To do so would destroy the parties' belief in his impartiality. Moreover, he should not do or say anything that will in effect strengthen the position of one party on a particular issue. As far as the search for agreement is concerned, the conciliator must be patient and systematically guide the parties over the issues involved in the dispute. He should not formally make his proposal at a joint meeting, without having first obtained the agreement of each of the parties separately. These principles, then, are among those that guide a conciliator in his attempts to settle a dispute between employers and the unions. Unfortunately a number of conciliators, either as a result of lack of experience or in anxiety to achieve results, break all or most of the rules during conciliation meetings. During the industrial unrest that followed the Udoji Commission's awards in 1975, the resources of the Ministry of Labour were so strained that many of the conciliators aggravated situations rather than improved them. Some in open joint meetings committed employers or unions to a course of action that they considered fair without prior consultation. This infuriated the party that the suggestion did not favour. In other cases, the apparently frustrated conciliators made some inappropriate and uncalled-for remarks that destroyed the whole basis of conciliation.

Yet, a reasonable number of disputes are settled at the conciliation stage. Where a settlement is reached within fourteen days of his appointment, the conciliator must report the fact to the Minister of Labour by forwarding to him a memorandum of the terms of settlement signed by the representatives of the parties. Such terms as agreed will be binding on both parties with effect from the date the agreement is signed.

Where settlement of the dispute is not reached within fourteen days of his appointment, or if, after attempting negotiation with the parties, he is satisfied that he will not be able to bring about a settlement, the conciliator will send a report to the Minister of Labour. Within fourteen days of the receipt of such a report, the Minister is obliged by law to refer the dispute to arbitration.

5.4.2 Arbitration

Arbitration into industrial disputes in Nigeria is undertaken by the Industrial Arbitration Panel (IAP). The IAP is a standing body that arbitrates over matters which have failed to be resolved at the conciliation stage. It is made up of a chairman, a vice-chairman and at least ten other members, two of whom are nominated by the employers' associations and two by the workers' organisations. The arbitral process may consist of a sole arbitrator selected from among the members of the Panel by the chairman; or a single arbitrator selected from among the members of the Panel by the chairman and assisted by assessors appointed by the Minister of Labour; or one or more arbitrators nominated by or on behalf of the workers concerned, from among the members of the Panel and presided over by the chairman or vice-chairman.

An arbitration tribunal, however constituted, must make its award within forty-two days of its constitution except where the Minister, in a particular case, allows a longer period. On receipt of an award of the tribunal, the Minister must publish the details of the award and allow some time (not more than twenty-one days) within which any of the parties to the dispute who may not be satisfied with the award may raise objections. If no notice of objection is given to the Minister within the time limit and in the manner specified in the original publication, the Minister will then publish in the *Government Gazette* a notice confirming the award and the award shall be binding on the employers and workers party to the dispute. If, however, a party to the dispute raises an objection to the award made by the tribunal, the Minister will refer the dispute for determination to the National Industrial Court.

Dr A. A. Adeogun has argued that the awards of IAP should become binding on the parties immediately upon publication, leaving it to the parties themselves to decide whether or not an appeal should be lodged with the National Industrial Court.[24] He seems to believe that the mere act of review leads to the erosion of the powers of the IAP, or at least a distrust of that body since its awards are subject to the confirmation of a higher authority. In such circumstances, the IAP may not be said to be performing its functions in a situation that can be described as being totally free. However, on the basis of experience, there is a case for the continued review of all awards by the Ministry of Labour. The IAP, sometimes out of enthusiasm, hands down decisions that are not in accord with practice in industry. Sometimes it makes an award such as the backdating of arrears, even when such backdating offends the provisions of the government's incomes policies. We believe that the involvement of the Minister of Labour is necessary to ensure that the award is not only fair and just but in accordance with government's economic parameters and industrial practice generally. Since the Minister has no power to alter the awards, such a review should be seen as a check on delegated powers. The government, through the Ministry of Labour, is the mediator in industrial disputes, and a review of awards affords the Ministry the opportunity of registering such awards for future experience. As the organ of government in charge of labour, it must be made aware of actions taken in law in the settlement of disputes.

Indeed, because the law does not vest the Minister of Labour with power to review and vary the awards of the Panel, embarrassing moments have been created for the government. For example, in the trade dispute *Management of the Nigeria Airways Limited* v. *Airline Pilots Association of Nigeria*,[25] the IAP (then IAT) awarded certain levels of salary scales and introduced certain conditions of service including allowances for pilots and flight engineers on 22 October 1975. In April 1976 the Federal Commissioner of Labour, not having received government objection within twenty-one days of the notice as provided for by law, confirmed the awards. Apparently the federal government was not happy with these awards as they considered the scales of salaries awarded too high. Moreover, there were protests from other sectors of the public service over the awards, considered too generous. In the circumstances the federal government, instead of appealing to the National Industrial Court (with uncertain result) promulgated a law, the Industrial Arbitration Tribunal (Variation of Certain Award) Act, 1979, under which the confirmation notice of the award was deemed to have lapsed and made void. Instead of the terms of the award, new terms were substituted. This approach seemed to have incensed the IAP, which was reported to have described the law as 'a bad law and should be repealed'.[26]

The question which arises is: has the IAP the right to query a law duly passed by the federal government, even if it does not agree with its intent? The duty of labour tribunals is simply to settle industrial disputes within a defined framework, they do not or ought not to make law or policy. Yet that is precisely what the IAP seems to be doing. For example, in 1978 the federal government in a policy measure decided that car loans should no longer be granted direct to an employer but that an employer may guarantee the employee's loan for the bank. The measure was designed to free money which car loans had hitherto tied down for other development purposes, and to drive it home to employees that there was really no reason why they should not go to the bank for a loan for a car just as they do for other purposes. This was a deliberate policy decision of the federal government. However, when in 1980 the Civil Service Union took the matter to the IAP, the Panel, using its own parameters, changed government policy. It decided that the government must continue with the old system of direct car loans, thus changing a fundamental labour policy of the country. That award, eventually confirmed by the National Industrial Court, has brought much inconvenience to both the federal and state governments. They just do not have the resources to finance such direct car loans. Implementation has therefore become difficult, which results in a sour industrial relations atmosphere. Such a situation might have been averted if the system provided for a review and where possible modification or outright rejection in the light of the nation's economy.

Since the creation of the Industrial Arbitration Panel (formerly Industrial Arbitration Tribunal) in 1969 the body has made much impact on industrial relations practices in the country. We can illustrate this role by the discussion of a few of the cases handled and the awards made by the Panel. Our first example is the dispute between the Nigerian Tobacco Company Limited and the Nigerian Tobacco

General Workers' Union. In 1970, the tenth year of Nigeria's independence, the federal government decided to make a loan equivalent to a month's salary to all its employees, to enable them to celebrate the occasion. In the statement put out to the Press on the matter, the government hoped that private employers would follow the government example, that is, to grant similar loans to employees in the private sector. Many employers in the country were taken by surprise and those who were not in a strong financial position, or who felt it was not their duty to grant interest-free loans to employees for merry-making, refused to do so. NTC was one such company. A dispute arose that led to a strike. At the end of the strike action which lasted for about a week, the NTGWU insisted that the workers went on strike because the company refused a government order. In the circumstances, they must be paid for the period of the strike. The NTC refused and the matter was referred to arbitration. During the proceedings, the lawyer to the union argued that the NTC was wrong not to have granted the loans because the government order was mandatory and it was the breach of that order that made the workers react in the way that they did. The employer should therefore be held responsible for all the consequences that followed. But the company's representatives submitted that the government statement had no force of law and that the principle of 'no work, no pay' must apply. In its award, the tribunal upheld the company's case and thus restored the important principle of employers not being obliged to pay workers for periods of strikes.

The second case was concerned with dismissals. Record Manufacturers (Nigeria) Limited had dismissed two employees, Messrs Adekunle and Peters, because of alleged negligence, in 1975. The union took up the issue with the company and a dispute arose that was referred to the tribunal. Having examined the evidence, the tribunal ruled that the dismissal of Mr Adekunle was fair. As regards Mr Peters, the tribunal held that the dismissal was unfair. However, because it would not be in the employee's interest to order reinstatement, a monetary award was made to compensate him for the loss of employment. Thus while it is possible under the common law to dismiss an employee under his contract of employment without ascribing any reason for it, the tribunal established in this and similar cases that such dismissals must be fair and on reasonable grounds.

Another example of the tribunal's impact on industrial relations practice is the dispute between Allied Workers Union and Michelin (Nigeria) Trading Limited. The union had approached the company to amend the procedural agreement already in existence so that welfare and other related matters could be included in the list of items that are negotiable. These matters included welfare matters, gratuity schemes, medical facilities, vehicle allowances, casual leave, departmental transfer, Christmas bonus, funeral expenses and a non-accident bonus for drivers. Now, in Nigeria, these matters are generally classified as items for discussion only. It was on the strength of this practice that the company refused the union's demand. Eventually the matter went to arbitration and in the award made in February 1975, the tribunal turned down the union's request, thus confirming the practice of separating negotiable and non-negotiable items between management and union.

5.4.3 The National Industrial Court

The court is made up of a president and four other members. All members are appointed by the federal Executive Council after consultation with the Advisory Judicial Committee. The president must have been a judge of the high court or have been a practising lawyer for at least ten years. The other members, known as 'ordinary members', need not be lawyers, but must be people with sufficient knowledge of economics, industry and trade. As in the case of high-court judges, members retire on the attainment of sixty-two years of age.

In addition to the five members of the Court, the law empowers the Minister of Labour to draw up a list of assessors, made up of employers' and workers' representatives. From among the assessors, the president of the court may appoint four to assist the court in dealing with any matter. Of this four, two shall be persons nominated by or on behalf of the employers and two by or on behalf of workers' organisations. The assessors are drawn upon in cases where the president of the court or members feel that a specialist opinion or evidence by both employers' and workers' representatives would be helpful to the court.

The court has exclusive jurisdiction in the following cases:

(a) to make awards for the purpose of settling trade disputes; and
(b) to determine questions as to the interpretation of: (i) any collective agreement; (ii) any award made by an arbitration tribunal or by the court itself; (iii) the terms of settlement of any trade dispute as recorded in any memorandum of agreement following conciliation.

The court's jurisdiction is mainly appellate, that is, issues that cannot be resolved by the Industrial Arbitration Panel are referred to it for ruling. However, the court has an original jurisdiction in two situations. If in the case of any trade dispute reported, the Minister of Labour is of the view that the dispute is one to which workers in any essential service are a party, or that in the circumstances of the case reference of the dispute to an arbitration tribunal would not be appropriate, he may within seven days of the receipt of such a report refer the dispute directly to the National Industrial Court. The NIC is the final court of appeal in all industrial disputes and no appeal lies to any other body or person from any determination of the court.

The practice and procedure of the court are governed by the National Industrial Court Rules 1979, and the supplementary provisions in Part IV of the Trade Disputes Act 1976. Both the supplementary provisions and the rules provide a mere skeleton for practice and procedure as these are largely determined as the court proceeds and are always informal. For example, s.27 of the supplementary provisions provides:

(3) Subject to the provisions of this Act, and any rules or regulations made under this section, a body to which this section applies –
   (a) may regulate its procedure and proceedings as it thinks fit, and shall not be bound to act in any formal manner; and
   (b) shall not be bound by any rules of evidence but may inform itself on any matters in such manner as it thinks just.

On the appearance of counsel, s.28 of the supplementary provisions stipulate thus: 'In the proceedings before the National Industrial Court or an arbitration tribunal ... either party may appear by a legal practitioner'.

Although the appearance of counsel is not mandatory, in practice, in all matters before the NIC and the IAP, legal practitioners take over the prosecution of cases from the parties directly involved. The court has power to compel the attendance of witnesses and or produce any document. Oral evidence may only be given on oath if the court so requires. The court, as pointed out above, does not follow the strict rules of evidence and neither are there rules as to what documents may or may not be put by way of documentary evidence. All judgements of the court must be delivered in writing and the court is empowered to enforce its judgements in any way it thinks fit. The court may, either of its own motion or an application by any of the parties to the proceedings, review any order made by it and may, on such a review, revoke or vary that order on the grounds that:

(a) the order was wrongly made as the result of an error on the part of the court staff;
(b) a party did not receive proper notice of the proceedings leading to the order:
(c) the order was made in the absence of a party entitled to be heard;
(d) new evidence has become available since the making of the order; or
(e) the interest of justice requires such a review.

In order to establish the typology of the disputes that come before the court, we analysed the twenty-nine published cases that the court handled in the years 1978–81. We grouped the cases into those that involved 'interest' claims and disputes over 'rights' as discussed above. The result of that analysis is shown in Table 5.2.

TABLE 5.2   Analysis of twenty-nine NIC judgements, 1978–81

'Interest' claims	
Claims regarding wages, hours and holidays	7
Claims regarding dismissals	8
	15
Disputes involving 'rights'	
Distinction between 'negotiation' and 'discussion'	4
Interpretation of written contracts	3
	7
Other cases	
Interpretation of previous award ...	3
Legal technicalities/jurisdiction of the court	4
	7
Total	29

It must not be imagined, however, that the cases analysed in Table 5.2 fall into neat categories. In a number of them the dispute may involve one or more independent items, while in yet others a claim may have ancillary disputes emanating from the main dispute. For example, in the dispute between the Federated Motor Industries and Automobile, Boatyard, Transport Equipment and Allied Workers Union,[25] already referred to, many issues were at stake. First, the management applied the principle of 'no work, no pay' for the period of the industrial action. Second, 403 of the workers were dismissed and new ones employed. The Industrial Arbitration Panel, which first considered the matter, recommended the reabsorption of the dismissed workers without preconditions and that where some of the workers could not be absorbed, such workers should be considered as redundant and be entitled to redundancy benefits. The company objected to the award and the matter was referred to the court. At the hearing, counsel for the company submitted that there was a distinction between a trade dispute and agitation. Since the workers were concerned with agitation that had nothing to do with their terms and conditions of employment, they were not protected by law. On the other hand, counsel for the union argued that the issue before the court was the alleged refusal of the workers to put in a full day's work for a full day's pay and not the demand for the removal of the works manager. It can be seen, therefore, that the original issue had developed into three, namely:

(a) demand for the removal of the works manager;
(b) industrial action followed by dismissals;
(c) redundancy claims.

The court sorted out the matter. It held that interaction between workers or their representatives and the works manager in a factory must, perforce, be connected with the workers' terms and conditions of employment. Accordingly, the 403 workers whom the company refused to take back but were quickly replaced with new hands, were entitled to severance pay.

Similarly, in the dispute between Vicenti Engineering Limited and the Civil Service Technical Workers' Union,[26] two independent items were contested. These were:

(a) that the company should pay workers their wages for the days declared as public holidays;
(b) that the company do grant its workers annual holidays with full pay as provided for in the Labour Act 1974.

The company, which is a construction one, had many workers who were on daily pay and as such were not regarded as qualifying for the benefits of public holidays and annual holidays. In its ruling the court held that the company was bound to pay for days declared as public holidays and that under s.17 of the Labour Act 1974, every worker was entitled to have an annual holiday with full pay.

An analysis of the cases reveals that the court is not prepared to disturb an agreement voluntarily reached by the parties provided that such an agreement does not offend public policy. This is so even if the agreement is a departure from the normal industrial practice. Thus, in spite of practice to the contrary, the court held that gratuity was negotiable at the company level in the case of the Nigerian Insurance (Employers) Association and the Nigerian Union of Bank, Insurance and Allied Workers,[27] because the company conceded the fact during the hearing. Similarly, in the dispute between the Nigerian Breweries Limited and the Nigerian Breweries Management[28] the company was able to establish that in dealing with their union items are classified into those for 'discussion' and those for 'negotiation', and that medical facilities fall into the ambit of the former. On the basis of this evidence, the court set aside a previous decision of the IAP to the effect that medical facilities should be negotiable between the company and the managers. This approach of ascertaining what the intentions of the parties are on what the parties themselves have agreed and resolving the dispute in that regard is commendable. A situation where the court decides on principles that it considers just and fair and applies them to disputes between employers and unions, without regard to the intentions of the parties, can only bring confusion into employer–employee relations.

In concluding the discussion on industrial arbitration in Nigeria, it is important to highlight one major problem area in the procedure. Rather than regard the arbitral process as a continuation of collective bargaining whereby the parties would be expected to state the facts and be 'guided' to accept a solution based on the practices and customs of the particular company, or industry in general, and in relation to the economy of the country, the tribunals in many cases and in many respects behave like courts of law. Indeed, the current chairman of the IAP has advocated the immediate integration of the arbitral tribunals (IAP and NIC) with the judicial system of the country for the 'purpose of their general recognition as the exclusive industrial tribunals of the land with the traditional authority of superior courts of record entrenched in the constitution of the land'.[29] This legalistic approach to the settlement of labour disputes manifests itself in several ways. Although the tribunals do not follow strictly the rules of evidence, they entertain, and regularly so so, the appearance of counsel. It is true that the law setting up the tribunals provides for the appearance of counsel, but there is some danger in the parties to a labour dispute being represented by counsel, as the proceedings are made to look like court proceedings. For instance, although the IAP is not a court, yet counsel always address the Chairman of the Panel as 'my Lord' and the parties are referred to as 'applicant' and 'respondent', while at the NIC they are referred to as 'appellants' and 'respondents'. These legal niceties have the effect of intimidating simple employers and workers, some of whom have never been involved in legal proceedings. By the use of these legal terms and by portraying a court-room atmosphere, the dispute is taken out of its industrial context. Moreover, some of the lawyers who appear for the parties are not familiar with industrial problems, and in consequence base their arguments on legal principles and technicalities rather than focus on the matter in dispute. A good example of this problem can be illustrated by the case of Western Textiles Industries Company Limited and Ado-Ekiti Westinco Workers' Union. Briefly, the facts of the case are as follows. The company was dissolved in 1975 by an Act. Before the dissolution, the union had a dispute with the company. After the dissolution of the company, the Industrial Arbitration Panel made an award in favour of the union, to which the company raised an objection. The objection, which was written on note paper bearing the dissolved company's name, was based on the fact that Western Textiles had been dissolved and there was therefore nobody or company to assume responsibility for the award made by the IAP. Later in 1977 the federal government transferred the assets of the dissolved company to Odua Investment Company Limited. At the hearing before the NIC, the counsel for the dissolved company appeared for Odua Investment Company Limited. But the counsel for the union objected to such appearance on the ground that Odua Investment Company Limited was not a party to the proceedings and that no application was made by Western Textiles Industries Company Limited to substitute Odua for Western Textiles. He argued further that the notice of objection by the company was bad in law as the proper application for a joinder of a party had not been made by Western Textiles. If the dissolved company had no relationship with the new company, then the objection should be struck out and it should not be entertained until it was amended or regularised. The two lawyers representing the parties 'battled' on these legal technicalities for a long time. But the question is: how does the pursuit of these technicalities help the case of the union? Clearly, if there were workers of the union present, as indeed they would be, they would be completely lost in those legal arguments. Yet the problem was their own. The court seemed to have appreciated the predicament to which the union would be put if this line of argument by both counsels were allowed to continue. Consequently, the court held that it would not like to stultify itself by giving an empty judgement that would be unenforceable. As there were persons running the business of the defunct Western Textiles at the time when the dispute occurred, such persons ought to be parties to the dispute and the court so ordered. This case does illustrate the danger inherent in a system that gives relatively minor roles to the parties directly involved while allowing others not so involved to play the leading role. In our view, a better approach would be actively to involve the parties themselves in the process. The tribunals (IAP and NIC) should merely concern themselves with the establishment of the facts, to enable them to recommend or decide upon a suitable or workable solution acceptable to all parties concerned.

5.4.4 Inquiry and investigation

The law empowers the Minister of Labour to set up a board of inquiry to inquire into or investigate disputes and other employment problems. This he may do where any trade dispute *exists* or is *apprehended*, without the formal consent of the parties. The power derives from s.23 of the Trade Disputes Act 1976 which provides:

(1) Where any trade dispute exists or is apprehended, the Minister may cause inquiry to be made into the causes and circumstances of the dispute and, if he thinks fit may refer any matter appearing to him to be connected with or relevant to the dispute to a board of inquiry appointed for the purpose by the Minister; and the board shall inquire into the matter referred to it and report thereon to the Minister.

(2) A board of inquiry appointed under this section shall consist of a chairman and such other persons as the Minister thinks fit to appoint or may, if the Minister thinks fit, consist of one person only.

The supplementary provisions in Part IV of the Trade Disputes Act 1976 that govern the National Industrial Court and arbitration tribunals also apply to the Boards of Inquiry. The procedure is informal, and the Boards are free to regulate their own procedures and practices. Parties to the dispute may either appear by themselves or be represented by counsel. Generally, the Board calls for memoranda from the parties concerned and other interested parties, before the hearing. Boards of Inquiry are rarely used, because they are not meant to duplicate the conciliation machinery or the arbitration tribunals.

Rather, they are used in cases where both conciliation and arbitration are considered unsuitable and where public interest is involved. A good example of a dispute involving public interest was the trade dispute that a Board of Inquiry investigated between the Elder Dempster Lines Limited and the Nigerian Union of Seamen, in 1959. This was a dispute involving allegations of racial discrimination. The union had alleged, among other things:

(a) that diluted beer was served to African crew;
(b) that there was discrimination in the food given to Europeans;
(c) that the company gave instructions to Customs Officers at Liver-
     pool for a special search of the personal effects of African crew
     members;
(d) that Mr J. Fishwick (a European), the second steward, regularly
     requested stewards under him to wash his car during working
     hours.

Such allegations of racial discrimination can become so emotional and blown out of proportion that the normal conciliation and arbitral process are not suitable. An inquiry, which may involve others not directly concerned with the dispute, is more appropriate. Also, where the dispute involves a government – state or federal – or a government agency, a Board of Inquiry may be more appropriate machinery. Thus when a dispute arose between the Lagos state government and the doctors working in the state in 1973, a Board of Inquiry was appointed. The Board was specifically charged to look into the dispute and ascertain, among other things:

(a) whether or not there is a need for the establishment of a hospital
     management board for government hospitals in Lagos State;
(b) whether or not any allowances or entitlements in the nature or
     fringe benefits shall be payable to the doctors and, if so, the nature,
     amount and extent of such benefits;
(c) what promotion prospects there are for the doctors in the service
     of the Lagos state government; and
(d) whether or not the doctors should engage in private practice and, if
     so, to what extent.

The crisis at the University of Lagos that erupted in October 1980 also necessitated the appointment of a Board of Inquiry, headed by Mr Justice Balonwu. In that dispute the vice-chancellor of the University had been accused of wrong-doing by some members of the academic staff who wanted him removed. The University Council met and asked the vice-chancellor to resign but he declined to do so. Meanwhile, the lecturers in the university went on strike and students demonstrated; law and order appeared to have broken down there. Neither conciliation nor arbitration would have been appropriate in this case. The dispute had become of concern to the public. As a result of the findings of the Board of Inquiry, the vice-chancellor was asked to resign, while the registrar and six professors were dismissed.

The composition of a Board of Inquiry appears to depend on the nature of the dispute. It may be made up of a chairman and other members, or it may just consist of an individual. The inquiry into the dispute between the West African Airways Corporation (Nigeria) Limited and the British Airline Pilots Association (West Africa) in 1959 was conducted by Mr H. U. Kaine, sitting alone. That dispute was concerned with the issue of compensating pilots who became redundant or whose services were terminated following the withdrawal of Ghana from the old West African Airways Corporation. The dispute involving Elder Dempster and the Nigerian Union of Seamen which we have already referred to had a chairman and two members. The chairman was T. E. A. Salubi, Industrial Relations Commissioner, Federal Ministry of Labour. The other members were Mr A. H. B. McClatchey, representing the employers, and Mr L. L. Borha, a trade unionist. The composition in the latter case appears to have been made to allay the fears of both the employers and the unions that the outcome of the proceedings will be fair.

The reports of the Boards of Inquiry are not binding, but the government generally issues a White Paper on such reports making the aspects that the government has accepted binding on the parties. Therefore, although the approach adopted in the appointment of these bodies is different from that of conciliation and arbitration, the effect on the parties is the same.

6 An Evaluation of the System

Our objective in this study was to determine the nature of the industrial relations system that has developed in Nigeria. The approach has been to trace and examine critically that development within a socioeconomic and political framework. By so doing, we have been able to establish that the Nigerian industrial relations system is a product of the country's history and environment. These peculiar circumstances influenced the move away from the imposed voluntaristic system of industrial relations to one that is production-oriented and integrative in approach. In this final chapter we shall summarise the main findings of the study and evaluate the current system in the light of Nigeria's economic development plans and labour policy.

6.1 SUMMARY

In Chapter 1, we examined four models of industrial relations: the Anglo-Saxon, the West German, the communist and that of the developing countries. The Anglo-Saxon model is based mainly on the British system with its emphasis on voluntarism. However, in recent years the state has become more active and the law plays quite a significant role. Thus the British system that developed under the *laissez-faire* philosophy in economic matters is becoming more and more like the model in developing countries with elements of both voluntarism and state control. As in the developing countries, the system is changing. The system in the USA is a modification of the British system, with emphasis on the role of law. For example, while the parties may engage in collective bargaining such agreements are legally enforceable. That system must be examined in the light of the philosophy that underlay the economic development of the USA, with its general acceptance of the free-enterprise system in which individualism, a spirit of enterprise and a desire for independence asserted themselves. The Australian experience of compulsory arbitration is another example of a country's attempt to minimise conflict and encourage economic and social development. The state, through its various arbitration boards, is actively involved in the collective bargaining process.

The West German model is a concealed semi-bargaining system embodied in law. Although the model provides for co-decision-making at the works level, it nevertheless prevents plant bargaining on wages and salaries from taking place. Such bargaining takes place between national unions and employers' associations. This aspect is similar to the Nigerian system which provides for collective bargaining at the national level. Also similar to the Nigerian system is the system of labour courts designed to integrate all parties in the industrial relations system. Perhaps Nigeria has much to learn in this respect, as the country is currently experimenting with the integrative as opposed to the former dysfunctional approach in industrial relations.

The communist model is state-directed and controlled. This model does not regard industrial relations as a separate sub-system within the total social system in the Dunlopian thesis, instead it is regarded as an integral part of the social system. Accordingly, both the state and communist party determine the direction of industrial relations.

In spite of the diversity of the developing countries, there is a discernible model that incorporates both the elements of voluntarism and those of state control. The Nigerian system has both elements but avoids the Senegalese example which is based essentially on a code.

In Chapters 2–5, we examined the development of the Nigerian industrial relations system, and we now summarise this below. The development of the system can be divided into four phases, corresponding approximately to major economic or political changes which have affected that development. These phases cover the periods 1900–37, 1938–56, 1957–65 and 1966 and after.

6.1.1   The first phase: 1900–37

The year 1900 marks a watershed in the historical development of Nigeria. In that year, the Protectorate of Southern Nigeria came into being and in 1906 it was merged with the colony of Lagos to form the colony and Protectorate of Southern Nigeria. In 1914 the Southern and Northern Protectorates were amalgamated to form the colony and Protectorate of Nigeria under British rule.

In spite of the paucity of industrial establishments, this phase witnessed the early stirrings of trade unionism starting with the Civil Service Union in 1912. While the development of these unions may have been influenced by developments outside Nigeria, we found no evidence of external initiative in this regard. Other than in the tin-mining industry, employers in the private sector were concerned mainly with the purchase of produce and other raw materials and the distribution of manufactured goods in the country. Consequently, trade unionism could not take root in these organisations as the workers were scattered throughout Nigeria. In the establishments where trade unionism existed, such as the railways, its existence was not officially recognised. As would be expected in such circumstances, no machinery was established either for joint consultation or collective bargaining. To achieve their objective during this phase, the unions had to resort to agitation. However, once trade unions started to develop, the British government was anxious that they should be channelled in the right direction away from 'improper and mischievous ends'. Pressure was therefore mounted on the colonial administration in Nigeria by the British government to recognise the development of unionism, which was to yield results in the next phase.

6.1.2   The second phase: 1938–56

This phase is marked by the passing of the Trade Union Ordinance in 1938. This law, which was enacted at the initiative of the British government, laid down the mode of registration of trade unions and prescribed the rights and obligations of trade unions in employer–employee relations. Thus the law recognised the existence of a union that fulfilled the minimum standard stipulated, and gave impetus to trade-union growth and development. This law together with the Trade Disputes Ordinance of 1941 and the Labour Code Ordinance of 1945 constituted the legal framework for industrial relations. However, in line with the British system of industrial relations that was imposed on the country at the time, these laws assigned a minimum role to the state. This inevitably hampered the effective development of the industrial relations system. First, under the colonial labour policy, employers were not obliged to recognise unions nor to deal with them. Union development was thereby stultified and the history of Nigerian unionism is one of small weak unions with poor leadership. Second, the situation bred frustrations which in turn generated conflict between employers' and workers' organisations.

Hence there were constant agitations during this period, culminating in the General Strike of 1945. By the close of this phase, no company in Nigeria had engaged in collective bargaining with its union.

6.1.3 The third phase: 1957–65

The first year of this phase, 1957, ushered in self-government for both the Western and Eastern Regions of Nigeria, while the Northern Region followed in 1959. The country itself gained independence from Britain in 1960. The phase marked the shift from commercial activities to industrialisation, and this in turn accounted for the growth of the wage-earning population. However, the shift to industrialisation had other implications for industrial relations. First, it brought many workers together in the same plant, a situation that fostered the growth of worker organisations. Accordingly, there was much union activity during this period. Second, school leavers were lured into the cities by the prospects of finding industrial employment. But industrial development did not keep pace with this migration, and this had the unpleasant result of high unemployment in the cities. The unfulfilled expectations of job seekers, the economic difficulties that the country experienced soon after independence because of the vagaries of world prices of agricultural products, etc., and the apparent indifference of politicians caused the General Strike of 1964. The unions continued to be in a poor state as a result of inefficient leadership, union ideological differences over international affiliation, lack of training and poor financial position, to name but a few of their woes. But the formation of the Nigeria Employers Consultative Association in 1957 brought some change into the development of industrial relations in the country. The NECA encouraged collective bargaining among its members with the implication of union recognition and improved conditions. A few employers, led by the UAC of Nigeria Ltd and the Nigerian Tobacco Company Ltd, introduced collective bargaining in their respective organisations. Their example was soon followed by other employers. The state kept 'aloof' from industrial relations but changed conditions of employment for its own employees through wage commissions.

6.1.4 The fourth phase: 1966 and after

The military take-over of the country in 1966 marked a turning point in Nigeria's political history. The events that followed the military *coup* swept away some of the old institutions and traditions. The harsh economic effects of the civil war that broke out in 1967, and the spate of strikes that followed in 1968, drove home to the military government the importance of carrying along all sections of the society if the nation was to survive economically. To do this, the workers and employers could not be left alone to solve their own problems as what they did affected other sections of the community. In response to the challenge, the military administration broke with the tradition of voluntarism and promulgated a decree banning strikes and lockouts. Arbitration was made compulsory and collective agreements became subject to the approval of the government. Thus the voluntary approach that was imposed in the mid-1930s and that had been the cornerstone of Nigerian industrial relations was abandoned.

The experience in intervention gained during the civil war (1967–70) strengthened the government's belief – even after the end of the civil war – that the state must no longer be an umpire in industrial relations but instead should be an active participant. This is the philosophy underlying the promulgation of the National Labour Policy in 1975. In line with this policy, the institutional framework for industrial relations was improved. Unions were grouped into industrial unions, the employers restructured themselves into federations, and the government's monitoring role became evident in the Industrial Arbitration Panel and the National Industrial Court. In addition to the monitoring role, the government also regulates collective bargaining through its incomes policies. Collective agreements are still subject to approval by the government. In our conclusions, we shall evaluate the new system of industrial relations in Nigeria and determine whether it fulfils the government policy of ensuring that the workers, employers and the government should regard themselves as partners in the economic and social development of the country.

6.2   CONCLUSIONS AND EVALUATION

The philosophy on which the Nigerian National Policy on Labour is based and which made the country move away from the voluntary ethic in industrial relations is that in a dynamic society no social policy can remain stagnant or be merely concerned with implementing a pre-established policy. In the development of the country, the unions, employers and government are partners, and therefore in its economic policy the government 'must not only shape and define its labour objectives in such a way as to keep pace with increasingly complex requirements of the people, but also to ensure that those changes, that is, social, political and economic, are directed towards the fulfilment of the aspirations of our people for a better life'. The objective therefore is to pursue a 'policy of guided democracy in labour matters'. This policy is said to be predicated upon 'the continued guarantee of freedom of association, the promotion of strong, stable and responsible workers' and employers' organisations, the establishment and development of a suitable institutional framework for the effective prevention and expeditious settlement of labour disputes, the promotion of labour/management co-operation and of consultation at appropriate levels between workers, employers and Government'.[1] What the government is saying can be summarised thus: *the state will allow employers and trade unions to conduct their own affairs subject to the supervision of the state. Such supervision is necessary because all three parties, the unions, the employers and the government, must work together for the development of Nigeria.*

The philosophy underlying the Nigerian labour policy is similar to the German one which adopts an integrative approach of incorporating the parties, the unions, employers and the state in industrial relations. In this approach an attempt is made to harness the efforts of all citizens in the over-all development of the country for the benefit of all. Therefore, to achieve this objective all three parties must be actively involved in industrial relations. In evaluating Nigerian industrial relations, we shall focus on three main elements of the system, namely: the institutional framework, collective bargaining and dispute settlement.

6.2.1 The institutional framework

The theories of industrial relations that we examined in Chapter 1 regard conflict as inevitable in industrial relations, as in other aspects of social life. It would seem, therefore, that the problem facing any viable industrial relations system is how to contain and control that conflict so that it does not destroy society. The *pluralist* approach would have it that concessions and compromises are the surest way of resolving conflicts, but there is no guarantee that such an approach would succeed indefinitely. Indeed, experience of countries like Britain show that conflict is thereby neither reduced nor eliminated.

In the case of Nigeria, the government has been seeking not only to avoid industrial conflict but also to develop a stable system of industrial relations that will mobilise all energies available to promote economic development. The attempt has been to develop a practical pattern of industrial relations that can stand the strains of the rapid changes that are taking place in the country as a result of industrialisation. The creation of industrial unions, for example, has improved the size and strength of unions, thus eliminating some of the endemic problems that had plagued the unions in the past. Moreover, the legal recognition of unions and the legislation on check-off provide a statutory framework in place of the purely voluntary relationships that had previously existed. These developments have enhanced the unions' ability to negotiate on an equal footing with employers. The developments in trade unionism have affected employers in terms of institutional rearrangements and practices. Employers within the NECA have been organised along industrial lines, similar to the unions, to ensure effective functioning of the system. This reorganisation has been followed by the establishment of National Joint Industrial Councils (NJICS) for industry-wide collective bargaining. The government's monitoring and regulatory role is evidenced by its incomes policies, approval of collective agreements and by the compulsory arbitration system. These developments can be considered positive and appear clearly to provide a more stabilised system of industrial relations in the country.

However, there are certain weaknesses inherent in the institutional framework. First, although in an attempt to establish stable and responsive institutions for collective bargaining the government has in the process created very powerful trade unions in the public sector, no machinery for collective bargaining has been established. This means that the govenment will continue to carry out its economic policies and make unilateral changes to conditions of employment of all its employees. This is a departure from the 'partnership-in-progress' doctrine enshrined in the National Labour Policy.

Second, having created powerful unions, the problem for the government is what to do with, or how to curb the powers of, these unions. As the government is committed to the growth of the Nigerian economy (as shown by its development plans) then there is need for increased investment, increased productivity and, most importantly, a stable political and industrial relations climate. At present, there is no guarantee that the government's economic strategies, aims and objectives will always coincide with those of labour. The problem therefore is how the government can reconcile its policy of creating viable industrial relations institutions with its objective of economic growth, as the unions can use their power to thwart the achievement of that objective.

We have argued in this study that trade unions in Nigeria should be encouraged to develop along lines different from those of the countries of the West. In the West, an assessment of the over-all effects of trade unions is based on their social and political, as well as economic, consequences. We believe that the role of trade unions in Nigeria, especially during this period of rapid industrialisation, should be to co-operate with the government in its efforts to improve the lot of all interest-groups in the society, without necessarily losing sight of the welfare of their members. Therefore, the assessment of the success or effectiveness of the trade unions in Nigeria should not be based solely on how much *pressure* they bring on government to make changes in the social, economic and political spheres, but rather on how much *influence* they are able to bring to bear in the process of economic growth and development. In Chapter 1 of this study we saw that each country's industrial relations system has been shaped by that country's history and events. For example, in Western Germany both employers and workers had to come together soon after the Second World War in order to rebuild the country. Co-determination in the country's industrial relations today is a result of that effort. Moreover, the labour-court system is a further attempt to ensure that industrial conflict is not allowed to disrupt the country's economic and social development. Australia moved away from the voluntary approach in industrial relations that it had earlier adopted into a compulsory arbitration system, following the crippling strikes of 1891–6. Similarly, the American unions became enmeshed in the capitalist system because of the economic philosophy that prevailed in the USA in the nineteenth century. In the same way, we think that the Nigerian industrial relations systems could develop features that may be peculiar to the Nigerian situation. Therefore, it will still be necessary in the future for the government to channel the course of that development in the direction it wants.

Indeed Chamberlain and Kuhn have suggested that the central problem for public policy in industrial relations is 'the legitimate exercise of group power in a democratic society'.[2] The processes by which group power is exercised in society must be subject to government supervision. This is necessary because the material well-being of the society could be frustrated by inter-group conflict. Thus the government should intervene in order to enforce what it believes to be in the public interest. 'Because there is no consensus in society as a whole on the priorities which should be observed by the parties to collective bargaining; it is almost impossible for any government to maintain for long the role of an impartial arbiter'.[3] It is true that in industrial relations laws are only one influence among many others, and they take their effect over time. However, we believe that the objective must be to make sure that the law points in the right direction in conformity with Nigeria's economic and social objectives.

6.2.2   Collective bargaining

While the employers and unions may establish their procedural and substantive rules through the collective bargaining process, that exercise must be subject to the control and regulation of government. The expanding role of government in the management of the economy and its commitment to the country's economic growth dictate that it must intervene in employer–employee relations. In a rapidly developing country like Nigeria, the high rate of inflation can be aggravated by uncontrolled wages. This in turn has consequences for industrial expansion. What is needed, therefore, is some form of regulatory measure which, in the Nigerian circumstances, must be preferred to a *laissez-faire* approach. Consequently, the determination of wages and salaries and other conditions of employment cannot be left entirely to the outcome of free collective bargaining.

Indeed, the Nigeria Employers Consultative Association believes that the government in Nigeria should play a significant role in industrial relations. In their submission to the federal government in January 1980, on the restoration of free collective bargaining, the Association said:

> While this Association fully supports the restoration of free collective bargaining by the Government, it strongly recommends that the Government should make it clear that its attitude and approach to the subject should not be interpreted to mean the return to a non-interventionist or *laissez-faire* policy. That consumer and society needs should be given adequate attention by trade unions and employers is hardly in dispute. It is therefore necessary that there should be in-built in the policy the condition that the public interest must be taken into account by the bargainers; that the frontiers of collective bargaining would be determined by the application of this consideration; and that the Government would intervene, whenever necessary, to ensure that this predetermined limit is observed.[4]

Since 1976 the government has regulated the collective bargaining process through its income policies. In most countries of the West, incomes policies, in spite of the limited success they have achieved, have become instruments of economic planning. This goes to confirm that some faith, however little, is still placed on them. However, the way incomes policies have been administered in Nigeria has satisfied neither the wage earner nor the consumer of goods produced. If incomes policies should become instruments of economic planning, then it would be necessary to overhaul the existing system. In respect of collective bargaining, a situation should be created where employers and trade unions are allowed a free hand to negotiate within wide parameters predetermined by government. The government's economic plans will naturally take into account such other interest-groups in the society as consumers, shareholders, peasant farmers and other self-employed persons. The policies to be adopted must focus not only on the movement of total incomes but also on the main components of income, including wages and profits. Also to be taken into account are prices of essential commodities, which have always had a dramatic effect on wage-earners' incomes. To this end, it will be necessary to ensure that the groups that will be mostly affected, that is, employers and workers, are consulted and their full participation secured. Some degree of success may be achieved only if all concerned are involved and committed to the policies.

Moreover, an effective incomes policy requires highly centralised employers' and trade-union organisations that have influence or recognised authority over their members. For, although escalating price increases may not be in the interest of workers and the community in general, many employers and unions may not see the immediate relationship between large wage settlements and high prices. As far as any particular union is concerned, there is nothing irrational or even immoral in pressing for large wage increases, even though they may lead to price increases. As both the NECA and the NLC now form effective central bodies, what is left is for the government to consult and associate them with every policy in this regard through the Prices, Productivity and Incomes Board. Unless the parties directly involved are closely associated with government policies, such policies will only lead to and encourage conflict.

With regard to the structure of collective bargaining, the removal of collective bargaining from the plant level to national level has certain distinct advantages. It makes it much easier for the government to monitor and regulate the collective bargaining process. Unlike in the past, when all companies that had concluded collective agreements had to send these to the federal Ministry of Employment, Labour and Productivity, currently only about thirty agreements (excluding the public-sector unions) are involved. Also, the change means that collective disputes arising out of the interpretation or implementation of collective agreements are thereby reduced.

However, it must not be assumed that the present structure of collective bargaining has swept away all the ills of the past. On the contrary, collective agreements are still voluntary agreements and a party can break any provision without any legal sanction. Perhaps, as in some of the systems we studied in Chapter 1 – for example the USA and Germany – the time has come for collective agreements to be made legally enforceable. This aspect may enhance the supervisory role of the state, by ensuring that the collective agreements that have been approved by the government are implemented by the parties concerned.

Moreover, as we pointed out in this study, branch-union executives who wielded power before now have been suddenly left without power as a result of the change. In order to show that they are still in charge, these union officials have called a number of wildcat strikes since 1978, without the sanction of their national union. The national unions have not been able to control these branch-union officials. The difficulty lies in the fact that the national unions are not strong enough yet to be able to control these branch unions. As Allan Flanders has correctly remarked, 'when trade unions are not strong enough to be able to act effectively as managers of conflict, then an essential part of the mechanism of social control, on which we rely for order in industry, breaks down'.[5] This situation creates a vicious circle, because a union that is internally weak is normally one that is also externally weak. Its success in bargaining with employers for improved terms and conditions is likely to be less and less impressive compared with the apparent gains that branch militants can achieve through unilateral action.[6] The danger in this is that, once the workers know that they can achieve what they want through local action, because they consider their national union ineffective, the collective bargaining process becomes fragmented. This is a situation that is likely to continue until the national union officials are properly trained to handle their own men and to be able to manage conflict situations.

6.2.3 Dispute settlement

It is difficult to say whether a particular national system of dispute settlement is efficient and where its weaknesses lie. As Thilo Ramm has remarked in relation to the German system, the concept of efficiency includes more than the mere working of the system, as all systems will more or less work.[7] Efficiency in this regard may be defined subjectively in terms of the confidence of all persons whom it affects – for example, whether employers, employees and unions believe in the usefulness of the system and are on the whole satisfied with the manner in which it operates. Or, it may be defined objectively as covering all labour disputes, for example the impact the system has on incidence of strikes, lockouts, and other forms of industrial action. Even here we are likely to meet with difficulties, because it is clearly wrong to regard every strike or lockout as evidence of a breakdown of the dispute settlement system, neither should the absence of strikes and lockouts be regarded as evidence that the system is working perfectly. In many cases, frequent strikes or lockouts may simply indicate that bad relations between employers and workers exist in the particular industries, while the dispute settlement system is functioning generally well. Conversely, a total absence of strikes or lockouts may indicate no more than that good relations exist between the employer and his workers or that one of the bargaining parties has gained such ascendancy over the other as to be able virtually to dictate the terms and conditions of employment, or perhaps that the state itself is in that position *vis-à-vis* the bargaining parties.[8] In these circumstances, any evaluation is fraught with difficulties because a comparison with other systems working under the same conditions is not available.

In the case of Nigeria, however, one important criterion of efficiency, or at least confidence in the system, is the fact that both employers and unions are willing to submit their issues for adjudication and to abide by the awards and decisions handed down.

In this study, it was established that most of the individual grievances are settled at the enterprise level through the grievance procedure. It was also established that both workers and managers believe that such procedures are useful for solving problems that otherwise would have escalated into industrial actions. In the case of collective disputes that are concerned with the interpretation or implementation of the whole or parts of collective agreements, most of the disputes reach the conciliation stage, out of which a number are referred to the Industrial Arbitration Panel (IAP). Currently, a small proportion of the awards of the IAP are appealed to the National Industrial Court (NIC), but that situation might change in the future. The court may well handle more cases in future. The system of industrial-dispute adjudication is new in Nigeria, and indeed the first judgements of the NIC were delivered only in 1978. It is therefore too early to hold firm views on the workings of the system. However, the observations we make here are intended to highlight what appear to us to be weaknesses that have begun to show in the system during its short life.

The conciliation stage of the statutory machinery appears to be weak because of a lack of experienced conciliators. The process envisages a pool of experienced labour officers from which the Ministry of Labour may draw. Unfortunately, the Ministry of Labour has manpower problems and, with the expansion of industrial establishments in the country, they are unable to cope. Consequently, one inexperienced labour officer may be assigned to several disputes at a time. The industrial disputes including strike actions that followed the Udoji Commission's awards of 1975 were so many that the Ministry of Labour simply could not cope.

Delay, especially at the arbitration stage of the system, causes both employers and employees much frustration in Nigeria. In any dispute settlement procedure, time is of the essence. The Nigerian National Policy on Labour has as one of its cardinal points the expeditious settlement of disputes, yet delays continue to be a frustrating feature of the IAP. In some cases, it takes up to one year or more before the awards are communicated to the parties. For example, it took twenty months before the awards of the IAP in the dispute between the Civil Service Union and the federal government regarding the granting of car loans and car-running allowances was published in February 1981. Some unions have gone on strike over these delays, arguing that the management had deliberately colluded with the IAP to slow down proceedings. One reason for the delay is the structure of the IAP. Although the chairman is empowered to appoint one or more members of the Panel to look into a particular dispute, in the main the whole Panel meets over an issue. There are no sub-panels on different disputes that can sit simultaneously over such issues. Therefore, all other disputes must wait until the one before the Panel is disposed of. The situation might improve if standing divisions are created out of the Panel. This may necessitate the enlargement of the body and possibly a change of title; the IAP is really an arbitration board. The problem of reconciling different opinions from the various divisions to be created over similar issues can be overcome if the NIC, like the Grosse Senat in the West German system, is made to review all its awards.

Moreover, in their proceedings the IAP and the NIC tend to adopt what has been referred to in another context as 'civil law thinking'.[9]

While the law allows the appearance of counsel for the parties, the disputes must not be taken out of their industrial context. Indeed, Professor Folke Schmidt has queried whether it is appropriate to apply judicial reasoning to disputes arising under collective agreements. He argues that the judge is supposed to apply an existing rule once the facts in issue have been established. Fundamentally, the method looks back to the past, because adjudication of vested rights means an application of rules that are supposed to exist and facts have to be proved which relate to the past. The judge is thus dependent upon precedents. This means that if the rules apply in a particular case and the facts are proved, the action will be sustained. In the case of negotiated settlements, there is always room for compromise. It is not all or nothing. Also, in the case of negotiations, the parties to the dispute may pay regard not only to possible vested rights, but also to circumstances making one solution preferable in view of situations that may arise in the future.[10]

However, one way of overcoming these problems is to ensure that each body, that is, the IAP and the NIC, is made up not only of professional judges but also of representatives of employers and workers who have had practical experience of industrial relations. While the composition of the IAP satisfies this criterion, that of the NIC, which is the final court of appeal for all industrial disputes, does not. This is the one major flaw in the system. The president of the NIC is a professional judge while the other ordinary members are people who are knowledgeable in economics and labour relations but not necessarily with the experience of employer and worker relations. Accordingly, decisions are handed down purely on the basis of 'principles'. If representatives of the parties were members of the court, they would at least keep some basic control over the proceedings of the professional judges in order to prevent a reversion to 'civil law thinking'. The effectiveness of this control, however, will depend largely on the expertise of the employers' and workers' representatives, as these organisations cannot supervise the activities of their representatives.

On the face of it, the statutory system of dispute settlement in Nigeria maintains the illusion of state control and supervision. However, on close examination, this control and supervision shows up as being superficial. Although the system is compulsory, conciliators can only forward to the Minister of Labour what the parties themselves have agreed. The Minister may only confirm such agreement; he has no power to vary it. In the case of awards made by the IAP, the

Minister's duty is to confirm the award of the Panel: such awards are not subject to review. Similarly, the judgements of the NIC are binding on the parties without further state sanction. What emerges from the system, therefore, is twofold: (i) what the parties themselves have agreed, which is then given a stamp of state authority, or (ii) what the IAP or NIC believes is the true solution, even if such a solution may not be in accord with what the government or either of the parties to the dispute may have wanted. Therefore, it would seem that the state has not gone far enough in ensuring that disputes are settled in a manner acceptable not only to the parties to the dispute but also to the state itself. Accordingly, it is our view that the Trade Disputes Act 1976 be amended to ensure:

(a) that both the IAP and the NIC regard themselves as continuation of the collective bargaining process and as such should be more concerned with fact finding rather than lay emphasis on legalism;
(b) that an award or decision does not conflict with established practice or policy, and where departure is intended for reasons of social change it should be in the form of recommendation; which should not be immediately binding;
(c) that where the Minister of Labour is satisfied that an award or ruling offends a major policy decision or law or any other administration order, he should direct the tribunal seized of the matter to re-examine it in the light of the new evidence.

Moreover, the Government must ensure that laws passed in respect of labour matters are enforced. For instance, the law on essential services and the one on 'no work, no-pay' have consistently been breached with impunity. Consistency and firmness are essential factors in industrial relations. The Government must give the lead to other employers in this regard.

Finally, Nigeria, like many other developing countries, has developed an industrial relations system in which the state plays an active role. Government involvement has become necessary, because it would appear that the free and voluntary system of industrial relations that was practised until 1968 could not cope adequately with the rapid social, economic and political changes taking place in the country. Moreover, there does not appear to be anything to show that an unregulated system will in the long run be in the best interest of all sections of the community. There has been a steady trend towards the creation of an elite working class whose level of income and standard of living is completely different from that of the self-employed peasant farmer. In order to carry out its development plans in the interest of all in society, it has become necessary that the government should be actively involved in industrial relations as a participant to ensure that employers and unions are associated with the development of the country. It is in the light of this that it has been suggested in this study that trade unions and workers, by education and persuasion, the law and enlighted self-interest, may be persuaded to accept that to improve the lot of their members they will have to co-operate with the government and the employers in ensuring a high level of productivity. This would ensure the growth of the economy and the availability of resources for all citizens, including the wage earners they represent. The government strategy, therefore, should be a reform of the industrial relations system to ensure that employers and trade unions are associated with the country's development plans. This will not be easy; it will require skilful and energetic political engineering but, if all the parties are drawn into the effort, it may succeed.

Appendices

A The New Forty-two Industrial Unions

1. AGRICULTURAL AND ALLIED WORKERS' UNION OF NIGERIA
   Agriculture and livestock production. Agricultural services including animal husbandry and horticulture, veterinary services, pest control and irrigation services. Forestry, logging, fishing and game reserves.
2. NATIONAL UNION OF AIR TRANSPORT SERVICES EMPLOYEES
   All employees of commercial airlines and travel agencies other than aircraft pilots and aircraft engineers.
3. NIGERIAN COAL MINERS' UNION
   Extraction of coal including prospecting for coal and preparing sites for the extraction of coal.
4. NATIONAL UNION OF ELECTRICITY AND GAS WORKERS
   Generation, transmission and distribution of electric light and energy for public consumption. Manufacture of gas in gasworks and other forms of energy.
5. MEDICAL AND HEALTH WORKERS' UNION OF NIGERIA
   All medical and health workers including the paramedical staff published in L.N. no. 30 in *Federal Gazette*, no. 28 (8 June 1972) but excluding medical doctors, pharmacists, radiographers, medical laboratory technologists, dental technologists, nurses and midwives.
6. NIGERIA UNION OF PHARMACISTS, RADIOGRAPHERS, LABORATORY AND DENTAL TECHNOLOGISTS
   All radiographers, pharmacists, dental technologists, medical and veterinary laboratory technologists qualified to be so classified in Nigeria.
7. PRECISION, ELECTRICAL AND RELATED EQUIPMENTS WORKERS' UNION
   Manufacture, assembly, sale and service of electronic, precision and electrical equipments and appliances, measuring, controlling, laboratory and scientific instruments, surgical, medical and dental instruments, optical and photographic goods; watches, clocks and other horological equipment, musical instruments; security equipment.
8. NATIONAL ASSOCIATION OF NIGERIA – NURSES AND MIDWIVES.
   All nurses and midwives of all grades and by whatever name called, qualified to register and practise in Nigeria.
9. NIGERIA UNION OF JOURNALISTS
   Newspaper editors, reporters, feature writers, newspaper and similarly classified workers in the newspaper industry. *Daily Times* Group of Companies Senior Staff Association.

10. NIGERIA UNION OF SEAMEN AND WATER TRANSPORT WORKERS
    All persons employed in the manning of ocean-going vessels or craft afloat, including fishing vessels but excluding persons in the officer cadre of such vessels or craft, civil-service employees of inland waterways, and employees of the Nigerian Ports Authority.
11. DOCK-WORKERS' UNION OF NIGERIA
    All dock-workers excluding those employed by the Nigerian Ports Authority.
12. NIGERIA PORTS AUTHORITY WORKERS' UNION
    All employees, excluding senior staff of the Nigerian Ports Authority.
13. NIGERIA UNION OF TEACHERS
    Teachers employed in educational institutions of all types excluding universities and associated institutions.
14. NIGERIA UNION OF RAILWAYMEN
    All categories of employees, excluding senior staff employed in railway transport.
15. NIGERIA CIVIL SERVICE UNION
    All junior employees of federal and state governments excluding customs, immigration, technical, typist and stenographic staff.
16. CIVIL SERVICE TECHNICAL WORKERS' UNION OF NIGERIA
    All junior staff employed in the civil services of the federal and state government classified as technical employees.
17. NIGERIA UNION OF CIVIL SERVICE TYPISTS, STENOGRAPHIC AND ALLIED STAFF
    All typists, stenographic and allied staff, by whatever name called, employed in the civil services of the federal and state governments.
18. RADIO, TELEVISION AND THEATRE WORKERS' UNION
    Employees in radio, television, theatre, motion picture production, distribution and projection. Operation of cinema services allied to the foregoing.
19. NATIONAL UNION OF BANKS INSURANCE AND FINANCIAL INSTITUTIONS EMPLOYEES
    Banks and closely related institutions, such as mortgage companies, industrial-loan institutions, agricultural-credit agencies, co-operative credit societies, investment companies and holding companies. Insurance carriers of all kinds; insurance agents and brokers; organisations servicing insurance carriers; consultants for policy holders; adjusting agencies; other closely related institutions not otherwise mentioned. All types of dealers in real estate.
20. NATIONAL UNION OF FOOD, BEVERAGE AND TOBACCO EMPLOYEES
    Manufacture of food for human consumption and of related products such as chewing gum, spices, prepared foods for animals and fowls. Slaughtering preparation and preservation of meat. Manufacture of dairy products. Canning and preserving of fruits and vegetables. Canning and preserving of fish and other sea foods. Manufacture of grain mill products. Manufacture of bakery products. Sugar factories and refineries. Manufacture of cocoa, chocolate and sugar confectionery and miscellaneous food preparations. Distilling, rectifying and blending of spirits. Wine industries, breweries and manufacturing of malt, manufacture of non-alcoholic

beverages such as soft drinks and carbonated mineral waters. Manufacture of tobacco products. Stemming, redrying and other operations connected with preparing raw tobacco leaf for manufacturing.

21. NATIONAL UNION OF HOTEL AND PERSONAL SERVICES WORKERS
Services generally involving the care of the person or his apparel – hotels, restaurants, cafés, taverns and other drinking and eating places. Rooming houses, camps and other lodging places. Laundries and laundry services, cleaning and dyeing. Barber and beauty shops. Domestic services. Portrait and commercial photographic studies. Shops and offices cleaning and related services.

22. NATIONAL UNION OF SHOP AND DISTRIBUTIVE EMPLOYEES
Wholesale and retail trade. The resale (sale without transformation) of goods to business units and to institutions and government. Importers and exporters. Manufacturers' sales offices and agents. Commission merchants and commodity brokers. Assemblers and buyers of farm products and co-operative agricultural marketing associations. Resale of industrial and construction materials, machinery and equipment, and business and professional equipments. Warehousing, grading and sorting, breaking bulk and repacking. Resale (sale without transformation) of goods for personal or household consumption or utilisation. Petrol-filling stations, consumer co-operatives.

23. PRINTING AND PUBLISHING WORKERS' UNION
Printing, lithographing and publishing newspapers, periodicals, books, maps, atlases, sheet music and directories. Commercial or job printing. Commercial lithographing. Manufacture of greeting cards. Book-binding, paper ruling and other work related to book-binding. Services for the printing trade such as typesetting, engraving, copper plates, making woodcuts, photo-engraving, electro-typing and stereo-typing.

24. NATIONAL UNION OF PAPER AND PAPER PRODUCTS WORKERS
Paper and paper-board mills and the manufacture of pulp, paper and paper-board. Manufacture of pulp from wood, rags and other fibres. Manufacture of pressed and moulded pulp goods, such as pulp plates and utensils, paper bags, boxes and other containers, cards, envelopes and stationery, wallpaper, toilet paper, straws and other articles, made of paper and paper-board.

25. NATIONAL UNION OF POSTAL AND TELECOMMUNICATION EMPLOYEES
Communication services rendered to the public whether by post, telegraph, telephone or radio including the installation and maintenance of such services.

26. NIGERIA UNION OF CONSTRUCTION AND CIVIL ENGINEERING WORKERS
Construction, repair and demolition of buildings, highways, streets and culverts. Heavy construction of such projects as sewers and water mains, railroads, piers, tunnels, subways, bridges, viaducts, dams, drainage projects, irrigation, flood control projects, hydroelectric plants, gas mains, pipelines and all other types of heavy construction. Marine construction such as dredging, land draining and reclamation, construction of harbours and waterways, airports, communication systems such as telephone and telegraph lines. All other construction. Special trade contractors in the field of construction, such as carpenters, plumbers, plasterers, electricians

civil, architectural, structural and soil engineering, surveying, and related services.

27. NATIONAL UNION OF FURNITURE, FIXTURES AND WOODWORKERS
Manufacture of household, office, public-building, professional and restaurant furniture. Office and store fixtures, window and door screens and shades, regardless of materials used. Sawmills and planning mills. Manufacture of lath, shingles, cooperage stock, veneers, plywood and excelsior. Wood preserving and manufacture of finished articles made entirely or mainly of wood, bamboo, can and cork. Manufacture of lumber, wooden building materials and prefabricated parts and structures. Manufacture of boxes, crates, drums, barrels and other wooden containers. Manufacture of baskets and other rattan reed or willow containers.

28. METAL PRODUCTS WORKERS' UNION OF NIGERIA
Manufacture of basic metal forms into finished products such as tin cans and other tin ware, hand tools, cutlery and hardware, hollow ware, metal stampings, lighting fixtures, fabricated wire products, metal shipping containers, safes and vaults, steel springs, bolts, nuts, washers, rivets, collapsible tubes, ordnance including small arms, and accessories. Fabrication of steelworks, including the erection of steelworks such as welding for bridges, industrial warehouses, tanks and motor lorry bodies. Industries engaged in enamelling, japanning and lacquering, galvanising, plating and polishing metal products, blacksmithing and welding. Manufacture of silverware and jewellery.

29. NATIONAL UNION OF PETROLEUM AND NATURAL GAS WORKERS
Oil-well and natural gas-well operations, including prospecting, drilling, crude oil and natural gas and petroleum products; also petroleum tanker drivers.

30. NATIONAL UNION OF CHEMICAL AND NON-METALLIC PRODUCTS WORKERS
Manufacture of basic industrial organic and inorganic chemicals, except products of petroleum and coal but including fertilisers. Explosives and fireworks, synthetic fibre and rubber, resins, plastics, elastomers and vegetable and animal oils and fats including the production of cake and meal by crushing or extraction from oilseeds and nuts. Manufacture of medicinal and pharmaceutical preparations, perfumes, cosmetics and other toilet preparations, soaps, and other washing and cleaning compounds including detergent. Polishes, inks, matches, candles and insecticides. Manufacture of clay products, such as bricks, tiles, pipes, crucibles, architectural terracotta, stove lining, chimney pipes and tops, and refractories. Manufacture of glass and glass products except the grinding of optical lenses. Pottery, china and earthenware. Manufacture of all types of hydraulic cement such as Portland. Manufacture of concrete, gypsum and plaster products, stone products. All other similar chemical and non-metallic products.

31. FOOTWEAR, LEATHER AND RUBBER PRODUCTS WORKERS UNION OF NIGERIA
Manufacture of all kinds of footwear, leggings and gaiters from leather, fabrics, plastics, wood and other materials. Tanning, currying, finishing, embossing and japanning of all kinds of hides and skins and the manufac-

ture of leather products (other than footwear and other wearing apparel) such as luggage, handbags, pocket-books, cigarette and key cases, coin purses, saddlery, harness, whips and other articles made of leather and leather products. Manufacture from natural or synthetic rubber of all kinds of rubber products such as tubes and tyres, vulcanised footwear, industrial and mechanical rubber goods and rubber sundries such as mats, gloves, sponges and other vulcanised articles. The reclaiming of rubber from used tyres, scrap and miscellaneous waste rubber. Rebuilding, retreading and vulcanising of tyres. Dipping, mixing, rolling, cutting and related processing of natural rubber, except on rubber plantations.

32. UNION OF SHIPPING, CLEARING AND FORWARDING AGENCIES WORKERS OF NIGERIA
All employees excluding senior staff engaged by shipping, clearing and forwarding agencies.

33. NATIONAL UNION OF TEXTILE, GARMENT AND TAILORING WORKERS
Manufacture of textiles including the preparation of textile fibre for spinning, weaving and finishing; knitting mills, cordage, rope, twine, and thread industries. Manufacture of wearing apparel and made-up textiles. Manufacture of carpets, rugs, oilcloth, linoleum, artificial leather, water-proofing fabric and jute mills.

34. NATIONAL UNION OF ROAD TRANSPORT WORKERS
Transportation of passengers and foods by road, excluding the transporta-tion of petroleum by road and transportation undertaken by self-employed persons.

35. IRON AND STEEL WORKERS' UNION OF NIGERIA
The manufacture of basic iron and steel products consisting of all proces-ses from smelting in blast furnaces to the semi-finished stage in rolling mills and foundries – that is, the production of billets, blooms, slabs or bars, re-rolling and drawing into basic forms such as sheets, plates, strips, tubes and pipes, rails, rods and wires, tinplate, rough castings and forgings, coke ovens associated with blast furnaces. The manufacture of basic non-ferrous metal products, consisting of all processes from smelting, alloying and refining, rolling and drawing, foundering and casting.

36. AUTOMOBILE, BOATYARD, TRANSPORT AND EQUIPMENT AND ALLIED WORKERS UNION OF NIGERIA
The manufacture and assembly of complete motor vehicles such as passenger automobiles, commercial cars and buses, trucks and truck trailers, universal carriers and special-purpose meter vehicles such as ambulances, taxi-cabs, etc. Manufacture of motor-vehicle parts and ac-cessories such as engines, brakes, clutches, axles, gears, transmissions, wheels and frames but excluding tyres and tubes. Repairs of motor vehicles. Manufacture of motor-cycles, scooters, bicycles, tricycles, pedicabs and parts, including animal-drawn and hand-drawn vehicles. Shipyards and boat yards engaged in building and repair work. Specialised marine and ship parts manufacturing and assembly. Ship-breaking yards. Manufacture and assembly of other types of transport equipment.

37. METALLIC AND NON-METALLIC MINES WORKERS' UNION
Extraction of metalliferous and non-metalliferous ores, excepting coal and petroleum but including prospecting and preparing sites for the

extraction of these ores. Also included are all supplemental operations for dressing and beneficiating ores and other crude minerals, such as breaking, milling, grinding, pulverising, washing, cleaning and grading. Quarrying, salt mining, chemical and fertiliser mineral mining are also included in this group.

38. RECREATIONAL SERVICES EMPLOYEES' UNION
Stadia employees and related workers. Recreation clubs by whatever name called, swimming pools, amusement centres including carnivals, circuses, zoological gardens and services similarly classified.

39. NON-ACADEMIC STAFF UNION OF EDUCATIONAL AND ASSOCIATED INSTITUTIONS
All non-academic staff employed in educational, research and associated institutions.

40. NATIONAL UNION OF LOCAL GOVERNMENT EMPLOYEES
Employees of Local Government Councils.

41. NATIONAL UNION OF PUBLIC CORPORATIONS EMPLOYEES
All junior employees of federal and state statutory corporations and companies other than Nigeria Railways, Nigeria Airways, Nigerian Ports Authority, National Electric Power Authority, Nigeria Coal Corporation, Broadcasting and Television Authorities and any other similar bodies already covered by industrial unions.

42. CUSTOMS, EXCISE AND IMMIGRATION STAFF UNION
All employees excluding senior staff of the Customs and Excise Department of the federal Ministry of Finance and the Immigration Service of the federal Ministry of Internal Affairs.

B Employers' Federations, 1981

1. Agricultural and Allied Industries
2. Air Transport Services
3. Electricity and Gas
4. Precision, Electrical and Related Equipment
5. Seafaring and Water Transport
6. Master Stevedores/Dock Labour Employers
7. Banking, Insurance and Finance Institutions
8. Food, Beverage and Tobacco
9. Hotel and Personal Services
10. Shop and Distributive Trades
11. Printing and Publishing
12. Paper and Paper Board
13. Construction and Civil Engineering
14. Furniture, Fixtures and Woodworking
15. Metal Products/Iron and Steel
16. Petroleum and Natural Gas
17. Chemical and Non-Metallic Products
18. Leather, Footwear and Rubber Manufacturers
19. Shipping, Shipping Agencies, Clearing and Forwarding
20. Textile, Garment and Tailoring
21. Road Transport
22. Automobile, Boatyards and Transport Equipment
23. Metallic and Non-Metallic Mining
24. Recreational Services
25. Advertising
26. Education, Training and Consultancy Services
27. Legal Services
28. Medical Services
29. Associate Members

C The National Policy on Labour*

1. INTRODUCTION

In a dynamic society, no social policy can remain stagnant, it will therefore be entirely wrong that our national system of labour administration, as expressed in the Third National Development Plan and the various labour legislation, should be merely concerned with implementing a pre-established policy. We are witnessing today such an acceleration of developments in the field of political, social and economic policy that there is an urgent need for the Government, not only to shape and define its labour objectives in such a way as to keep pace with the increasingly complex requirements of the people, but also to ensure that these changes, that is, social, political and economic, are directed towards the fulfilment of the aspirations of our people for a better life. The new conept of development oriented administration and greater Government involvement in social and economic development have contributed tremendously to the transformation of the social and economic life of our country. Workers' and employers' organisations play a crucial role in this development. It is therefore manifest that the trade unions and the Government are partners in the development of the country.

2. THE OBJECTIVES AND PRINCIPLES OF THE POLICY

It is with this consideration in mind that the Federal Military Government has decided that the time is opportune to formulate a new labour policy which will have the following principal objectives:

   (i)   the need to give a new sense of direction and a new image to the trade-union movement in Nigeria;
   (ii) the desirability of removing completely from the trade-union arena ideological or external influences which have plagued Nigerian trade-union unity for more than a quarter of a century;
   (iii) the need to rationalise the structure and organisation of trade unions and to ensure that they are self-sufficient financially in future, and not dependent upon foreign sources for finance;

*The policy was announced to representatives of the unions and the Nigeria Employers Consultative Association by the federal Commissioner for Labour, Brigadier H. E. O Adefope (as he then was) on 4 December 1975.

(iv)   the need to provide facilities for trade-union education in order to improve the quality of trade-union leaders and the general knowledge and understanding of the purposes of trade unions by the rank and file members of these organisations;

(v)   the need to strengthen the labour administration system in the country through the provision of adequate material and human resources for the Ministry of Labour for the enforcement of labour laws and regulations, and the enhancement of institutions established by the Government for the purpose of promoting effective labour administration in the country; and

(vi)   the need for the continued support of the principles and objectives of the International Labour Organisation (ILO) and the Organisation of African Trade Union Unity (OATUU) subject to the over-riding interests of the Government and the people of Nigeria.

With these objectives in mind, the Federal Military Government has decided on a new National Labour Policy which will involve limited government intervention in certain areas of labour activity in order to ensure industrial peace, progress and harmony. The Federal Military Government does not believe in politicising the trade-union movement. On the other hand, the union activity especially at the central level is so important in our economic and social life that Government has of necessity to be involved to some extent.

In its new dimensions, the Federal Military Government is pursuing the policy of guided democracy in labour matters. This policy is predicated on the continued guarantee of freedom of association, the promotion of strong, stable and responsible workers' and employers' organisations, the establishment and development of a suitable institutional framework for the effective prevention and expeditious settlement of labour disputes, the promotion of labour/management co-operation and of consultation at appropriate levels between workers, employers and Government, and the vigorous enforcement of the provisions of labour legislation relating to minimum conditions of employment, social security, safety, health and welfare at work.

3. MAJOR ELEMENTS OF THE POLICY

3.1 Structure of trade unions

The present structure of the Nigerian trade-union movement is irrationally proliferated and out-dated. The Government would therefore adopt conscious and positive measures to restructure trade unions preferably along industrial lines, in accordance with the provisions of the Trade Unions Decree no. 31 of 1973, in order to accelerate the formation of amalgamations and federations of registered trade unions into bigger and more viable organisations. One of the measures which the Government will take to streamline the structure of the trade-union movement will be to legalise, by appropriate legislation the de-registration of unions of self-employed persons registered under the repealed Trade Unions Act who are not 'workers' as defined in the Trade Unions Decree no. 31 of 1973.

3.2   Trade-union finance

The ability of a trade union to make its way in the field of industrial relations depends primarily on its capacity to marshal adequate human and financial resources to sustain its organisation and operational programmes. This may take a variety of forms but they are usually made up almost exclusively of contributions paid by members. The extent to which these are paid regularly by all members is therefore a matter of great importance to the viability of a workers' organisation. Inadequate or irregular contributions are likely to impede the growth of a trade union and prevent it from taking effective action in the interests of its members. Accordingly, legislation will be introduced to make the 'check-off' system compulsory. The compulsory introduction of the 'check-off' system will, however, be accompanied by necessary checks and balances to ensure that the more ample supply of funds to trade unions is used judiciously to finance their legitimate aims and objectives, including, in particular, welfare provisions for their members and their dependants.

3.3   Trade-union education

The education and training of management have been accorded their proper place in the scheme of things. In contrast to this not much has been done by the government in the area of workers' education. There is neither conflict nor paradox in educating workers and management. They are partners together in the development of out society. Strength cannot negotiate with weakness nor order and discipline with anarchy and chaos. The employer who is abreast of the times is the first to recognise the value of sound, independent and responsible trade unions, capable of representing effectively the interests of their members. Education, by imparting understanding, can help reduce the area of labour–management conflict and promote the substitution of reasoning and conciliation for emotions and force. Trade-union members need education not only in the exercise of their freedom, rights and privileges, but equally in their duties and responsibilites as trade unionists and citizens. To attain this objective, workers and union leaders must have knowledge and skills, courage and resources, and ability to think independently so as to make free, mature and intelligent judgement.

The Government has therefore decided to:

(i)   establish a National Institute for Labour Studies during the Third National Development Plan period for the purpose of equipping, through education, officials and members of trade unions to take their place in Nigerian society and to fulfil effectively their social and economic functions and responsibilities as trade unionists and citizens; and

(ii)   take over immediately all foreign-sponsored labour institutions established and operating in Nigeria.

3.4   Affiliation with international organisations

The concern of the Federal Military Government in labour matters emanates as much from its obligations to safeguard the interests of workers and employers as to ensure orderly social conduct since labour matters affect also the social, economic and political goals of the Government. To regulate the relations of trade unions with employers and other organisations in desirable channels is a function which the Government has responsibility to perform. Above all, the Government has the right to take the necessary measures to guarantee public order and national security.

The Federal Military Government has therefore decided to exclude completely the influence, and proscribe the activities of, international trade-union organisations and trade secretariats in Nigeria with the exception of the International Labour Organisation (ILO), the Organisation of African Trade Union Unity (OATUU) and any other organisation specifically approved by the Government.

3.5 Labour inspection and enforcement of labour laws

The inspection functions of the Ministry of Labour including Factory Inspection, have the following objects in view, namely:

  (i)   to secure the enforcement of the Legal Provisions relating to conditions of work and the protection of workers while engaged in their work;
  (ii) to supply technical information and advice to employers and workers concerning the most effective means of complying with the legal provisions; and
  (iii) to bring to the notice of the Government defects and abuses not specifically covered by existing legal provision.

Labour and Factory Inspectors therefore perform the four-fold task of enforcement officers, education officers, promoters of social justice and 'keepers of the Social Peace'. The great importance attached to inspection work hardly needs any emphasis.

The Federal Military Government will henceforth enforce rigorously the provisions of existing labour legislation prescribing minimum conditions of employment and processes of collective bargaining. In this connection, the provisions of the Labour Decree no. 21 of 1974 relating to the protection of wages, contracts of employment, and terms and conditions of employment will be rigorously enforced in order to ensure that workers are not exploited by unscrupulous employers of labour. To this end the personnel and necessary material resources of the Federal Ministry of Labour will be reinforced.

3.6 Employment service

The Federal Military Government will adopt an employment policy which will ensure that employment service of the Federal Ministry of Labour is organised as an integral part of the national programme for the achievement and maintenance of a high level of employment and the development and use of its productive resources by encouraging the full use of the employment exchanges and the professional and executive registeries, on a voluntary basis, by employers in both the public and private sectors.

It may be necessary to review the policy regarding the employment service if employers do not make adequate use of the facilities.

3.7 International labour relations

The Federal Military Government re-affirms its support for the principles of the International Labour Organisation, of which Nigeria is a member, as enshrined in its Constitution and will continue to apply those international conventions and recommendations which it has ratified or adopted in so far as they are consistent with the interests and aspirations of the Nigerian Government and people.

D The Growth of Trade Unions, 1940–77

Year	No. of unions	Total membership
1940	14	4 337
1941	36	17 144
1942	77	26 346
1943	83	27 284
1944	91	30 000
1945	97	n.a.
1946	100	52 747
1947	109	76 362
1948	127	90 864
1949–50	140	109 998
1950–1	144	144 358
1951–2	124	152 230
1952–3	131	143 282
1953–4	152	153 089
1954–5	177	165 130
1955–6	232	175 987
1956–7	270	198 265
1957–8	298	235 742
1958–9	318	254 097
1959–60	347	259 072
1960–1	360	274 126
1961–2	402	281 124
1962–3	435	324 203
1963–4	502	352 790
1964–5	540	369 991
1965–6	578	379 184
1966–7	631	387 990
1967–8	662	393 671
1968–9	659	648 060
1969–70	725	684 498
1970–1	751	705 712
1971–2	881	759 322
1972–3	843	725 204
1973–4	878	741 055

Year	No. of unions	Total membership
1974–5	929	755 802
1975–6	936	772 751
1976–7	896	724 697

Sources: *Annual Reports of the Department of Labour and Federal Ministry of Labour, 1947–71;* the Records of the Registrar of Trade Unions.

Notes and References

PREFACE

1. P. Kilby, 'Industrial Relations and Wage Determination: Failure of the Anglo-Saxon Model', *Journal of Developing Areas*, vol. 1 (1967) pp. 489–520.
2. In U. G. Damachi and H. D. Seibel (eds), *Social Change and Economic Development in Nigeria* (Praeger, 1973).
3. V. P. Diejomaoh, 'Industrial Relations in a Development Context: The Case of Nigeria', in *Industrial Relations in Africa*, ed. U. G. Damachi *et al.* (Macmillan, 1979).

CHAPTER 1

1. K. Marx and F. Engels, *Selected Works* (Foreign Languages Publishing House, 1958) p. 36.
2. R. Miliband, *The State in Capitalist Society*, (Quartet, 1975).
3. R. Hyman, *Industrial Relations: A Marxist Introduction*, (Macmillan, 1975) p. 121.
4. Ibid, pp. 11–12.
5. H. A. Clegg, 'Pluralism in Industrial Relations', *British Journal of Industrial Relations*, vol. 13, no. 3 (1975) pp. 309–16.
6. A. Fox, 'Industrial Sociology and Industrial Relations', in Royal Commission on Trade Unions and Employers' Associations, Research Paper no. 3 (HMSO, 1966) p. 6.
7. P. Drucker, *The New Society* (Heinemann, 1951) p. 81.
8. J. T. Dunlop, *Industrial Relations Systems* (Henry Holt, 1958) p. 6.
9. A. Flanders, *Industrial Relations: What is Wrong with the System?* (Faber & Faber, 1965).
10. Ibid, p. 10.
11. C. J. Margerison, 'What Do We Mean by Industrial Relations? A Behavioural Science Approach', *British Journal of Industrial Relations*, vol. 7 (1969) pp. 273–86.
12. B. C. Roberts, *Labour in the Tropical Territories of the Commonwealth* (Bell, 1964) p. 3.
13. Ibid, p. 4.
14. Sidney Webb and Beatrice Webb, *The History of Trade Unionism* (Kelley, 1920) pp. 25–6.

15. H. Pelling, *A History of British Trade Unionism*, 3rd edn (Macmillan, 1976) p. 16.
16. S. and B. Webb, *Trade Unionism*, p. 63.
17. Pelling, *A History*, p. 23.
18. Flanders, *Industrial Relations*, ch. 3.
19. Ministry of Labour, *Industrial Relations Handbook*, pp. 134–5.
20. O. Kahn-Freund, 'Labour Law', *Law and Opinion in England in the Twentieth Century* (Stevens, 1959) pp. 262–3.
21. Flanders, *Industrial Relations*, p. 29.
22. See P. L. Davies, 'Arbitration and the Role of Courts: The Administration of Justice in Labour Law (United Kingdom)', *Report and Proceedings of the 9th International Congress of International Society for Labour Law and Social Security*, pp. 281–346.
23. A. Flanders, 'The Tradition of Voluntarism', *British Journal of Industrial Relations*, vol. 12, no. 3 (Nov 1974) p. 365.
24. Roberts, *Labour in the Tropical Territories*, p. 5.
25. See Flanders, 'The Tradition of Voluntarism', p. 367.
26. K. F. Walker, 'Australia', in *Comparative Labour Movements*, ed. W. Galenson, (Prentice-Hall, 1952) p. 173.
27. Pelling, *A History*, p. 32. The most famous of these were the 'Tolpuddle Martyrs' of 1834.
28. Walker, 'Australia', p. 175.
29. K. F. Walker, *Australian Industrial Relations Systems* (Harvard University Press, 1970) p. 19.
30. Ibid, p. 14.
31. P. Taft, 'Germany', in *Comparative Labour Movements*, ed. W. Galenson (Prentice-Hall, 1952) pp. 245–60.
32. M. Stewart, *Trade Unions in Europe* (Gower Press, 1974) p. 100.
33. L. Erhard, 'Labour and German Prosperity', *Current History*, vol. 37 (Aug 1959) p. 65.
34. Thilo Ramm, 'Labor Courts, Grievance Settlement in West Germany', in *Labor Courts and Grievance Settlement in Western Europe*, ed. B. Aaron (University of California Press, 1971) p. 92.
35. Ibid, p. 156.
36. E. C. Brown, *Soviet Trade Unions and Labour Relations* (Harvard University Press, 1966) p. 2.
37. D. A. Dyker, *The Soviet Economy* (Staples, 1976) p. 5.
38. Ibid, p. 112.
39. S. M. Schwarz, 'Trade Unions in the Soviet State', *Current History (Aug 1959) p. 83*.
40. *ILO, The Trade Union Situation in the USSR* (Geneva, 1960) p. 39.
41. Ibid, p. 56.
42. Brown, *Soviet Trade Unions*, pp. 234–5.
43. C. A. Myers, *Labor Problems in the Industrialization of India* (Harvard University Press, 1958) p. 64.
44. C. A. Myers and S. Kannappan, *Industrial Relations in India*, 2nd edn (Asia Publishing House, 1970) p. 147.
45. Cited by M. A. Bienefeld, 'Trade Unions and Peripheral Capitalism: The

220   *Notes and References*

Case of Tanzania', *Institute of Development Studies Discussion Paper*, DP 112 (June 1977).
46. Ibid, p. 6.
47. See W. H. Friedland, *Vuta Kamba: The Development of Trade Unions in Tanganyika* (Hoover Institution Press, 1969).
48. R. B. Davison, 'Labour Relations and Trade Unions in the Gold Coast', *Industrial and Labour Relations Review*, vol. 7, no. 4 (July 1954) pp. 599–600.
49. U. G. Damachi, *The Role of Trade Unions in the Development Process: With a Case study of Ghana* (Praeger, 1974) p. 14. See also L. N. Trachtman, 'The Labour Movement of Ghana: A Study in Political Unionism', *Economic Development and Cultural Change*, vol. 10 (Jan 1962).
50. Roberts, *Labour in the Tropical Territories*, p. 278.
51. Elliot Berg, 'French West Africa', in *Labor and Economic Development*, ed. W. Galenson (John Wiley, 1959) pp. 186–254.
52. M. Mackintosh, 'Industrial Relations in the Republic of Senegal', *Institute of Development Studies Discussion Paper*, no. 81 (Sept 1975) p. 59.
53. G. Pfeffermann, *Industrial Labor in the Republic of Senegal* (Praeger, 1968) p. 82.
54. Ibid, p. 94.
55. Pfeffermann, *Industrial Labor in the Republic of Senegal*, p. 98.
56. Constitution of 1963, Article 20.
57. K. Marx, *Capital* (Allen & Unwin, 1887) p. xvii.

CHAPTER 2

1. J. S. Coleman, *Nigeria: Background to Nationalism* (University of California Press, 1965) p. 4.
2. A detailed account of these developments is contained in K. O. Dike, *Trade and Politics in the Niger Delta, 1830–1885* (Clarendon Press, 1956).
3. Coleman, *Nigeria*, p. 42.
4. Later, after the Southern Camerouns left Nigeria in 1961 to join the Cameroun Republic it became the National Convention of Nigerian Citizens.
5. L. Schatzl, *Industrialisation in Nigeria: A Spatial Analysis* (Weltforum Verlag, 1973) p. 15.
6. R. O. Ekundare, *An Economic History of Nigeria: 1860–1960* (Methuen, 1973) pp. 21–3.
7. Schatzl, *Industrialisation in Nigeria*, p. 17.
8. Ibid, p. 54.
9. *The Economic Development of Nigeria: A Report of a Mission Undertaken by the International Bank for Reconstruction and Development at the Request of the Governments of Nigeria and the United Kingdom* (Lagos, Government Printer, 1954) p. 6.

10. T. M. Yesufu, *An Introduction to Industrial Relations in Nigeria* (Oxford University Press, 1962) p. 5.
11. *Third National Development Plan 1975–80*, p. 147.
12. O. O. Vincent, *The Nigerian Economy and the Role of Public and Private Organizations in its Development: An Address Delivered by the Governor of the Central Bank of Nigeria at the Second National Conference on Management Development*, held in Kaduna, 13–15 October 1977.
13. *Third National Development Plan, 1975–80*.
14. All those I spoke to on the issue, including university lecturers and government officials, confirm the view.
15. This Act replaced that of 1972, which was considered inadequate.
16. *The Second National Development Plan, 1970–74*, p. 32.
17. *Third National Development Plan, 1975–80*, Table 2.6.
18. Schatzl, *Industrialisation in Nigeria*, p. 25.
19. P. Kilby, *Industrialisation in an Open Economy: Nigeria 1945–1966* (Cambridge University Press, 1969) p. 15.
20. See S. J. Ukpanah and U. Udo-Aka, 'The Impact of Nigeria's Third National Plan on the Personnel Function', a paper presented at the conference of the Institute of Personnel Management of Nigeria held in Lagos, 30–31 October 1975, p. 6.
21. The word 'family' has two meanings; it may mean (i) members of a household, parents and children, or (ii) all descendants of a common ancestor, house or lineage. We use the word here in the second sense.
22. This custom has changed over the years. Grown-up children may now earn their living from the proceeds of sales.
23. F. A. Wells and W. A. Warmington, *Studies in Industrialization: Nigeria and the Camerouns* (Oxford University Press, 1962) p. 5.
24. See C. A. Myers and S. Kannappan, *Industrial Relations in India* (Asia Publishing House, 1970) ch. 3.
25. F. H. Harbison, 'Egypt', in *Labor and Economic Development*, ed. W. Galenson (John Wiley, 1959) pp. 146–85; see also R. D. Lambert, 'Labor in India', *Economic Development and Cultural Change*, vol. 8 (1959) p. 209.
26. Ibid, p. 3.
27. E. J. Berg, 'French West Africa', in *Labour and Economic Development*, pp. 186–254.
28. H. D. Seibel, 'The Process of Adaptation to Wage Labour', in *Social Change and Economic Development in Nigeria*, ed. U. G. Damachi and H. D. Seibel (Praeger, 1973) pp. 3–10.
29. Ibid, p. 6.
30. P. Kilby, 'Some Determinants of Industrial Productivity in Nigeria', *Proceedings of the Nigerian Institute of Social and Economic Research* (Dec 1960) pp. 171–80.
31. Kilby, *Industrialisation in an Open Economy*, p. 217.
32. National Manpower Board, Lagos, *Labour Force Sample Survey 1966/67*.
33. *Third National Development Plan, 1975–80*, p. 64.
34. See V. Diejomaoh, 'The Structure and Nature of Nigeria's Manpower Resources', *Management in Nigeria* (June–July 1977) pp. 23–39.

35. U. G. Damachi, 'Manpower in Nigeria', in *Social Change and Economic Development in Nigeria*, pp. 81–95.
36. The commission was chaired by Chief J. Udoji, a retired civil servant. A total amount of ₦859.3 million was spent on the payment of arrears throughout the country. See 'A Survey of the Effects of Udoji Salary/Wages Awards', Research Department Central Bank of Nigeria, Lagos, a paper prepared for the Anti-Inflation Task Force. Unpublished (Oct 1976).
37. T. M. Yesufu, 'Consumption Patterns and Living Conditions of Employees of the Nigerian Tobacco Company Ltd', unpublished study, (1967).

CHAPTER 3

1. J. I. Roper, *Labour Problems in West Africa* (Penguin, 1958) p. 49.
2. T. M. Yesufu, *An Introduction to Industrial Relations in Nigeria* (Oxford University Press, 1962) p. 33.
3. *Report of the Commission of Inquiry into the Disorders in the Eastern Provinces of Nigeria* (Fitzgerald Report) Colonial, no. 256, 1950, para. 21.
4. Ibid, pp. 33–4.
5. P. C. W. Gutkind *et al.*, *African Labour History* (Sage Publications, 1978) p. 37.
6. Ibid, p. 38.
7. M. A. Tokunboh, 'The Changing Pattern of Industrial Relations in Nigeria', *Management in Nigeria*, vol. 2, no. 4 (Nov–Dec 1966).
8. See B. C. Roberts, *Labour in the Tropical Territories of the Commonwealth* (Bell, 1964) p. 178.
9. *Report of the Tudor Davies Commission into the Cost of Living in the Colony and Protectorate of Nigeria* (HMSO, 1945) p. 27.
10. Mr M. A. Tokunboh was for many years a labour officer in the Federal Ministry of Labour. He has now retired, having served as Permanent Secretary in several ministries, including the Ministry of Labour.
11. See Appendix D for the growth of unions between 1940 and 1977.
12. This came out clearly in the Report of the Tribunal of Inquiry into the Activities of the Trade Unions (Lagos: Federal Ministry of Information, 1977).
13. *Annual Report of the Federal Ministry of Labour*, 1962–3, para. 68.
14. See R. Melson, 'Nigerian Politics and the General Strike of 1964', in *Protest and Power in Black Africa*, ed. R. I. Rotberg and A. A. Mazrui (Oxford University Press, 1970) pp. 771–87.
15. Ibid, p. 776.
16. *Annual Report of the Federal Ministry of Labour*, 1963–4, p. 62.
17. The negotiations were so called because Chief F. S. Okotie-Eboh, the then Minister of Finance, was the chairman.
18. *The Daily Times* (24 September 1974).
19. These were Aliyu Dangiwa, who later became the General Secretary of

the new NLC; O. Sonubi, a senior lecturer in industrial relations at the University of Ibadan; and J. O. Emodi, legal adviser to the Nigerian Railway Corporation.

20. I was a member of the Nigerian delegation, representing the employers.
21. The forty-two industrial unions are shown in Appendix A. Each grouping encompasses all companies that are engaged in similar activities and they follow closely the international classification of such activities.
22. *The Daily Times* (28 February 1978).
23. M. O. Abiodun, *Restructuring Trade Unions in Nigeria: 1976–78* (Salama Press, 1978) p. 8.
24. *Annual Report of the Federal Ministry of Labour*, 1961–2, para. 78.
25. *Second and Final Report of the Wages and Salaries Review Commission* (Lagos: Federal Ministry of Information, 1970–1) p. 46.
26. The model constitution of the NLC drawn up by the government deliberately played down the political role of unions.
27. A. J. Peace, *Choice, Class and Conflict: A Study of Southern Nigerian Factory Workers* (Harvester Press, 1979) chs 5 and 6.
28. O. Oloko, 'Industrial Unions: Their Effects on Industrial Relations in the Nigerian Economy', paper presented at the Institute of Personnel Management conference, Lagos (30 October 1980).
29. *The Adebiyi Tribunal Report* of 1977 has many instances of deviations from union rule books by union officials.
30. J. F. Weeks, 'A Comment on Peter Kilby: Industrial Relations and Wage Determination', *Journal of Developing Areas*, vol. 3 (Oct 1968) pp. 7–18.
31. E. J. Berg, 'Urban Real Wages and the Nigerian Trade Union Movement, 1939–60: A Comment', *Economic Development and Cultural Change*, vol. 17 (1969) pp. 604–17.
32. P. Kilby, 'Industrial Relations and Wage Determination: Failure of the Anglo-Saxon Model', *Journal of Developing Areas*, vol. 1 (July 1967) pp. 489–520.
33. W. M. Warren, 'Urban Real Wages and the Nigerian Trade Union Movement, 1939–60', *Economic Development and Cultural Change*, vol. 15 (1966) pp. 21–36.
34. The NLC seems to have derived its inspiration from the report of the World Employment Conference on Basic Needs, organised by the ILO and held in Geneva, 4–17 June 1976.
35. It took about one year before the National Assembly decided to take action on the matter which the Executive was obliged under the constitution to refer to it.
36. See the Fitzgerald Commission Report, already referred to. Some authorities consider union agitation as 'political' while others, including Kilby (1968) and Cohen (1974) (see the Bibliography), believe that the Wages Commissions in Nigeria had been set up as a result of unions' political action and that political parties improved workers' wages in order to win their electoral votes.
37. J. S. Coleman, *Nigeria: Background to Nationalism* (University of California Press, 1965) p. 256.
38. R. Cohen, *Labour and Politics in Nigeria* (Heinemann, 1974) p. 161.

224   *Notes and References*

39. W. Ananaba, *The Trade Union Movement in Nigeria* (Ethiope Publishing Corporation, 1969) p. 93.
40. R. V. Grillo, 'The Tribal Factor in an East African Trade Union', in *Tradition and Transition in East Africa*, ed. P. H. Gulliver (University of California Press, 1969) p. 320.
41. I. C. Imoisili, 'Nigerian Managers as Trade Unionists: An Empirical Survey', *Perman, Journal of the Institute of Personnel Management of Nigeria* (Sept 1979) p. 13.
42. G. Travernier, 'The Militant Managers', *International Management*, vol. 33, no. 2 (Feb 1978) pp. 12 and 15.
43. Yesufu, *Industrial Relations*, p. 47.
44. See Appendix B.
45. The Fitzgerald Report. Despatch dated 15 May 1950 from the Governor of Nigeria to the Secretary of State for the Colonies, pp. 2–3.
46. *Annual Report of the Department of Labour*, 1952–3, para. 106.
47. *Annual Report of the Department of Labour*, 1950–1, p. 26.
48. The Fitzgerald Report, para. 21.
49. *Annual Report of the Department of Labour*, 1947, p. 13.
50. *Annual Report of the Department of Labour*, 1956–7, p. 13.
51. B. C. Roberts and L. Greyfié de Bellecombe, *Collective Bargaining in African Countries* (Macmillan, 1967) pp. 37–9, 60–1.
52. The Fitzgerald Report, para. 23.
53. *Annual Report of the Department of Labour*, 1954–5, para. 20.
54. *Annual Report, Federal Ministry of Labour*, 1960–1, para. 92.
55. The text of the policy is covered in Appendix C.
56. Address by the Federal Commissioner for Labour, Major-General H. E. O. Adefope, to the inaugural conference of industrial unions held in Lagos, Kaduna, Ibadan, Benin and Enugu between 31 October 1977 and 12 November 1977.
57. Address by the Minister of Employment, Labour and Productivity, at the 24th Annual General Meeting of the NECA, on 19 December 1980.
58. C. P. Kindleberger, *Economic Development* (1958) p. 223, cited by K. Schweinitz Jr, 'Industrialisation, Labour Control and Democracy', *Economic Development and Cultural Change*, vol. 7, no. 4 (1959) p. 385.
59. C. Kerr *et al.*, 'The Labour Problem in Economic Development', *International Labour Review*, vol. 71 (1955)
60. A Mehta, 'The Mediating Role of the Trade Union in Underdeveloped Countries', *Economic Development and Cultural Change*, vol. 6 (Oct. 1957) pp. 16–23.
61. A. Sturmthal, 'Unions and Economic Development', *Economic Development and Cultural Change*, vol. 8 (1959) pp. 199–205.
62. W. Galenson (ed.), *Labor and Economic Development* (John Wiley, 1959) p. 13.
63. W. H. Friedland, *Vuta Kamba: The Development of Trade Unions in Tanganyika* (Hoover Institution Press, 1969) p. 58.
64. T. Burns (ed.), *Industrial Man* (Penguin, 1969) p. 7.
65. A. Tevoedjre, 'A Strategy for Social Progress in Africa and the ILO's Contribution', *International Labour Review*, vol. 99, no. 1 (Jan. 1969) p. 77.

CHAPTER 4

1. The section provides: 'Any person who, with any of the intents in the preceding section mentioned, assaults any other person or anyone in whom he is interested, is guilty of a felony, and liable to imprisonment for five years.'
2. Per Goddard, L. J. (as he then was) in *Evans* v. *National Union of Printing, Bookbinding and Paper Workers* (1938) 4 A11 ER 51.
3. *National Coal Board* v. *Galley* (1958) 1 WLR 26.
4. Per Lord Wright, in *Crofter Handwoven Harris Tweed* v. *Veitch* (1942) AC 435 at p. 463.
5. Lord Denning M.R., in *Morgan* v. *Fry* (1968) IQB 521.
6. Suit NSC 88/1964.
7. See the award of the IAT (Now IAP) in the case of *N.T.C. General Workers Union and N.T.C. Ltd (1972) and Union of P. & T. Workers of Nigeria* v. *the Attorney-General of the Federation of Nigeria*, Suit no. LD/142/58.
8. In a paper prepared entitled 'Free Collective Bargaining'. Unpublished (Feb 1980). This definition is based on that of the ILO. See their *Collective Bargaining* (Geneva, 1960) p. 3.
9. See NECA's memorandum on 'collective bargaining' sent to the federal Ministry of Employment, Labour and Productivity, dated 3 April 1980.
10. Most of the employees surveyed would prefer these items negotiated at the enterprise level. It is, however, too early to assess the success or otherwise of the new system.
11. O. Oloko, 'Industrial Unions: Their Effects on Industrial Relations in the Nigerian Economy', paper presented at the Institute of Personnel Management Conference, Lagos (30 Oct. 1980). Unpublished.
12. Department of Labour, 'Short Report on Joint Consultative Committee in Nigeria, 31 March, 1957', mimeographed. Unpublished.
13. Ibid, p. 2.
14. NECA's view was put forward by its director, Mr G. C. Okogwu, at a meeting held on 23 April 1980.
15. *Report of the Commission on the Review of Wages, Salary and Conditions of Service of the Junior Employees of the Governments of the Federation and in Private Establishments, 1963–64* (Lagos: Federal Ministry of Information, 1964).
16. At p. 35.
17. Wages and Salaries Review Commission, 1970–71 (Lagos: Federal Ministry of Information, 1971).
18. Public Service Review Commission, Main Report (Lagos: Federal Ministry of Information, Sept. 1974).
19. This came out in answers to a questionnaire.
20. In a memorandum sent to the federal government through the PPIB, ref. 2/70, dated 29 January 1980.

CHAPTER 5

1. National Industrial Court, Suit no. NIC/1/79.
2. This dispute is discussed further in this chapter.

3. Suit no. NIC/1/78.
4. Suit no. NIC/1/79.
5. K. G. J. C. Knowles, *Strikes–A Study in Industrial Conflict* (Basil Blackwell, 1952) p. 11.
6. J. E. T. Eldridge, *Industrial Disputes* (Routledge & Keegan Paul, 1968) p. 70.
7. R. Hyman, *Strikes*, 2nd edn (Fontana/Collins, 1976) p. 35.
8. *Report of the Royal Commission on Trade Unions and Employers' Associations 1965–68*, Cmd 3623 (HMSO, 1968) p. 111.
9. A. Kornhauser *et al.*, *Industrial Conflict* (McGraw-Hill, 1954) p. 8.
10. Hyman, *Strikes*, p. 35.
11. H. A. Turner *et al.*, *Labour Relations in the Motor Industry* (Allen & Unwin, 1967) pp. 118–19.
12. Knowles, *Strikes*, p. 278.
13. Hyman, *Strikes*, p. 36.
14. Kornhauser *et al.*, *Industrial Conflift*, p. 8.
15. *The Daily Times* (8 October 1968).
16. *West Africa* (16 November 1968) p. 1362.
17. Federal Ministry of Labour, *Annual Report*, 1968–9, p. 2.
18. The jump in the number of strikes in 1970–1 and 1974–5 followed the reports of the Adebo Commission and the Udoji Commission, respectively.
19. V. P. Diejomaoh, 'Industrial Relations in a Development Context: The Case of Nigeria', *Industrial Relations in Africa*, ed. U. G. Damachi *et al.* (Macmillan, 1979) p. 195.
20. All twenty companies surveyed for this study each had a grievance procedure.
21. The role of the mediator is discussed in detail further on in this Chapter, under the section on statutory procedure.
22. A. A. Adeogun, 'Trade Unions and the Settlement of Trade Disputes', Paper delivered at the 1977 National Conference on Industrial Relations at the University of Ibadan. Unpublished.
23. Ref. no. ML. Ac/231/Con., dated 21 February 1974.
24. A. A. Adeogun, 'Towards a Better System of Settling Trade Disputes', *Nigerian Law Journal*, vol. 10 (1976) p. 5.
25. No. 6, LN 29 of 1976.
26. *The Punch* (21 March 1982) p. 16.
27. Suit no. NIC/1/79.
28. Suit no. NIC/23/78.
29. Suit no. NIC/17/78.
30. Suit no. NIC/17/78.
31. M. O. Efueye, 'The Role of Arbitration Tribunal in Industrial Relations'; lecture given at the ILO/SIDA/NECA seminar held in Lagos, 1–5 March 1982, p. 8.

CHAPTER 6

1. See Appendix C.
2. N. Chamberlain and J. W. Kuhn, *Collective Bargaining*, 2nd edn (McGraw-Hill, 1965) p. 265.

3. K. Hawkins, 'The Decline of Voluntarism', *Industrial Relations Journal,* vol. 2, no. 2 (1971) p. 29.
4. In a letter dated 29 January 1980, addressed to the federal government through the Productivity, Prices and Incomes Board.
5. A. Flanders, *Management and Unions* (Faber & Faber, 1970) p. 246.
6. Ibid.
7. Thilo Ramm, 'Labor Courts and Grievance Settlement in West Germany', in *Labor Courts and Grievance Settlement in Western Europe,* ed. B. Aron (University of California Press, 1971) p. 155.
8. For example, the law that banned strikes in 1969 had the effect of creating a peaceful industrial atmosphere for a time.
9. Ramm, 'Labor Courts and Grievance Settlement in West Germany' p. 149.
10. Folke Schmidt, 'The Settlement of Employment Grievances in Sweden', in *Labor Courts and Grievance Settlement in Western Europe,* pp. 244–5.

Bibliography

Aaron, B. (ed.), *Labor Courts and Grievance Settlement in Western Europe* (University of California Press, 1971).

Abiodun, M. O., *Restructuring of Trade Unions in Nigeria: 1976–78* (Salama Press, 1978).

Adeogun, A. A., 'The Legal Framework of Industrial Relations in Nigeria', *Nigerian Law Journal*, vol. 3 (1969) pp. 13–40.

—— 'Towards a Better System of Settling Trade Disputes', *Nigerian Law Journal*, vol. 10 (1976).

Aire, J. U., 'Emerging Patterns and Trends of Industrial Relations in Nigeria', *Perman, Journal of the Institute of Personnel Management of Nigeria*, vol. 1, no. 1 (1974) pp. 20–9.

Akerele, A., 'The Environment of Industrial Relations: Participants and Influencing Factors', *Nigerian Journal of Economic and Social Studies*, vol. 17, no. 3 (1975).

Akpala, A., 'Labour Policies and Practices in Nigeria', *Journal of Industrial Relations*, vol. 13 (1971) pp. 274–90.

Allen, V. L., 'The Meaning of the Working Class in Africa', *Journal of Modern African Studies*, vol. 10 (1972) pp. 169–89.

Ananaba, W., *The Trade Union Movement in Nigeria* (Ethiope Publishing Corporation, 1969).

Anderman, S. D., 'Central Wage Negotiation in Sweden: Recent Problems and Developments', *British Journal of Industrial Relations*, vol. 5 (1967) pp. 322–37.

Arrighi, G., and Saul, J. S., *Essays on the Political Economy of Africa* (Monthly Review Press, 1973).

Ashenfelter, O., and Johnson, G. E., 'Bargaining Theory, Trade Unions and Industrial Strike Activity', *American Economic Review*, vol. 54 (1969) pp. 35–49.

Austin, D. G., and Rathbone, R. J. A. R., 'Trade Unions and Politics in Ghana', *Collected Seminar Papers on Labour Unions and Political Organizations*, no. 3 (University of London Institute of Commonwealth Studies, Jan–May 1967).

Babbie, E. R., *Survey Research Methods* (Wadsworth Publishing Company, 1973).

Bain, G. S., and Clegg, H. A., 'A Strategy for Industrial Relations Research in Great Britain', *British Journal of Industrial Relations*, vol. 12 (1974) pp. 91–113.

Baldwin, G. B., 'Labour Problems in a Developing Economy', *Current History*, vol. 37 (1959) pp. 91–5.

Banks, J. A., *Marxist Sociology in Action: A Sociological Critique of the Marxist Approach to Industrial Relations* (Faber & Faber, 1970).

—— *Trade Unionism* (Collier-Macmillan, 1974).

Barbash, J., 'The Elements of Industrial Relations', *British Journal of Industrial Relations*, vol. 2 (1964) pp. 66–78.

Barret, R. J., 'The Role of Trade Unions in Underdeveloped Countries', *Labour Law Journal*, vol. 13 (1962) pp. 1047–59.

Beling, W. A. (ed.), *The Role of Labor in African Nation-Building* (Praeger, 1968).

Bell, D., *The End of Ideology*, revised edn (The Free Press, 1962).

Bendix, R., 'A Study of Managerial Ideologies', *Economic Development and Cultural Change*, vol. 5 (1957) pp. 118–28.

Berg, E. J., *The Role of Trade Unions in African Economic Development* (Harvard University Press, 1963).

—— 'French West Africa', in *Labor and Economic Development*, ed. W. Galenson (John Wiley, 1959).

—— 'Major Issues of Wage Policy in Africa', in *Industrial Relations and Economic Development*, ed. A. M. Ross (Macmillan, 1966).

—— 'Urban Real Wages and the Nigerian Trade Union Movement, 1939–60: A Comment', *Economic Development and Cultural Change*, vol. 17 (1969) pp. 604–16.

—— and Butler, J., 'Trade Unions', in *Political Parties and National Integration in Tropical Africa*, ed. J. S. Coleman and C. G. Rosberg (University of California Press, 1970).

Bienefeld, M. A., 'Trade Unions and Peripheral Capitalism: The Case of Tanzania', *Institute of Development Studies Discussion Paper*, DP112 (June 1977).

Blain, A. N. J., and Gennard, J., 'Industrial Relations Theory – A Critical Review', *British Journal of Industrial Relations*, vol. 8 (1970) pp. 389–407.

Bolin, B., *Sweden: A Trade Union Approach to an Active Labour Market*, International Institute for Labour Studies, Bulletin 1 (Oct 1966) pp. 22–35.

Braundi, E. R., and Lettieri, A., 'The General Strike in Nigeria', *International Socialist Journal*, vol. 1 (1964) pp. 598–609.

Braverman, H., *Labor and Monopoly Capital* (Monthly Review Press, 1974).

Brotherton, C. J., and Stephenson, G. M., 'Psychology in the Study of Industrial Relations', *Industrial Relations Journal*, vol. 6, no. 3 (1975) pp. 42–50.

Brown, D., and Harrison, M. J., *A Sociology of Industrialisation* (Macmillan, 1978).

Brown, E. C., 'Labour Relations in Soviet Factories', *Industrial and Labour Relations Review*, vol. 11 (1958) pp. 183–202.

—— *Soviet Trade Unions and Labour Relations* (Harvard University Press, 1966).

Burkitt, B., and Bowers, D., *Trade Unions and the Economy* (Macmillan, 1979).

Burns, T. (ed.), *Industrial Man* (Penguin, 1969).

Chamberlain, N. W., *The Labor Sector* (McGraw-Hill, 1965).
—— and Kuhn, J. W., *Collective Bargaining*, 2nd edn (McGraw-Hill, 1965).
Chandrashekar, B. K., 'Labour Relations in India', *British Journal of Industrial Relations*, vol. 8 (1970) pp. 369–88.
Clarke, T., and Clements, L., *Trade Unions under Capitalism* (Fontana/Collins, 1977).
Clegg, H. A., *The Changing System of Industrial Relations in Great Britain* (Blackwell, 1979).
—— 'Pluralism in Industrial Relations', *British Journal of Industrial Relations*, vol. 13, no. 3 (1975) pp. 309–16.
Cohen, R., *Labour and Politics in Nigeria* (Heinemann, 1974).
—— 'Further Comment on the Kilby/Weeks Debate', *Journal of Developing Areas*, vol. 5 (1971) pp. 155–64.
Coleman, J., *Nigeria: Background to Nationalism* (University of California Press, 1965).
Cox, R. W., 'Trade Unions, Employers and the Formation of National Economic Policy', in *Industrial Relations and Economic Development* (Macmillan, 1966).
Crouch, C., *The Politics of Industrial Relations* (Fontana/Collins, 1979).
Cullingford, E. C. M., *Trade Unions in Germany* (Wilton House Publications, 1976).
Damachi, U. G., *The Role of Trade Unions in the Development Process: With a Case Study of Ghana* (Praeger, 1974).
—— 'Government, Employers and Workers in Ghana: A Study of the Mutual Perception of Roles', *British Journal of Industrial Relations*, vol. 14, no. 1 (1976) pp. 26–34.
—— and Seibel, H. D. (eds), *Social Change and Economic Development in Nigeria* (Praeger, 1973).
—— *et al.* (eds), *Industrial Relations in Africa* (Macmillan, 1979).
Davis, I., *African Trade Unions* (Penguin, 1966).
Davison, R. B., 'Labour Relations and Trade Unions in the Gold Coast', *Industrial and Labour Relations Review*, vol. 7, no. 4 (July 1954) pp. 593–604.
—— 'Labour Relations in Ghana', *The Annals of the American Academy of Political and Social Science* (March 1957) pp. 133–41.
Deutscher, I., *Soviet Trade Unions* (Royal Institute of International Affairs, 1950).
Deyrup, F. J., 'Organized Labour and Government in Under-developed countries: Sources of Conflict', *Industrial and Labour Relations Review*, vol. 12 (1958) pp. 104–12.
Diejomaoh, V. P., 'Industrial Relations in a Development Context: The Case of Nigeria', in *Industrial Relations in Africa*, ed. U. G. Damachi *et al.* (Macmillan, 1979).
—— 'The Structure and Nature of Nigeria's Manpower Resources', *Management in Nigeria* (June–July 1977) pp. 23–39.
Dike, K. O., *Trade and Politics in the Niger Delta 1830–1885* (Clarendon Press, 1956).

Dore, R. P., 'Industrial Relations in Britain, Japan, Mexico, Sri Lanka, Senegal', *Institute of Development Studies Discussion Paper*, no. 61 (Aug 1974).

Drucker, P., *The New Society* (Heinemann, 1951).

Dunlop, J. T., *Industrial Relations Systems* (Henry Holt, 1958).

—— 'Political Systems and Industrial Relations', *IILS Bulletin*, no. 9 (1972) pp. 99–116.

—— and Healy, J. J., *Collective Bargaining* (Irwin, 1955).

Dyker, D. A., *The Soviet Economy* (Staples, 1976).

Edelman, M., 'Labour Policy in a Democracy', *Current History*, no. 216 (Aug 1959) pp. 96–100.

Ekundare, R. O., *An Economic History of Nigeria 1860–1960* (Methuen, 1973).

Eldridge, J. E. T., *Industrial Disputes* (Routledge & Kegan Paul, 1968).

Engels, F., *The Condition of the Working Class in England* (Progress Publishers, 1885).

Erhard, L., *'Labour and German Prosperity'*, *Current History*, vol. 17, no. 216 (Aug 1959) pp. 65–7.

Fanon, F., *The Wretched of the Earth* (Penguin, 1963).

Fashoyin, T., 'The Impact of the Trade Disputes Decrees of 1968 and 1969 on Strike Activity', *Quarterly Journal of Administration* (Oct 1978) p. 59.

Fatchett, D., and Whittingham, W. M., 'Trade and Developments in Industrial Relations Theory', *Industrial Relations Journal*, vol. 7 (1976) pp. 50–60.

Fisher, P., 'The Economic Role of Unions in Less-developed Areas', *Monthly Labour Review* (Sept 1961) pp. 951–6.

Flanders, A., *Industrial Relations: What Is Wrong with the System?* (Faber & Faber, 1965).

—— *Management and Unions* (Faber & Faber, 1970).

—— 'Collective Bargaining: A Theoretical Analysis', *British Journal of Industrial Relations*, vol. 6 (1968) pp. 1–25.

—— (ed.), *Collective Bargaining* (Penguin, 1969).

—— 'The Tradition of Voluntarism', *British Journal of Industrial Relations*, vol. 12, no. 3 (Nov 1974) pp. 352–70.

Fox, A., 'Industrial Sociology and Industrial Relations', in Royal Commission on Trade Unions and Employers' Associations, Research Paper no. 3 (HMSO, 1966).

—— *The Sociology of Industry* (Heinemann, 1971).

—— 'Managerial Ideology and Labour Relations', *British Journal of Industrial Relations*, vol. 4 (1966) pp. 366–78.

—— 'Collective Bargaining, Flanders and the Webbs', *British Journal of Industrial Relations*, vol. 13 (1975) pp. 151–71.

—— and Flanders, A., 'The Reform of Collective Bargaining from Donovan to Durkheim', *British Journal of Industrial Relations*, vol. 7, no. 2 (1966) pp. 151–80.

Friedland, W. H., *Vuta Kamba: The Development of Trade Unions in Tanganyika* (Hoover Institution Press, 1969).

Galenson, W. (ed.), *Comparative Labor Movements* (Prentice-Hall, 1952).

——(ed.), *Labor and Economic Development* (John Wiley, 1959).

Giddens, A. (ed.), *Emile Durkheim: Selected Writings* (Cambridge University Press, 1972).

Goodman, J. F. B. *et al.* (eds), 'Rules in Industrial Relations Theory: a Discussion', *Industrial Relations Journal*, vol. 6, no. 3 (1975) pp. 14–30.

Grillo, R. D., 'The Tribal Factor in an East African Trade Union', in *Tradition and Transition in East Africa*, ed. P. H. Gulliver (University of California Press, 1969).

Grunfeld, C., 'Australian Compulsory Arbitration: Appearance and Reality', *British Journal of Industrial Relations*, vol. 9, no. 3 (1971) pp. 330–52.

——*Modern Trade Union Law* (Sweet & Maxwell, 1966).

Gulick, C. A., and Bers, M. K., 'Insight and Illusion in Perlman's Theory of the Labour Movement', *Industrial and Labour Relations Review*, vol. 6, no. 4 (1953) pp. 510–31.

Gutkind, P. C. W. *et al. African Labour History* (Sage Publications, 1978).

Hill, S., and Thurley, K., 'Sociology and Industrial Relations', *British Journal of Industrial Relations*, vol. 12 (1974) pp. 147–70.

Hinchcliffe, K., 'Labour Aristocracy – Northern Nigeria Case Study', *Journal of Modern African Studies*, vol. 12 (1974) pp. 57–67.

Hodder, B. W., *Economic Development in the Tropics* (Methuen, 1968).

Hopkins, A. G., 'The Lagos Strike of 1897: An Exploration in Nigerian Labour History', *Past and Present*, vol. 35 (1966).

Hoselitz, B. F., 'The Development of a Labour Market in the Process of Economic Growth' in *International Labor Movements in Transition*, ed. A. F. Sturmthal (University of Illinois Press, 1973).

Hyman, R., *Industrial Relations: A Marxist Introduction* (Macmillan, 1975).

——*Marxism and the Sociology of Trade Unionism* (Pluto Press, 1971).

——*Disputes Procedure in Action* (Heinemann, 1972).

——'Inequality, Ideology and Industrial Relations', *British Journal of Industrial Relations*, vol. 12 (1974) pp. 171–90.

——*Strikes* (Fontana/Collins, 1972).

——and Brough, I., *Social Values and Industrial Relations* (Basil Blackwell, 1975).

Imoagene, S. O., 'Psycho-Social Factors in Rural–Urban Migration', *Nigerian Journal of Economic and Social Studies*, vol. 14 (1967) pp. 375–80.

Imoisili, C., 'Nigerian Managers as Trade Unionists: An Empirical Survey', *Perman, Journal of the Institute of Personnel Management of Nigeria* (Sept 1979) p. 13.

International Labour Office, *Collective Bargaining* (1960).

——*The Trade Union Situation in the United Kingdom* (1961).

——*The Trade Union Situation in the United States* (1960).

——*The Trade Union Situation in the USSR* (Geneva, 1960).

——*The Trade Union Situation in Sweden* (1961).

——*The Role of Trade Unions in Developing Societies* (1978).

——*African Labour Survey* (Geneva, 1962).

James, R., 'Politics and Trade Unions in India', *Far Eastern Survey*, vol. 27 (1958) pp. 41–5.

Johns, S. W., 'Trade Union, Political Pressure Group or Mass Movement? The Industrial and Commercial Workers Union of Africa', in *Protest and Power in Black Africa*, ed R. I. Rotberg and A. A. Mazrui (Oxford University Press, 1970).

Johnston, T. L., *Collective Bargaining in Sweden* (Allen & Unwin, 1962).

Kassalow, E. M., 'Union Organization and Training in Emerging Labor Movements', *Monthly Labour Review*, vol. 85 (1962) pp. 1010–15.

—— *Trade Unions and Industrial Relations* (Random House, 1969).

—— and Damachi, U. G. *The Role of Trade Unions in Developing Societies* (International Institute for Labour Studies, 1978).

Kennedy, V. D., 'The Conceptual and Legislative Framework of Labour Relations in India', *Industrial and Labor Relations Review*, vol. 11 (1958) pp. 487–505.

Kerr, C. *et al.* (eds), *Industrialism and Industrial Man* (Harvard University Press, 1960).

—— *et al.* (eds), 'The Labour Problem in Economic Development', *International Labour Review*, vol. 71 (1955) pp. 223–35.

—— and Siegel, A., 'The Structure of the Labor Force in Industrial Society', *Industrial and Labor Relations Review*, vol. 8, no. 2 (1955) pp. 151–68.

Kilby, P., *Industrialization in an Open Economy: Nigeria 1945–1966* (Cambridge University Press, 1969).

—— 'Some Determinants of Industrial Productivity in Nigeria', *Proceedings of the Nigerian Institute of Social and Economic Research* (Dec 1960) pp. 171–80.

—— 'Trade Unionism in Nigeria, 1938–66', in *The International Labor Movement in Transition*, ed. A. Sturmthal *et al.* (University of Illinois Press, 1973) pp. 228–58.

—— 'Industrial Relations and Wage Determination: Failure of the Anglo-Saxon Model', *Journal of Developing Areas*, vol. 1 (July 1967) pp. 489–520.

—— 'African Labour Productivity Reconsidered', *Economic Journal*, vol. 71 (1961) pp. 273–91.

—— 'A Reply to John F. Weeks's Comment', *Journal of Developing Areas*, vol. 3 (1968) pp. 19–25.

Knowles, K. G. J. C., *Strikes – A Study in Social Conflict* (Basil Blackwell, 1952).

Kornhauser, A. *et al.*, *Industrial Conflict* (McGraw-Hill, 1954).

Kuhn, J., 'Grievance Machinery and Strikes in Australia', *Industrial and Labour Relations Review*, vol. 8, no. 2 (1955) pp. 169–76.

Laffer, K., 'Industrial Relations – its Teaching and Scope: An Australian Experience', International Institute for Labour Studies, bulletin (Nov 1978).

Lambert, R. D., 'Labor in India', *Economic Development and Cultural Change*, vol. 8 (1959) pp. 206–13.

Lenin, V. I., *What Is To Be Done?* (International Publishers, 1929).

Lichtblau, G. E., 'The Politics of Trade Union Leadership in Southern Asia', *World Politics*, vol. 7 (Oct 1954) pp. 84–101.

Lorwin, L. L., *The American Federation of Labor* (Brookings Institution, 1933).

234   *Bibliography*

Losche, P., 'Stages in the Evolution of the German Labour Movement', in *The International Labor Movement in Transition*, ed. A. Sturmthal and J. B. Scoville (1973).

Lozovsky, A., *Marx and the Trade Unions* (Laurence, 1935).

—— (ed.), *Handbook on the Soviet Trade Unions* (Cooperative Publishing Society, 1937).

Lynd, G. E., *The Politics of African Trade Unionism* (Praeger, 1968).

Macdonald, D. F., *The State and the Trade Unions* (Macmillan, 1976).

Mackintosh, M., 'Industrial Relations in the Republic of Senegal', *Institute of Development Studies Discussion Paper*, no. 81 (Sept 1975).

McLellan, D. (ed.), *Karl Marx: Selected Writings* (Oxford University Press, 1977).

Margerison, C. J., 'What Do We Mean by Industrial Relations? A Behavioural Science Approach', *British Journal of Industrial Relations*, vol. 7 (1969) pp. 273–86.

Marx, K., and Engels, F., *The Manifesto of the Communist Party* (Progress Publishers, 1952).

—— *Selected Works* (Progress Publishers, 1969).

Mehta, A., 'The Mediating Role of the Trade Union in Underdeveloped Countries', *Economic Development and Culture Change*, vol. 6 (Oct 1957) pp. 16–23.

Melson, R., 'Nigerian Politics and the General Strike of 1964', in *Protest and Power in Black Africa*, ed. R. I. Rotberg and A. A. Mazrui (Oxford University Press, 1970).

Meynaud, J., and Bey, A. S., *Trade Unionism in Africa* (Methuen, 1967).

Miliband, R., *The State in Capitalist Society* (Quartet, 1975).

Millen, B. H., *The Political Role of Labor in the Developing Countries* (Brookings Institution, 1963).

Mitchell, C. J., *An Outline of the Sociological Background to African Labour* (Ensign Publishers, 1961)

Morris, M. D., 'Labour Discipline, Trade Unions and the State in India', *Journal of Political Economy*, vol. 63 (1955) pp. 293–308.

Mukerjee, R., *The Indian Working Class*, 3rd edn (Hind Kitabs, 1951).

Munns, V. G., and McCarthy, W. E. J., 'Employers Associations', *Royal Commission Research Paper*, no. 7 (1967)

Myers, C. A., *Labor Problems in the Industrialization of India* (Harvard University Press, 1958).

Nigeria, Federal Republic of, 'Labour–Management Relations in the Coal Industry in Nigeria', *Inter-African Labour Institute*, bulletin (May 1963) pp. 198–206.

—— *Report of the Commission on The Review of Wages, Salary and Conditions of Service of the Junior Employees of the Governments of the Federation and in Private Establishments* (Federal Ministry of Information, 1964).

—— *Second and Final Report of the Wages and Salaries Review Commission, 1970–71* (Federal Ministry of Information, 1971).

—— *Public Service Review Commission Main Report* (Federal Ministry of Information, 1974).

—— *Second National Development Plan 1970–74* (Federal Ministry of Information, 1970).

—— *Third National Development Plan 1975–80* (Federal Ministry of Information, 1975).

—— *Report of the Tribunal into the Activities of the Trade Unions* (Federal Ministry of Information, 1977).

—— *Annual Reports, 1947–72, Federal Ministry of Labour.*

Nisbert, R. A., *Emile Durkheim* (Prentice-Hall, 1965).

Okogwu, G. C., 'New Dimensions in Government Policy on Industrial Relations in Nigeria', Lecture delivered on 3 August 1976 at the National Conference on Industrial Relations, University of Ibadan.

—— 'Industrial Unions in a Developing Economy', A paper delivered at a seminar organised by the Federal Ministry of Labour in Lagos from 10–11 August 1973.

—— 'Industrial Relations in the 1980s', A paper delivered at a seminar organised by the Nigerian Tobacco Company Limited for its managers, February 1980.

Olaloku, F. A. *et al.*, *Structure of the Nigerian Economy* (Macmillan, 1979).

Orde-Browne, G. St. J., *Labour Conditions in West Africa Report*, Cmd 6277 (HMSO, 1941).

Orr, C. A., 'Trade Unionism in Colonial Africa', *Journal of Modern African Studies*, vol. 4 (1966), pp. 65–81.

Oxnam, D. W., 'Industrial Arbitration in Australia: Its Effects on Wages and Unions', *Industrial and Labour Relations Review*, vol. 9, no. 4 (1956) pp. 610–28.

Parsons, J., *The Social System* (The Yale Press, 1951).

Peace, A. J., *Choice, Class and Conflict: A Study of Southern Nigeria Factory Workers* (Harvester Press, 1979).

—— 'Industrial Protest at Ikeja, Nigeria', in *Sociology and Development*, ed. E. de Kadt and G. P. Williams (Tavistock Publications, 1974).

Peil, M., *The Ghanian Factory Worker: Industrial Man in Africa* (Cambridge University Press, 1972).

Pelling, H., *A History of British Trade Unionism*, 3rd edn (Macmillan, 1976).

Perlman, M., *Labour Union Theories in America* (Peterson, 1958).

Perlman, S., *A Theory of Labour Movement* (Kelley, 1928).

Peterson, R. B., 'The Swedish Experience with Industrial Democracy', *British Journal of Industrial Relations*, vol. 6 (1968) pp. 185–203

Pfeffermann, G., *Industrial Labor in the Republic of Senegal* (Praeger, 1968).

Phelps-Brown, E. H., *The Growth of British Industrial Relations* (Macmillan, 1959).

—— 'New Wine in Old Bottles: Reflections on the Changed Working of Collective Bargaining in Great Britain', *British Journal of Industrial Relations*, vol. 11 (1973) p. 329.

Reder, M. W., *Labor in a Growing Economy* (John Wiley, 1957).

Rimmer, D., 'The New Industrial Relations in Ghana', *Industrial and Labour Relations Review* (Jan 1961) pp. 206–26.

Roberts, B. C., *Labour in the Tropical Territories of the Commonwealth* (Bell, 1964).
—— (ed.), *Industrial Relations: Contemporary Issues* (Macmillan, 1968).
—— *Trade Union Government and Administration in Great Britain* (Bell, 1956).
—— and Bellecombe, L. G., *Collective Bargaining in African Countries* (Macmillan, 1967).
Roberts, I. L., 'The Works Constitution Acts and Industrial Relations in West Germany: Implications for the UK'. *British Journal of Industrial Relations,* vol. 11 (1973) pp. 338–67.
Roper, J. I., *Labour Problems in West Africa* (Penguin, 1958).
Ross, A. M., *Industrial Relations and Economic Development* (Macmillan, 1966).
Routh, G., *Occupation and Pay in Great Britain 1906–79,* 2nd edn (Macmillan, 1980).
Sandbrook, R., and Cohen, R., *The Development of an African Working Class* (Longman, 1975).
Saposs, D. J., 'The Impact of Labour Ideology on Industrial Relations', *Monthly Labour Review,* vol. 85 (1962) pp. 1100–4.
Schatzl, L., *Industrialisation in Nigeria: A Spatial Analysis* (Weltforum Verlag, 1973).
Schwarz, S. M., 'Trade Unions in the Soviet State', *Current History* (Aug 1959) pp. 79–84.
Schweinitz, K. de (Jnr), 'Industrialization, Labour Controls and Democracy', *Economic Development and Cultural Change,* vol. 7, no. 4 (July 1959) pp. 385–404.
Somers, G. C. (ed.), *Essays in Industrial Relations Theory* (Iowa State University Press, 1969).
Standing, G., *Labour Force Participation and Development* (ILO, 1978).
Stephens, L., 'Impressions of Industrial Relations in Nigeria and Ghana', *Personnel Management,* vol. 41 (1959) pp. 28–33.
Stewart, M., *Trade Unions in Europe* (Gower Press, 1974).
Sturmthal, A., 'Industrial Relations Strategies', in *The International Labor Movement in Transition,* ed. A. Sturmthal and J. B. Scoville (1973), pp. 1–33.
—— 'Unions and Economic Development', *Economic Development and Cultural Change,* vol. 8 (1959) pp. 199–205.
—— and Scoville, J. (eds) *The International Labor Movement in Transition* (University of Illinois Press, 1973).
Taft, P. 'Germany', in *Comparative Labour Movements,* ed. W. Galenson (Prentice-Hall, 1952).
Tannenbaum, A. S., 'Systems of Formal Participation', in *Organizational Behaviour: Research and Issues,* ed. Strauss, G. *et al.* (Industrial Relations Research Association, University of Wisconsin, 1974).
Tannenbaum, F. A., *A Philosophy of Labor* (Alfred A. Knopf, 1951).
Tevoedjre, A., 'A Strategy for Social Progress in Africa and the ILO's Contribution', *International Labour Review,* vol. 99, no. 1 (Jan 1969).

Tokunboh, M. A., 'The Changing Pattern of Industrial Relations in Nigeria', *Management in Nigeria*, vol. 2, no 4 (Nov–Dec 1966) pp. 153–5.

Trachtman, L. N., 'The Labour Movement of Ghana: A Study in Political Unionism', *Economic Development and Cultural Change*, vol. 10 (Jan 1962) pp. 183–200.

Turner, H. A., *Wage Trends, Wage Policies and Collective Bargaining: The Problems for Under-developed countries* (Cambridge University Press, 1966).

——*Labour Relations in the Motor Industry* (Allen & Unwin, 1967).

Ubeku, A. K., *Personnel Management in Nigeria* (Ethiope Publishing Corporation, 1975).

United Kingdom, *Industrial Relations Handbook* (HMSO, 1961).

—— *Report of the Royal Commission on Trade Unions and Employers' Associations*, 1965–68, Cmd 3623 (HMSO, 1968).

Walker, K. F., *Australian Industrial Relations Systems* (Harvard University Press, 1970).

——'Towards Useful Theorising About Industrial Relations', *British Journal of Industrial Relations*, vol. 15, no. 3 (1977) pp. 307–15.

——'The Comparative Study of Industrial Relations', *International Institute for Labour Studies*, bulletin, no. 3 (1967).

——'Australia', in *Comparative Labour Movements*, ed. W. Galenson (Prentice-Hall, 1952).

Walker, P. (ed.), *Between Labour and Capital* (Harvester Press, 1979).

Warmington, W. A., *A West African Trade Union* (Oxford University Press, 1960).

Warren, W. M., 'Urban Real Wages and the Nigerian Trade Union Movement, 1939–60', *Economic Development and Cultural Change*, vol. 15 (1966) pp. 21–36.

——'Urban Real Wages and the Nigerian Trade Union Movement 1939–60: Rejoinder', *Economic Development and Cultural Change*, vol. 17 (1969) pp. 618–33.

Webb, S., and B., *The History of Trade Unionism* (Longman, 1920).

——*Industrial Democracy* (Longman, 1920).

Wedderburn, K. W., *The Worker and the Law* (Penguin, 1965).

Weeks, J. F., 'A Comment on Peter Kilby: Industrial Relations and Wage Determination', *Journal of Developing Areas*, vol. 3 (Oct 1968) pp. 7–18.

——'Further Comment on the Kilby/Weeks Debate: An Empirical Rejoinder', *Journal of Developing Areas*, vol. 5 (1971) pp. 165–74.

——'The Impact of Economic Conditions and Institutional Forces on Urban Wages in Nigeria', *Nigerian Journal of Economic and Social Studies*, vol. 13 (1971) pp. 313–39.

Wells, F. A., and Warmington, W. A., *Studies in Industrialization: Nigeria and the Cameroons* (Oxford University Press, 1962).

Windmiller, J. P., 'External Influence on Labour Organizations in Underdeveloped Countries', *Industrial and Labour Relations Review*, vol. 16 (1953) pp. 539–75.

Woddis, J., *Africa: The Lion Awakes* (Lawrence & Wishart, 1959).

Wood, S. J., *et al.*, 'The Industrial Relations Concept as a Basis for Theory in Industrial Relations', *British Journal of Industrial Relations*, vol. 13, no. 3 (1975) pp. 291–307.

Wootton, B., *The Social Foundations of Wage Policy* (Allen & Unwin, 1962).

Yesufu, T. M., *An Introduction to Industrial Relations in Nigeria* (Oxford University Press, 1962).

—— 'The State and Industrial Relations in Developing countries', in *Industrial Relations and Economic Development*, ed. A. M. Ross (Macmillan, 1966).

—— 'Consumption Patterns and Living Conditions of Employees of the Nigerian Tobacco Company Ltd.' Unpublished Study (1967).

Index

All references are to Nigeria unless otherwise indicated.

244 *Index*